Geniuses Together

Books by Humphrey Carpenter

J. R. R. Tolkien: A Biography

The Inklings: C. S. Lewis, J. R. R. Tolkien,
Charles Williams, and Their Friends

W. H. Auden: A Biography

The Letters of J. R. R. Tolkien

Secret Gardens: A Study of the Golden Age
of Children's Literature

River Seine

RUE DE RIVOLI

To Montmartre

RIGHT BANK

ÎLE DE LA CITÉ

20)

PLACE
ST-MICHEL

Notre Dame

ÎLE ST
-LOUIS

QUAI DE ANJOU

BOULEVARD SAINT MICHEL

LATIN
QUARTER

AIN

Q. DE MONTBELLO

River Seine

QUAI DE LA TOURNELLE

Three Mountains
Press (William Bird)
and "transatlantic
review" office

BOULEVARD SAINT GERMAIN

Sorbonne
(University of Paris)

Panthéon

Hemingway's apartment (1922-3)
and Bal Musette (No. 74)

Jardin

des Plantes

PLACE DE LA
CONTRESCARPE

RUE MOUFFETARD

BOULEVARD DE PORT ROYAL

BOULEVARD SAINT MARCEL

Geniuses Together

American Writers in Paris in the 1920s

Humphrey Carpenter

Houghton Mifflin Company

Boston   1988

Library of Congress Cataloging-in-Publication Data

Carpenter, Humphrey.
 Geniuses together.

 Bibliography: p.
 Includes index.
 1. Authors, American—20th century—Biography.
2. American literature—20th century—History and
criticism. 3. American literature—France—Paris—
History and criticism. 4. Paris (France)—Intellectual
life—20th century. 5. Montparnasse (Paris, France)—
Intellectual life. 6. Americans—France—Paris—
Biography. I. Title.
PS129.C27   1987   810'.9'00912   87-21521
ISBN 0-395-46416-1

Printed in the United States of America

D 10 9 8 7 6 5 4 3 2 1

First American edition 1988

Contents

Illustrations

Foreword

This is the story of the longest-ever literary party, which went on in Montparnasse, on the Left Bank, throughout the 1920s.

Writers tend to huddle in gangs for self-protection; hence Bloomsbury, the Transcendentalists of Concord, the Auden Generation. Most of them are 'movements' to which we ourselves would not greatly wish to have belonged; we would have found Virginia Woolf terrifying, Ralph Waldo Emerson daunting, W. H. Auden overpowering. The American literary goings-on in Paris during the 1920s are a different matter.

'I went to a marvellous party,' runs the first line of a Noël Coward song, and evidently that was how it felt to have been a young American writer – or would-be writer – in the Montparnasse district of Paris after the First World War. It is hard to read about life in 'the Quarter', as they all called Montparnasse, without wishing to have tasted it oneself – to have bumped into Ernest Hemingway in a bar, to have drunk away the night with Robert McAlmon, to have been caught up in the intrigues of the expatriates and participated in their long *fiesta*. It was far from being the most productive 'movement' in literary history; but to live in Paris is always a delight, and to live there when life seems full of possibilities and tomorrow you might turn out to be a genius – well, to quote another song,* 'Who could ask for anything more?'

This book, its title shamelessly stolen from Robert McAlmon's memoirs of Paris in the 1920s, *Being Geniuses Together* (1938), is chiefly a collage of Left-Bank expatriate life as it was experienced by the Hemingway generation – the Lost Generation, as Gertrude Stein named them in a famous remark to Hemingway. There had been Americans in Paris for nearly 150 years before this particular crowd arrived, and I have prefaced the story with a brief history of the special relationship between the USA and the French capital. Next, I have supplied brief portraits of the three women – Gertrude Stein, Natalie Clifford Barney, and Sylvia Beach – who, arriving in Paris before the First World War, provided in their different ways meeting points and vital introductions for the exiles of the 1920s. But the main narrative concerns the years 1921 to 1928, because these saw the arrival and departure of Hemingway and most of his Paris associates.

---

*'I Got Rhythm', by the Gershwin brothers, from the film *An American in Paris* (1951).

Even within this short period I have been highly selective. The volume of the *Dictionary of Literary Biography* devoted to American writers in Paris between the two World Wars* contains nearly 100 entries, and Robert McAlmon could think of 250 expatriates connected with the arts in Montparnasse during the 1920s. I have concentrated on those I believe to be the most intriguing (in both senses of that word), and have allowed only a comparatively small number of the others to flit in and out of the narrative; even so, the 'Biographies in Brief' at the end of the book may be needed to help identify minor characters. The epilogue, dealing with the years after 1928, is short. There were American writers haunting the Dôme, the Sélect, and other Montparnasse cafés long after the Lost Generation had gone home, but the period 1921 to 1928 was when the party was at its wildest.

*For details of this and other books referred to in the narrative, see the bibliography and notes at the end of the book.

A denser civilisation than our own

In the seventeenth *arrondissement* of Paris, roughly half-way between the Arc de Triomphe and the railway lines that sprout north-westwards from the Gare St Lazare, lies the rue de Chazelles, where in former times stood the iron foundry of Monduit et Béchet. Here, during the year 1883, passers-by had their attention diverted by a curious spectacle.

The first that could be seen of it, projecting above the foundry walls, was a hand of stupendous proportions, grasping a gigantic torch, of which the rim was so broad as to permit several workmen to stand upon it. A few weeks later the hand had risen level with the second storey of the neighbouring apartment blocks, and a face could be seen frowning over the foundry, its forehead topped with a spiked corona. Thereafter, month by month, the colossus relentlessly raised its robed torso, until it dominated the surrounding streets with their little *tabacs* and wine-shops. All the time there was the sound of hammering.

The foundry and its formidable iron figure soon became a favourite Sunday resort for Parisian strollers. Wine-stalls were set up in the street, and leaflets were distributed by the Committee which had proudly given birth to the giantess. She was called (so read the Parisians) *La Liberté éclairant le monde*, and she was to be a gift from the French people – or such as cared to contribute to her cost – to their republican brethren across the Atlantic. The noted sculptor Monsieur Bartholdi had designed her; the ingenious framework beneath the iron sheets of her skin was the work of the up-and-coming engineer Monsieur Eiffel; and the entire project was the brainchild of the distinguished historian Monsieur Laboulaye, who had conceived it as a commemoration of the centenary of the American nation's Declaration of Independence.

Admittedly the project had been so long in gestation that the centenary had come and gone, and it was true that the American Congress had shown itself somewhat hesitant about the gift. But a splendid site, on an island at the entrance to New York harbour, had been granted, so that future generations of emigrants to the New World would be greeted by *La Liberté*, a symbol of that Franco-American amity which had begun in 1776. Plans were already being made to transport her, piece by piece, by train from the Gare St Lazare to the harbour at Rouen, whence she would take ship to her new home. Some disappointment was expressed in the newspapers that so splendid a creation would not be remaining in Paris.

*

A hundred and seven years earlier, on 5 July 1776, Paris had received its first official American visitor. His name was Silas Deane, and he did not know that he was technically an American. News had not yet come that a Declaration of Independence had been signed, and Deane, a Connecticut congressman, regarded himself as still a subject, though an unwilling one, of the British Crown. He was the first member of a delegation sent to win the support of France for the colonies' War of Independence to arrive in Paris.

He was not well equipped for the task: he could scarcely speak half a dozen words of French, and on principle he would not address any Frenchman who claimed an aristocratic title. By October he had managed to buy arms from France, but he had hardly attracted the notice of the Parisians. However, by Christmas another member of the delegation had joined him, and suddenly Paris was agog.

Benjamin Franklin was seventy years old, and in many ways typified the founding fathers of the USA. As a youth he had made his way from Boston to Philadelphia, where he set himself up as a printer. He made his fortune and fame by publishing almanacs full of self-help maxims ('He that riseth late must trot all day'), and by the age of forty-two could afford to retire and devote himself to public works and scientific experiments. He established a Free Library and a university in Philadelphia; he also invented the lightning-conductor, and devised much of the electrical terminology that we still use today, including 'positive', 'negative', and 'battery'. He served in Congress, made a trip to London to conduct some tricky Government business, and soon after the Declaration of Independence was chosen as a commissioner to the Court of France. It was hoped that he could secure economic and military assistance for the Americans, and raise French sympathy for their cause. France was chosen for this mission because it was the traditional enemy of England.

Franklin had never before set foot in Europe, but had spent hours in the reading room of his own Free Library in Philadelphia teaching himself French, and had corresponded with French scientific societies. His lightning-conductor had already been adopted all over France. The French were looking forward to meeting him in person.

He arrived in Paris in mid-December 1776, putting up in a mansion on the rue de l'Université, and was immediately besieged by Paris intellectuals and fashionable persons who wished to inspect this distinguished emissary of the New World. After a few weeks he escaped to the comparative quiet of Passy, a little village on the road to Versailles. He was given quarters free of charge in the mansion of one Monsieur de Chaumont, supplier of uniforms to the French army, who hoped that in return for hospitality he might be rewarded with a grant of land in the USA. Five years later, when Franklin was still staying in the house and no land had been offered, Monsieur de Chaumont thought he had better charge rent after all.

Franklin was thoroughly amiable, and women and children adored him, especially women. A young American visitor to Passy describes one of the de Chaumont girls approaching the old man as if she were his own daughter, tapping him playfully on the cheek and calling him 'Papa Franklin'. Franklin himself reported to a niece in Boston: 'This is the civilest Nation upon Earth . . . 'Tis a delightful people to live with.' He had brought his two grandsons with him; the younger boy was sent to school in Passy, while the elder acted as secretary to his grandfather.

Franklin was amazed by the extravagant costume and manners of the French aristocracy, who filled their noses with tobacco, dressed their heads so elaborately that their hats would not stay on, and therefore had to walk about with them under their arms. But unlike Silas Deane he was amused rather than outraged by it all, while for their part the aristocrats reciprocated his kindly curiosity, admiring his shrewdness and lack of artifice rather than being affronted by his rough ways. One French count wrote enviously of Franklin's 'almost rustic attire, the simple but proud attitude, the free and direct language, the hair-style without trappings or powder', and judged him more genuinely civilised than his French counterparts; it was as if one of Plato's friends had suddenly strolled into 'the weak and servile civilisation of the eighteenth century'.

Franklin himself perfectly understood the effect he was having, and played on it. He described himself as 'very plainly dressed, wearing my thin, gray straight hair, that peeps out from under my only *coiffure*, a fine fur cap, which comes down on my forehead almost to my spectacles. Think how this must appear among the powdered heads of Paris!' The fur cap, acquired during a journey to Canada a few months earlier, seemed a good middle course between the aristocratic hairstyles and the headgear of the poor. Franklin also wore bifocal glasses (another of his own inventions) and found that he particularly needed them when talking to Frenchmen, since 'when one's Ears are not well accustomed to the Sounds of a Language, a Sight of the Movement in the Features of him that speaks helps to explain; so that I understand French better by the help of my Spectacles'. Even with them on, he did not always understand everything. Attending a meeting of the French Academy of Sciences, he decided it was safest to clap whenever his neighbour did – and so applauded loudest and longest when he himself was being eulogised.

From the outset, Paris adored him. After only three weeks it had become the mode for everyone to have his picture over the mantelpiece. His face appeared on trinkets and snuff-boxes, on vases, even on chamber-pots, and ladies began to arrange their wigs in imitation of his fur cap. A medallion of him was put on sale, bearing the legend B. FRANKLIN – AMERICAIN.

Silas Deane went home and was replaced by the young American statesman John Adams; some time later Thomas Jefferson was sent over to join the delegation. Both men brought their families. An American colony was establishing itself in Paris, for along with the diplomats there was now a trickle of merchants, artists, and young men in search of an education. Soon the trickle became a flow, and they all expected Franklin to invite them to dinner. He tried to keep at least part of his weekend free for 'my grandson Ben with some of the American children from his school', but Americans were always turning up at Passy, and he felt obliged to entertain them.

Despite the warm welcome the Parisians had given him, Franklin found it an uphill task to negotiate a firm Franco-American alliance. The two countries could scarcely have differed more in religion and method of government, and there was also the snag (said Franklin) that the French *noblesse*, 'who always govern here', thought it 'indiscreet and improper' even to mention Trade.

Meanwhile the British suspected the worst of Franklin's negotiations. They planted a spy in his household at Passy, who sent a hair-raising report that Franklin and the French were plotting to construct some giant mirrors. These would be set up at Calais, and would reflect the heat of the sun on to the Royal Navy across the Channel, burning it up as it lay at anchor. While the fire was blazing, said the spy, Franklin would have a huge chain carried across to Dover, and by means of 'a prodigious electrical machine of his own invention' would 'convey such a shock as will entirely overturn our whole island'.

Franklin's real business in Paris was rather more prosaic. On 20 March 1778 treaties of alliance and commerce were signed by him and Louis XVI. Franklin had a wig specially made for the occasion, but it did not fit, so he decided to meet the King in his own hair and without a ceremonial sword. One of the French aristocracy who was present said that 'but for his noble face' one would have supposed him to be 'a big farmer'. The King told Franklin: 'Assure Congress of my friend-ship. I hope this will be for the good of the two nations.'

*

Franklin finally went back to Philadelphia in 1785, after nearly nine years in Paris, taking with him several crates of mineral water, and leaving the Paris mission in the charge of Thomas Jefferson, who had been in public service since his mid-twenties and was an example of a new type of American. He took grand quarters in the Champs-Élysées, engaged his own *maitre d'hôtel*, acquired a carriage, powdered his hair, and frequented the smartest salons. During working hours he set about negotiating further commercial deals with the French, in the hope of shifting the main part of American overseas trade from Britain to France.

He was helped by the Marquis de Lafayette, who had joined

Washington's army in the War of Independence and had proved a daring and capable commander of volunteer French troops. Now a citizen of several of the States, Lafayette had christened his two children Virginia and George Washington, and had taught them to sing American songs. He had also adopted two American Indian boys, and in the study of his Paris mansion had hung a framed copy of the Declaration of Independence; next to it was a blank frame, which Lafayette said was 'waiting for the declaration of the rights of France'.

Even with Lafayette's support, Jefferson could not cut his way very far through the jungle of tax-farming that tangled the French economic system and made negotiation practically impossible, while with the end of the American War of Independence against Britain, trade had automatically begun to flow again between those two countries. Jefferson ruefully admitted that there were links that bound the USA to the British, 'whether we will or no'.

For all his keenness to adopt the manners of the Parisians, Jefferson was not very impressed with what he called, with a slight sneer, 'the vaunted scene of Europe'. As a self-styled 'savage from the mountains of America', he said he found the general fate of humanity in the European countries 'most deplorable'; Voltaire had been right to judge that every man there must be either the hammer or the anvil. Admittedly Europeans were still far ahead of Americans in manners and the arts, but, 'My God!' said Jefferson, 'how little do my countrymen know what precious blessings they are in possession of, and which no other people on earth enjoy. I confess I had no idea of it myself.'

He also feared the influence of Europe on young Americans who came abroad. He noticed how in Paris they acquired a 'fondness for European luxury and dissipation', even 'a spirit of female intrigue'. It was all very un-American; he wished their parents would not send them.

This did not stop him enjoying Paris to the full. He would work all morning, ride in the Bois de Boulogne, then sometimes explore the bookshops on the Left Bank; when he eventually went back to the USA the books he had bought in Paris required 250 feet of shelves. Dinner in mid-afternoon was followed by the theatre, the opera or a concert, then a visit to some glittering salon. He was introduced to Madame de Staël, and became particular friends with Lafayette's aunt, the Comtesse de Tessé, who shared his passion for gardening. He had a friendly dispute with the naturalist Buffon about the size and appearance of the American moose. Since Buffon could not be persuaded that it looked quite different from a reindeer, Jefferson sent over for a specimen to prove his point. Eventually a giant skeleton arrived; the creature had been specially hunted down and shot by a New Hampshire general, who enclosed his bill.

Over in Jefferson's home state of Virginia they wanted a new Capitol building for Richmond, the seat of government, and they wrote to ask for Jefferson's advice. He recommended that they copy a Roman building he had seen on his travels around France, the Maison Carré at Nimes. They agreed; he sent a French architect over to Richmond to supervise the job, and the result was so successful that it was copied in American public buildings until the First World War.

By contrast, when Jefferson went to England for the first time in 1786 he was impressed by nothing except the mechanical inventions and the landscape gardening. His notes on his English travels rarely ran to more than a bare statement of accounts: 'For seeing house where Shakespeare was born, 1s.; seeing his tomb-stone, 1s.'

★

As the French Revolution approached, Jefferson felt himself to be more than an onlooker, knowing that the USA had provided a model for the French republican movement. He hoped the final settlement in France would resemble the English constitutional monarchy, rather than aiming for full-scale democracy all at once, and was fearful that in attempting too much the revolutionaries would lose everything.

In the spring of 1789 he sketched out a proposed Charter of Rights for France, largely modelled on the US Constitution, hoping that Louis XVI might sign it. There was provision in it for habeas corpus and a free press; legislation would be in the hands of the Estates General (nobility, clergy, and bourgeoisie), with the King's consent; fiscal privileges were to be abolished. But another American on the scene, the conservative-minded Pennsylvania statesman Gouverneur Morris, who in 1787 had been responsible for much of the final wording of the Constitution, thought Jefferson was far too radical and democratic in his attitude to the French insurrection. Morris admired French royalty and was alarmed by the mob.

Up to now, American politics had been conducted mostly by consensus; there were two factions, but they usually managed to agree. Suddenly, the execution of Louis XVI and France's declaration of war against Britain caused a rift between them. The conservative element had always implicitly opposed the French Revolution, and now (said Jefferson) they were 'open-mouthed against the murderers of a sovereign'. The more democratic faction were alarmed by events in France, but still regarded the Revolution as a laudable extension of the USA's own. Jefferson observed, not altogether with regret, that the French had 'kindled' American politics, had stirred up the two factions to an 'ardour' which internal affairs alone had not managed to excite.

The French Revolutionary Government sent an envoy over to the USA, Citizen Genêt, and he had a mixed welcome. At Philadelphia the crowd donned red caps and sang the 'Marseillaise', but when someone showed George Washington a broadsheet depicting his own head being chopped off on the guillotine, Genêt's recall was demanded. Jefferson sadly described all this as 'liberty warring on itself', while to the French, the USA no longer seemed an unshakeable ally. Genêt's successor wrote: 'Jefferson, I say, is an American and, as such, he cannot be sincerely our friend. An American is the born enemy of all the peoples of Europe.'

In 1796 John Adams succeeded Washington as President, and the country came near to declaring war on France and making an alliance with Britain. When Jefferson himself took over the Presidency in 1801 he studiously embraced neutrality. He said he was determined to avoid 'implicating' the USA with Europe, 'even in support of principles which we mean to pursue'.

The emergence of Napoleon further diminished American enthusiasm for the French cause. For a time, the victorious Bonaparte, who had made Spain cede Louisiana back to France, planned an expedition to New Orleans to take power there. But it never sailed, and eventually Louisiana was sold to the Americans for $15 million, a purchase that almost doubled the size of the USA.

The two-and-a-half-year war between Britain and America, which broke out in 1812, achieved nothing beyond reinforcing the American belief in neutrality; the Monroe Doctrine of 1823 warned Europe that the United States were 'henceforth not to be considered as subjects for future colonization', while American policy towards the outside world was now simply 'not to interfere'. Yet though isolationism had become the dominant note in official circles, a steady stream of Americans continued to cross to Europe, many of them on cultural Grand Tours. Among literary men, Washington Irving came to Paris in 1804, the scholar George Ticknor in 1819, James Fenimore Cooper and Henry Wadsworth Longfellow in 1826, Ralph Waldo Emerson in 1832, and Nathaniel Hawthorne in 1858. The first young American to study painting at the École des Beaux-Arts in Paris, John Vanderlyn, came in 1796, and many others followed. Doctors, clergymen, and bankers came too; and in 1844 P. T. Barnum brought General Tom Thumb to perform before Louis Philippe. In 1858 an American Church was established in the rue de Berri for members of the nonconformist congregations; and in the 1880s the Episcopalians built themselves a cathedral off the Champs-Élysées. An American newspaper magnate, James Gordon Bennett, established a European edition of his *New York Herald* in Paris in 1887, while the *Chicago Tribune*, not to be outdone, set up its own Paris edition a little later.

*

Alongside this solidly respectable American community of the Right Bank, with its smart hotels, cathedrals, and newspapers, another Paris began to attract its share of American attention. It was this 'alternative' Paris that would draw writers to the French capital in such droves after the First World War.

The Latin Quarter, on the Left Bank opposite Notre Dame, came to be so called in medieval times because it housed the university, and students who flocked there from all over Europe used Latin rather than French as their *lingua franca* in the streets. By the late nineteenth century it was the only part of central Paris to retain much of its medieval layout, for during the 1850s Baron Haussmann, Prefect of the Seine under Napoleon III, had been commissioned to plan a drastic reconstruction of the city, sweeping away most of the narrow alley-ways and lanes where criminals and insurgents could hide out – as described in Victor Hugo's *Les Misérables* (1862) – and which had helped to foment uprisings like those of 1830 and 1848. Haussmann's brief was to drive broad boulevards through the huddle. This he did, ruthlessly. But the Latin Quarter remained comparatively untouched, and soon began to attract tourists who came in search of its celebrated *vie bohème*.

The life-style of the *Quartier Latin* had always been bohemian – as is demonstrated by the careers of two early members of the University of Paris, Peter Abelard and the rakish poet François Villon – but nobody seemed to consider this of much interest until the 1840s, when a book about Latin Quarter life suddenly became a bestseller. It was written by a concierge's son, a hack writer named Henri Murger, who preferred to call himself Henry Mürger, and had abandoned his clerk's job in the hope of becoming a poet and painter. The result was his *Scènes de la Bohème*,* serialised in a Paris magazine during the 1840s and staged there in 1849. Fifty years later, Mürger's book was sentimentalised in Puccini's *La Bohème*.

Mürger's Bohemia – an exaggeration, though not a gross one, of the real thing – is a Latin Quarter inhabited by art students, would-be poets, and literary hacks employed by mysterious periodicals. They occupy garrets, avoid paying their rent, and borrow wherever they can, so as to eat in such pot-houses as Mother Cadet's, 'famous for its rabbit-stew, its genuine *choucroute* and a watery white wine with a flavour of musket flints'. Garret life consists largely of cutting up one's furniture and burning it to keep warm. The hack writer Rodolphe, the book's hero, dwells at the top of an old building near the Place de la Contrescarpe, close to the river and the Sorbonne. In order to keep his fire stoked, Rodolphe has cut up everything except the bed and two chairs, which are made of iron; sometimes he takes to burning his own manuscripts. Yet there is never any real hardship. Creditors are out-witted, forgotten dinner invitations surface just when the stomach

* Later known as *Scènes de la vie de Bohème*.

demands attention, and loans are raised from skinflint uncles. When the worst comes to the worst, Rodolphe sleeps at an address on the Avenue de Saint-Cloud, 'in the third tree on the left'.

He picks up his first girl, Louise, in a dance hall. She is one of the tribe of *grisettes*, apprentice seamstresses and milliners who wear grey work-dresses in the daytime and minister to the fancies of the students and other bohemians at night. Mürger calls her 'one of those birds of passage that nest, as fancy or often as necessity dictates, for a day, or rather for a night, in the garrets of the Latin Quarter, and readily stay for a few days in one place, if they can be detained by a whim – or by ribbons'. Sex is part of the backdrop in the Latin Quarter, and is treated with the same brisk humour as are the young men's financial scrapes:

Marcel's door . . . half opened and Rodolphe was confronted with the spectacle of a young man wearing only glasses and a shirt. 'I cannot receive you,' he told Rodolphe.
  'Why not?'
  A woman's head poked out from behind a curtain. 'There's the answer,' said Marcel.
  'She's not at all good looking,' said Rodolphe, as the door was shut in his face.

Rodolphe, evicted from his garret, is immediately taken in by its next tenant, the eighteen-year-old *grisette* Mimi, 'with whom Rodolphe had at one time done a little billing and cooing'. She is described as 'an adorable creature with a voice like the clash of cymbals'. (Another of the *grisettes* is known as Musette because she sounds like a bagpipe.)

When neither borrowing money nor bedding their girls, Rodolphe and his friends – 'Gustave Colline, the great philosopher, Marcel, the great painter, Schaunard, the great musician' – loll about in the Café Momus. The *patron* complains that they drive away all other customers: they steal the newspapers, monopolise the *trictrac* board, paint pictures, make coffee in their own percolator, and refuse to pay the bill.

Rodolphe is working endlessly on a play, while Marcel the painter labours at a canvas entitled *The Crossing of the Red Sea*, which has been offered for exhibition so many times that 'if it had been put on wheels, it could have gone to the Louvre by itself'. The picture is eventually sold to a grocer, who has a steam-boat and the words *Marseille Harbour* painted on it and hangs it up as his shop sign. Marcel is delighted.

Rodolphe and his friends have a thoroughly un-solemn attitude to the arts. An evening of festivities announced by them includes the following events:

8.30 pm. M. Alexandre Schaunard, distinguished Virtuoso, will perform on the piano 'The Influence of Blue upon the arts', a mimetic symphony . . .

9.30 pm. M. Gustave Colline, hyperphysical philosopher, and M. Schaunard will embark upon a comparative discussion of philosophy and metaphysics. To prevent collision between the antagonists, they will be tied together . . .

N.B. All persons desirous to read or recite poems will be immediately expelled from the Rooms and handed over to the police.

Much fun is poked at the serious literary aspirations of one Carolus Barbemuche, who wants to join the bohemians, and tells them solemnly: 'In my view, art is a sacred calling.' Rodolphe writhes in an agony of boredom when Barbemuche reads to him from one of his manuscripts.

Mimi deserts Rodolphe for a nobleman; Rodolphe publishes a poem about her, and when her new lover sees it he throws her out. Dying of tuberculosis, she returns to Rodolphe and his friends; but her demise is treated briskly and without melodrama, and the book ends with Rodolphe and Marcel determining to buy themselves a slap-up meal.

Scènes de la Bohème was translated into English, but was too *risqué* to catch on in the drawing rooms of Kensington and Boston, Massachusetts. The great popularity of the Latin Quarter 'bohemian' image in the English-speaking world by the early twentieth century owed something to Puccini's bowdlerised operatic version of the story, but just as much to a novel by an Englishman. A few years after the *Scènes* had first been published in Paris, a twenty-two-year-old English painter of French descent, George du Maurier, came to the Latin Quarter to study art. He eventually became well known as a *Punch* cartoonist, but at the end of his life he turned novelist. His *Trilby* (1894), loosely based on his own experiences as a Paris art student, was a runaway success on both sides of the Atlantic, playing no small part in attracting young Americans to Paris in the years that followed.

Du Maurier's Latin Quarter is scarcely recognisable as Mürger's. His bohemians are affluent young Englishmen of the upper class, with mutton-chop whiskers and top hats. Far from needing to burn their furniture, they live in mid-Victorian splendour and according to mid-Victorian morals. Du Maurier's appallingly named hero, Little Billee, is 'innocent of the world and its wicked ways; innocent of French especially, and the ways of Paris and its Latin Quarter'. He exults in the company of his 'glorious pair of chums', Taffy and the Laird, and has an 'almost girlish purity of mind'. His friends walk everywhere arm in arm with him as if he were their *grisette*.

The heroine, Trilby O'Ferrall, an artist's model of Irish birth, is equally ambiguous sexually. Du Maurier gravely informs us that she 'would have made a singularly handsome boy', and his drawings emphasise her masculinity. Though she poses for artists 'in the alto-gether' – it makes Little Billee 'sick' to think of this – she is described in sexless, religious terms: Little Billee perceives in her 'a well of sweetness . . . the very heart of compassion, generosity, and warm sisterly love', and hopes to turn her into the sort of girl who could be 'his sister's friend and co-teacher at the Sunday school'. Du Maurier admits that Trilby's life so far has not been exactly 'virtuous', but emphasises that she has 'followed love for love's sake only,' and persuades himself that 'she might almost be said to possess a virginal heart, so little did she know of love's heartaches'.

Having cut himself off from Mürger's themes – the comedy of poverty and the ups and downs of sexual entanglements – du Maurier is obliged to cobble together a plot combining Dickens with stage melodrama. Svengali, the Jewish mesmerist and musician who catches Trilby in his snare, is Fagin revived, 'a tall bony individual . . . of Jewish aspect . . . His thick, heavy, languid, lustreless black hair fell down behind his ears on to his shoulders, in that musician-like way that is so offensive to normal Englishmen.' He mesmerises Trilby into becoming a great singer, but then dies, whereupon she fades away.

Silly as the story is, 'people went *Trilby* mad,' writes Gerald du Maurier, the author's son, 'especially in America'. The novel was still well known, at least by hearsay, among the Americans who came to Montparnasse in the 1920s. One of them, Kay Boyle, had been called Trilby by one of her boyfriends back home.

*

Among the subsidiary characters in *Trilby* is a figure named in the published book as 'Antony, a Swiss', but who in the original serial publication (in *Harper's*) is called 'Joe Sibley' and is an American:

. . . the idle apprentice, *le roi des truands* . . . to whom everything was forgiven, as to François Villon . . . Always in debt . . . a most exquisite and original artist, and also somewhat eccentric in his attire . . . When the money was gone, then would [he] hie him to some beggarly attic in some lost Parisian slum, and write his own epitaph . . . decorating [it] with fanciful designs . . . On the third day or thereabouts, a remittance would reach him from some long-suffering sister or aunt . . . or else the fickle mistress or faithless friend (who had been looking for him all over Paris) would discover his hiding-place, the beautiful epitaph would be walked off in triumph to le père Marcas in the Rue du Ghette and sold for twenty, fifty, a hundred francs; and then . . . back again to Bohemia . . . *époi, da capo!*
And now that his name is a household word . . . he loves to remember all this.

This was du Maurier's reminiscence of James McNeill Whistler, who did not love to remember it in the least, but threatened to sue; hence the change of name and nationality when *Trilby* appeared as a book.

Du Maurier had crossed paths with Whistler during art-student days in Paris, and despite the expurgation of *Trilby*, Whistler's features can be detected among the background figures in several illustrations in the book – long-haired, monocled, and in dandy's clothes. Born in Lowell, Massachusetts, in 1834, the son of a railway engineer, Whistler had set off at the age of twenty-one to study painting in Paris, in the *atelier* of the Swiss artist Charles Gleyre, who also instructed Renoir. Whistler soon became known as a natural Paris bohemian; he acquired his first *grisette* – a hot-tempered girl known as Fumette or La Tigresse – and, unlike du Maurier and his friends, entered completely into Latin Quarter life. Behaving like any *rapin* (art student), he would pawn his jacket on hot days to buy cool drinks, and attend classes at Gleyre's only when he felt like it. He dressed with panache, reviving a florid style of costume that had first appeared in the 1830s. It is said that he had not merely read *Scènes de la Bohème* but knew much of the book by heart.

After a journey to Alsace in the summer of 1858, Whistler produced his first successful work, a group of etchings known as *The French Set*. The following year he abandoned Paris for London. He was often back there, but from then on avoided the Latin Quarter, no longer regarding himself as a penurious bohemian; Montmartre was his preferred place of residence.

His attitude to Paris is striking. There could be no greater contrast with the British reserve of the du Maurier set, who when they wanted an evening out would generally go to an English restaurant where they could dine off roast beef and beer. Whistler, far from conforming to his national background, was rejecting the whole American Puritan tradition from which he had emerged, a tradition embodied by his picture of his pious mother sitting in the gloom. He was also the first American in Paris to achieve a reputation as a trouble-maker. On one occasion he struck a workman for accidentally dropping some plaster on him; the American Minister in France had to be called to court to smooth out the affair. He also had a fight with a Paris cab-driver, and knocked his brother-in-law through a plate-glass window.

*

Henry James said his first memory was of the Place Vendôme, on the Right Bank near the Place de la Concorde, when he was six months old. His first important trip to Paris was a dozen years later, just as Whistler was in the middle of his year at Gleyre's (1855–56). This visit was the result of James's father's determination to take his sons and daughter abroad from New York for a year, 'to absorb French and German and get a better sensuous education'. In Paris they stayed first in a house rented from an American who divided his year between Louisiana and France; Henry remembered shiny floors, a perilous staircase, ormolu vases, gilded panels, brocaded walls, endless mirrors.

The James boys were provided with a French tutor, Monsieur Lerambert, who wore a tight black coat and spectacles, and Henry endured endless mornings of lessons rendering La Fontaine into English. In the afternoons a governess, Mademoiselle Danse, would take them for walks. There was Guignol (Punch and Judy) in booths on the Champs-Élysées, and a warren of little streets and squares to wander through, for Haussmann's reconstruction of the city was far from complete. Later, Henry and his elder brother William began to attend school in a somewhat curious institution, part classroom, part *pension*, in the rue Balzac, where what Henry later called 'ancient American virgins' drifted in from the dining room to learn French alongside the children.

Henry James made his first independent trip to Europe after studying at Harvard Law School. He spent some time in Paris in the autumn of 1872, finding it so thronged with American society – the Lowells, the Nortons, and other blue-blooded Bostonians – that it seemed almost 'Massachusetts-on-Seine'. He wrote to his father that he and James Russell Lowell had 'tramped over half Paris and into some queer places . . . There is a good deal of old Paris left still.' He told Charles Eliot Norton that he would probably stay on for some weeks, 'unless indeed M. Thiers [the current President] and the Assembly between them treat us to another revolution'. James's fear of insurrection was understandable; it was only eighteen months since the terrible struggles of the Paris Commune, in which 20,000 people had been killed and the Tuileries palace burnt to the ground. But Thiers and the Third Republic managed to retain control, and James's 1872 Paris stay was peaceful. Writing to his brother William, he described how he usually spent his day:

Mornings and very often evenings in my room; afternoons in the streets, walking, strolling, *flânant*, prying, staring, lingering at bookstalls and shop-windows; six o'clock dinner . . . *De temps en temps* the theatre . . . I walked to the Odéon in the rain (it hasn't stopped in three weeks) and enjoyed through the flaring dripping darkness from the Pont du Carrousel the great spectacle of the movement, the enormous *crue* of the Seine . . . It stretched out from quay to quay, rushing tremendously and flashing back the myriad lights from its vast black bosom like a sort of civilised Mississippi.

The letter continues by observing that, as a crowd, 'the Americans in Paris (as observed at Munroe's, the Grand Hotel etc.) excite nothing but antipathy.' On the other hand, 'I enjoy very much in a sort of chronic way which has every now and then a deeper throb, the sense of being in a denser civilization than our own. Life at home has the compensation that there you are a part of the civilization, whereas here you are outside it. It's a choice of advantages.'

The French nobleman who in 1776 had regarded Benjamin Franklin

as the equal of the ancient Athenians might have been surprised to find
Henry James, a century later, judging Paris 'a denser civilization' than
the USA: at the dawn of its independence, the latter had seemed to
promise so much. But the nineteenth century had not deepened and
enriched the quality of life in the USA; the civilised outlook of a
Franklin or a Jefferson was becoming the exception rather than the rule
in public and even intellectual circles, as the national energies bent
themselves almost exclusively on the amassing of personal wealth, and
the simple fact was that Europe, the Old World, was 'denser' in culture
simply by virtue of its vastly longer history. James, on his walks about
Paris in the rain, did not miss that point.

Coming back to Paris in 1875, he began to work his observations of
the differences between the two societies into his second novel, *The
American* (1877). The story was serialised in the *Atlantic* while it was
being composed, and was largely based on his own daily experiences in
Paris, sometimes scarcely assimilated into fictional form. Its hero
Christopher Newman, a wealthy young American visiting France, is
almost a caricature of the national type, 'the superlative American'. He
'had never tasted tobacco . . . His complexion was brown and the arch
of his nose bold and well-marked . . . He had the flat jaw and the firm,
dry neck which are frequent in the American type.'

Speaking no French, Newman blunders when dealing with the
Parisians, but gets away with it through sheer nerve. He admits that,
though he has made his pile back home, in Paris 'it's as if I were as
simple as a little child, and as if a little child might take me by the hand
and lead me about'. He makes the acquaintance of Tristram, an
American who lives with his wife 'behind one of those chalk-coloured
façades which decorate with their pompous sameness the broad
avenues distributed by Baron Haussmann over the neighbourhood of
the Arc de Triomphe'. Mrs Tristram, discovering that Newman wants a
wife, introduces him to a half-English, half-French widow, Claire de
Cintré, and the novel is thereafter chiefly concerned with his tortuous
relations with her family, the de Bellegardes. But there are passing
portraits of other American expatriates and tourists, such as the
Unitarian minister Babcock, whose 'digestion was weak and he lived
chiefly on Graham bread and hominy – a regimen to which he was so
much attached that his tour seemed to him destined to be blighted
when, on landing on the Continent, he found these delicacies fail to
flourish under the *table d'hôte* system'. Mr Babcock claims to be fond
of pictures and churches, 'but nevertheless in his secret soul he detested
Europe'.

Newman takes French lessons at the first opportunity, and soon
acquires a thoroughly sophisticated and European style of conversation. Claire de Cintré's brother is duly admiring of this, but is more
impressed by Newman's unchanging Americanness. 'It's a sort of air

you have,' he tells Newman, 'of being imperturbably, being irremovably and indestructibly (that's the thing!) at home in the world . . . I seem to see you move everywhere like a big stockholder on his favourite railroad. You make me feel awfully my want of shares. And yet the world used to be supposed to be ours. What is it I miss?'

*

James's view, then, was that each side – Americans and Europeans – had something to learn from the other; a judgement that would doubtless have been shared by the promoters of the Statue of Liberty. The appeal for funds for the statue opened in 1876, just as James was writing *The American* and moving from Paris to England.

The statue did not owe its inception only to a desire to express Franco-American friendship. Relations between the two countries had, after all, been diplomatically cool since the 1790s. *La Liberté* was intended by her French promoters not just as a gift to the USA, but as a subtle reproach to France herself for not achieving the high ideals of liberty and democracy which her Revolution had promised, and which the American struggle for independence did seem to have achieved.

The French did not realise that from the USA the picture looked rather different: that Americans were beginning to feel themselves trapped in a shallow and materialistic society, and that they would soon begin to turn towards Europe, the land that seemed to them to offer a true sense of liberation.

PART ONE

The Introducers

1

Slowly I was knowing that I was a genius

Some eighteen months after Henry James's departure for London, an American-Jewish mother and her five children arrived in Paris and settled for a while in Passy, which was now a suburb in the sixteenth *arrondissement*. The husband, Daniel Stein, had made a success in the clothing and textile business in the USA. In 1874 he had taken his wife and children on business to his native Europe. They spent about three years in Vienna; then Daniel had to return to the USA and his wife Milly came to Paris for a while with the children, Michael (aged thirteen), Simon, Bertha, Leo, and four-year-old Gertrude.

'Gertrude Stein,' writes Gertrude Stein in *The Autobiography of Alice B. Toklas*,

remembers a little school [in Paris] where she and her elder sister stayed and where there was a little girl in the corner of the school yard and the other little girls told her not to go near her, she scratched. She also remembers the bowl of soup with french bread for breakfast and she also remembers that they had mutton and spinach for lunch and as she was very fond of spinach and not fond of mutton she used to trade mutton for spinach with the little girl opposite. She also remembers all her three older brothers coming to see them at the school and coming on horse-back. She also remembers a black cat jumping from the ceiling of their house at Passy and scaring her mother and some unknown person rescuing her.

The Stein family stayed at Passy for about a year, then returned to the USA, settling in California. The mother died when Gertrude was fourteen, the father three years later; but in any case Gertrude already depended emotionally on her brother Leo.

She went to live with an aunt on the East Coast, studying at the 'Harvard Annex', the women's college at Cambridge, Massachusetts, which was soon renamed Radcliffe. There she was taught philosophy and psychology by Henry James's brother William, with whom she hit it off entirely. 'It was a very lovely spring day,' she writes,

Gertrude Stein had been going to the opera every night and going also to the opera in the afternoon and had been otherwise engrossed and it was the period of the final examinations, and there was the examination in William James' course. She sat down with the examination paper before her and she just could not. Dear Professor James, she wrote at the top of the paper, I am sorry but really I do not feel a bit like an examination paper in philosophy today, and left.

The next day she had a postal card from William James saying, Dear Miss Stein, I understand perfectly how you feel I often feel like that myself. And underneath it he gave her work the highest mark in his course.

She did not, however, read his brother's novels. Later she developed a great admiration for Henry James and called him her 'forerunner, he being the only nineteenth century writer who being an american felt the method of the twentieth century'. But when she was young he seemed to belong too much to the elder generation. 'The parents are too close,' she writes, 'they hamper you, one must be alone.'

At Radcliffe her written work rarely did her justice. 'She never wrote good English and grammar meant nothing to her,' says a contemporary. But she was full of vitality and seemed to be unselfconscious about her rotund and dumpy appearance. She often went for walks in the country with another girl: 'We said if we have any trouble with a man Gertrude will climb out on the furthest limb of a tree and drop on him.'

Leaving Radcliffe in 1897, she decided to pursue a career in medicine, with an emphasis on psychology, and began to attend the Johns Hopkins medical school in Baltimore. She spent her summer vacations travelling in Europe with Leo, and largely thanks to what she saw there she began to lose interest in her medical studies, offering no resistance when her professors told her they would 'flunk' her. One of her women friends pleaded that she would be letting down the feminist cause, but Gertrude answered: 'You don't know what it is to be bored.' She had been especially bored by abnormal psychology, of which she writes: 'The abnormal . . . is so obvious . . . The normal is so much more simply complicated and interesting.'

She began to realise that her own psychology was 'abnormal', at least by contemporary standards. In 1903 she wrote a novella, *Q.E.D.* (eventually published posthumously as *Things as They Are*). Based on events in her life, it describes the passionate relationship between Adele – a modified self-portrait – and the tall, slender Helen. Adele is the more passive partner, but observes of the possibility of a sexual affair: 'It is something one ought to know. It seems almost a duty.' The drama, played out in America and Europe, is complicated by Helen's feelings for another girl, Mabel. The book is never explicit about actual sexual relations, but seems to imply that Adele has difficulty in responding physically: 'Helen demanded of her a response and always before that response was ready. Their pulses were differently timed. She could not go so fast and Helen's exhausted nerves could no longer wait.'

Meanwhile Leo Stein had chosen to settle in Europe; he spent some time in the Florentine household of the American art connoisseur Bernard Berenson, but Berenson found him a tiresome bore and said he was 'for ever inventing the umbrella' – that is, had no sensibilities. Leo had hoped to become an art historian, but was discouraged by Berenson and went to Paris to reconsider his life. Over dinner with the musician Pablo Casals he suddenly decided he himself was 'growing into an artist'. He rushed back to his hotel room, took off all his clothes, sat in front of the mirror, and began to draw himself. The result pleased him enough to send him off to the Louvre to sketch statues, and he enrolled as an art student at the Académie Julien, an institution favoured by aspiring Americans who could not get into the École des Beaux-Arts. Deciding that he needed a studio but abhorring the idea of a search, he consulted his uncle Ephraim, an expatriate American sculptor, who recommended 27 rue de Fleurus, a house in a quiet side-street near the Jardin du Luxembourg, on the northern edge of Montparnasse. Leo inspected it, found that there was a good studio adjacent to the garden *pavillon*, and rented both the studio and the two-storey *pavillon* itself.

He settled into rue de Fleurus during the early months of 1903, hanging the few pictures he had dared to buy, mostly Japanese prints. Gertrude joined him for a holiday in North Africa and Spain, then, when the autumn came, agreed to live with him in Paris. 'She said,' writes Leo, 'she could stay there only on condition of a visit every year to America. I said she'd probably get used to it, but Gertrude is naturally dogmatic and said no, she was like that, and that was like her, and so it must be. That year she went to America for a visit and thirty-one years later she went again. No one really knows what is essential.'

At rue de Fleurus, the studio now became the living room, and a servant was engaged to look after brother and sister, who ate and slept in the *pavillon*. They quickly found that, thanks to having economised by setting up house together, funds from their shares in the family business in the USA were fast accumulating in the bank. They began to spend the spare money on pictures.

Gauguin, Cézanne and Renoir featured in their early purchases. Leo quickly showed himself perceptive of what was worthwhile among recent painting; he was one of the few people who had so far recognised the achievement of Cézanne (then nearing the end of his life) and virtually the only one able to write and talk articulately about it. Gertrude reported the purchases in the folksy style of letter she preferred at this date: 'We is doin business . . . We are selling Jap prints to buy a Cézanne . . . Leo . . . don't like it a bit and makes a awful fuss about asking enough money but I guess we'll get the Cézanne.'

In *The Autobiography of Alice B. Toklas*, Gertrude describes how they acquired their first Cézanne from the Paris dealer Vollard:

It was an incredible place. It did not look like a picture gallery. Inside there were a couple of canvases turned to the wall, in one corner was a small pile of big and little canvases thrown pell mell on top of one another, in the centre of the room stood a huge dark man glooming. This was Vollard cheerful. When he was really cheerless he put his huge frame against the glass door that led to the street . . . Nobody thought then of trying to come in . . .

They told Monsieur Vollard they wanted to see some Cézanne landscapes . . . Oh, yes, said Vollard looking quite cheerful and he began moving about the room, finally he disappeared behind a partition in the back and was heard heavily mounting steps. After quite a long wait he came down again and had in his hand a tiny picture of an apple with most of the canvas unpainted. They all looked at this thoroughly, then they said, yes but you see what we wanted to see was a landscape. Ah yes, sighed Vollard and he looked even more cheerful, after a moment he again disappeared and this time came back with a painting of a back, it was a beautiful painting there is no doubt about that but the brother and sister were not yet up to a full appreciation of Cézanne nudes and so they returned to the attack. They wanted to see a landscape. This time after even a longer wait he came back with a very large canvas and a very little fragment of a landscape painted on it . . .

Just at this moment a very aged charwoman came down the same back stairs, mumbled, bon soir monsieur et madame, and quietly went out of the door, after a moment another old charwoman came down the same stairs, murmured, bon soir messieurs et mesdames and went quietly out of the door. Gertrude Stein began to laugh and said to her brother, it is all nonsense, there is no Cézanne. Vollard goes upstairs and tells these old women what to paint and he does not understand us and they do not understand him and they paint something and he brings it down and it is a Cézanne. They both began to laugh uncontrollably . . .

They got their landscape ('a wonderful small green landscape . . . it covered all the canvas, it did not cost much'), and came back again and again. Vollard explained to his friends that their laughter annoyed him, 'but gradually he found out that when they laughed most they usually bought something.' He sold them 'a tiny little Daumier . . . Cézanne nudes . . . a very very small Manet . . . two tiny little Renoirs . . . two Gauguins'.

In another gallery they saw, and fell for, Matisse's *La Femme au Chapeau*, though visitors were ridiculing it. The price was 500 francs; they offered 400, but this was refused so they paid the full amount. At the time, Matisse was unknown and in penury, but his wife had guessed that anyone who offered 400 francs would probably give the full price if they only waited, and the 100 francs would make a huge difference. When Gertrude and Leo became friends with the Matisses and heard this story, they were delighted.

In the daytime, Leo attended his painting classes. Gertrude would sleep late, rising at noon and walking around Paris in the afternoon. During the evenings and nights she sat up writing. Soon after arriving in

Paris she began work on *Three Lives*, a trio of novellas about two German servant girls and a black woman in the American South. The project was partially suggested by Flaubert's *Trois Contes*, and also, she claimed, by the *Femme au Chapeau*, beneath which she sat as she wrote. The language and syntax were very queer and idiosyncratic, often mimetic of the oddities of German and Negro speech of the characters:

Anna led an arduous and troubled life.

Anna managed the whole little house for Miss Mathilda. It was a funny little house, one of a whole row all the same kind that made a close pile like a row of dominoes that a child knocks over, for they were built along a street which at this point came down a steep hill. They were funny little houses, two storeys high, with red brick fronts and long white steps.

This one little house was always very full with Miss Mathilda, an under servant, stray dogs and cats and Anna's voice that scolded, managed, grumbled all day long . . . Gradually it came to Anna to take the whole direction of their movements, to make all the decisions as to their journeyings to and fro, and for the arranging of the places where they were to live.

Leo was convinced that Gertrude's literary style was due to nature rather than artifice. He once remarked: 'Gertrude does not know what words mean.'

A prominent characteristic of the style, now and later, was the mannered repetition of certain words and phrases. Her own term for this was 'insistence'. Here it is at work in 'Melanctha', another of the *Three Lives*:

Melanctha was pale yellow and mysterious and a little pleasant like her mother, but the real power in Melanctha's nature came through her robust and very unendurable black father . . . Melanctha Herbert almost always hated her black father, but she loved very well the power in herself that came through him. And so her feeling was really closer to her black coarse yellow father, than her feeling had ever been toward her pale yellow, sweet-appearing mother. The things she had in her of her mother never made her feel respect.

The first publishers to whom the book was submitted thought it must be the work of somebody only dubiously fluent in English. It eventually got into print in 1909.

*

The quality of the Steins' growing Post-Impressionist collection began to attract visitors to 27 rue de Fleurus. 'Matisse brought people,' writes Gertrude, 'everybody brought somebody, and they came at any time and it began to be a nuisance . . . So the Saturday evenings began.' Saturday was instituted as a formal salon for visitors, with or without

invitation. They might call, inspect the canvases, and be received by
Gertrude. Among those who regularly put in appearances was Pablo
Picasso.

Early in the Steins' Paris sojourn, Leo had come across paintings by
the young and penurious Spaniard. He particularly wanted to buy
Picasso's *Jeune fille aux fleurs* from a circus clown turned picture dealer
named Sagot, but Gertrude thought there was 'something rather
appalling' in the stark depiction of the naked pre-pubescent awkwardly
clutching her basket of flowers, so Sagot told her: 'But that is all right, if
you do not like the legs and feet it is very easy to guillotine her and only
take the head.' They bought the entire picture.

Gertrude thought Picasso 'a good-looking young bootblack'. At the
dinner table, writes Gertrude, she 'took up a piece of bread. This, said
Picasso, snatching it back with violence, this piece of bread is mine. She
laughed and he looked sheepish. That was the beginning of their
intimacy.'

Gertrude and Leo introduced Picasso to Matisse – they had never
met before. Indeed, Gertrude was becoming more and more of an
introducer. She writes sarcastically of a man named Roché as 'one of
those characters that are always to be found in Paris . . . a general
introducer. He knew everybody . . . and he could introduce anybody to
anybody.' But the same could be said of her.

Picasso started to paint her portrait; neither of them could remember
whose suggestion it had been. She sat amid the cheerful disorder of his
Montmartre studio, and Fernande, his current mistress, offered to read
La Fontaine aloud while she posed. The portrait came at the end of
Picasso's 'Rose Period' (harlequins and circus subjects) and hints a little
at his future Cubism. It was abandoned for a time; Gertrude writes that
one day Picasso obliterated the entire head, saying 'I cannot see you any
longer when I look.' He eventually finished it during 1906 without the
sitter. As completed, it greatly sharpens Gertrude's features, giving an
impression of quickness of mind and concentration. The real Gertrude
Stein was more fleshly, with a rounder, less energetic but more
humorous face. Picasso himself commented of the picture: 'Everybody
thinks she is not at all like her portrait but never mind, in the end she
will manage to look just like it.' He gave it to Gertrude as a present –
which later American collectors found hard to believe or understand.

*

Gertrude did not grow to look like the portrait; by the time Picasso had
finished it she was fast putting on weight. A 1914 photograph of her in
the studio at rue de Fleurus shows a much more corpulent figure than in
the painting. Corpulence was a feature, too, of her next book, *The*

Making of Americans, written between 1906 and 1911 but not published in full until 1925; Edmund Wilson has said that it suffers from 'a sort of fatty degeneration of her imagination and style'. Here is a typical passage:

The children of all three of them by her possession of the mother of them and a little of the father of them had cut off from them in their later younger living a part of them and they had then a right to their sore feeling at her possession of their mother and a little of the father of them. There will be now more history of Madeleine Wyman in this possession.

This is part of a section which attempts to describe a family's relationship with its governess, and it exemplifies the three principles on which the book was written. First, like *Three Lives*, the book's style was intended to reflect the language and minds of the people it portrays – in this case an American German-Jewish family, the Herslands. Second, the absence of punctuation and the repetition or 'insistence' of certain phrases, sometimes even whole sentences, was meant (as Gertrude explained) as an attempt to get to 'the bottom nature in people' by 'hearing how everybody said the same thing over and over again with infinite variations'. Third, the actual narrative technique tries to convey an endless series of instant pictures of the present moment, rather than a historical and cumulative presentation. Possibly it owed something to Gertrude's studies with William James, who, she said, had taught her that 'science is continuously busy with the complete description of something'. A more obvious influence is Cubism, a movement born while she was at work on the book.

Though the aims of *The Making of Americans* are laudable, what results is quite different. The book is subtitled *The Hersland Family*, and underneath all the experimental writing it is an American family novel in the genre pioneered by Louisa M. Alcott and her imitators. The narrative is spattered with observations which, if conventionally punctuated, could come from the pages of the Alcott imitators, or at better moments from Henry James or even Jane Austen. Here are two pieces from it, with nineteenth-century punctuation added:

Henry Dehning was a grown man, and, for his day, a rich one, when his father died...He was strong, and rich, and good tempered, and respected; and he showed it in his look; that look that makes young people think older ones are very aged.

Mrs Dehning was the quintessence of loud-voiced, good-looking prosperity ...a woman whose rasping insensibility to gentle courtesy deserved the prejudice one cherished against her; but she was a woman, to do her justice, generous and honest; one whom one might like the better the more one saw her less.*

The Making of Americans appears, then, to be rather false modern-ism, an attempt to seem avant-garde when the underlying plan and material are somewhat conventional. It seems that Gertrude Stein was really trying to write 'the great American novel' – an expression she sometimes used – while disguising it as experimental.

The resemblance to James was noticed by the book's typist: 'Of course my love of Henry James was a good preparation for the long sentences.' The lady at the typewriter was Alice Babette Toklas, then aged thirty, two years Gertrude's junior, recently arrived in Paris. The name Alice B. Toklas sounds like one of Gertrude's queer inventions in *Three Lives* or *The Making of Americans*; and Alice eventually became a shadow of Gertrude, to the extent that it was hard to believe she had ever had an independent existence.

She came from a very similar background: she was the daughter of a Polish-Jewish businessman in California, and, like Gertrude, her mother had died when she was in her teens. Alice received a college education, and thereafter drifted through a life of ladylike amusement in San Francisco. When she was thirty she went on vacation to Paris with a friend, Harriet Levy, and while she was there, Gertrude's brother Michael Stein, whom Alice knew from San Francisco, intro-duced her to Gertrude.

Alice was no beauty. She had a perceptible moustache and an impassive, rather sullen expression. Mabel Dodge, a wealthy American friend of Gertrude's, found her thoroughly disconcerting, 'like Leah, out of the Old Testament, in her half-Oriental get-up ... her barbaric chains and jewels – and her melancholy nose'. But Gertrude fell for her instantly.

Alice writes of their first meeting, in September 1907, in Michael Stein's apartment:

It was Gertrude Stein who held my complete attention, as she did for all the many years I knew her until her death ... She was a golden brown presence, burned by the Tuscan sun and with a golden glint in her warm brown hair. She was dressed in a warm brown corduroy suit. She wore a large round coral brooch and when she talked, very little, or laughed, a good deal, I thought her

---

* Similarly, one can achieve something rather like the Stein effect by taking a passage of Henry James and removing the punctuation: 'And it belongs to this reminiscence for the triviality of which I should apologize did I find myself at my present pitch capable of apologizing for anything that I had on the very spot there one of those hallucinations as to the precious effect dreadful to lose and yet impossible to render which interfused the aesthetic dream in presence of its subject with the mortal drop of despair as I should insist at least didn't the despair itself seem to have acted here as the preservative.' This is from *The Middle Years.*

voice came from this brooch. It was unlike anyone else's voice – deep, full, velvety like a great contralto's... She was large and heavy with delicate small hands and a beautifully modelled and unique head.

This is one of the brighter passages from Alice's real autobiography. *What is Remembered* (1963). Most of the book reads like a pale imitation of Gertrude, without any of the humour, vitality, or perception.

Gertrude's own version of their first meeting, which she apparently means the reader to take seriously, has Alice coming to a swift judgement about her new friend: 'I may say that only three times in my life have I met a genius and each time a bell within me rang and I was not mistaken... The three geniuses... are Gertrude Stein, Pablo Picasso and Alfred Whitehead... In no one of the three cases have I been mistaken.' (Ezra Pound said that Gertrude told him the Jews had produced three geniuses: herself, Spinoza, and Jesus Christ.)

Gertrude invited Alice to a Saturday salon at rue de Fleurus, and to dinner with her and Leo beforehand. When Alice arrived she found Picasso and Fernande among the other guests. In *The Autobiography of Alice B. Toklas*, Gertrude has Alice say of this: 'Fernande was the first wife of a genius I was to sit with. The geniuses came and talked to Gertrude Stein and the wives sat with me.'

Alice took an apartment for herself and her friend Harriet, but Gertrude set about undermining Harriet's influence on Alice. When Harriet got religious mania, Gertrude advised her to kill herself. 'This upset me more than it did Harriet,' writes Alice. Gertrude then turned psychologist, analysing Alice according to her own terminology, and, says Alice,

diagnosed me as an old maid mermaid which I resented, the old maid was bad enough but the mermaid was quite unbearable. I cannot remember how this wore thin and finally blew away entirely. But by the time the buttercups were in bloom [summer 1908], the old maid mermaid had gone into oblivion and I had been gathering wild violets.

This appears to be a reference to sexual initiation, and some lines in one of Gertrude's poems suggests that a fairly happy physical relationship was soon established:

> Pussy how pretty you are ...
> Kiss my lips. She did
> Kiss my lips again she did.
> Kiss my lips over and over again she did.

'Then my friend went back to California, and I joined Gertrude Stein in the rue de Fleurus.' So writes Gertrude on behalf of Alice in the

Autobiography, but it was more complicated than this. Harriet was still with Alice in the summer of 1908, so Gertrude invited them both down to Fiesole in Tuscany, fixed them up with a villa, then persuaded Alice to abandon Harriet and come away with her on a walking tour. On this journey, Gertrude would, as always, refuse to get up before midday, so they invariably set out when the sun was at its highest, Gertrude having donned her usual brown corduroys although she sweated profusely. Alice tagged along patiently. 'The sun was giving a torrid heat,' she writes of one such walk, from Perugia to Assisi, 'so under some bushes I discarded my silk combination and stockings. It was all I could do.' (Gertrude's version has Alice say: 'I gradually undressed . . . but even so I dropped a few tears before we arrived.') Another time they walked in Spain, where the peasants assumed that Gertrude's corduroys were the habit of a religious order. Alice meanwhile 'always wore a black silk coat, black gloves and a black hat, the only pleasure I allowed myself were lovely artificial flowers on my hat'.

Still Harriet clung to Alice, and when they all got back to Paris after the 1908 trip, Alice and Harriet resumed apartment life together, despite heavy hints from Gertrude. In one of the 'word-portraits' Gertrude had begun to write of her acquaintances, there is a description of Harriet's indecision and failure to understand when Gertrude and Alice had pointedly asked her what were her plans for the summer: 'She said she did not have any plans for the summer. No one was interested in this thing in whether she had any plans for the summer. That is not the complete history of this thing, some were interested in this thing in her not having any plans for the summer . . .' Finally, when Harriet took a trip back to California, Alice sent her a message that there was little point in coming back to Paris, as she was moving in with Gertrude.

'And with that,' says Alice, 'I moved over to the rue de Fleurus.' Leo does not seem to have minded; he gave up his study so that she could have a bedroom. He was currently involved in a lengthy courtship of a much-bedded artist's model, Nina Auzias. He said he had no physical feelings for her, but regarded her as a 'psychological study', taking a voyeuristic interest in her sexual affairs. They were eventually married in 1921.

Leo sometimes wrote burlesques of his sister's word-portraits, but this was scarcely necessary, for the originals often seem to set out to parody themselves. For example this is what Gertrude has to say about Picasso:

This one always had something being coming out of this one. This one was working. This one always had been working. This one was always having something that was coming out of this one . . . *(etc.)*

Which is far less illuminating than her rough notes for the piece:

Do one about Pablo his emotional leap and courage as opposed to lack of courage in Cézanne and me. His laziness and lack of continuity and his facility too quick for the content. Too lazy to do sculpture . . .

Nevertheless the word-portraits are far more genuinely experimental than *The Making of Americans* – a real attempt at Cubism in prose. When some of them were published in Gertrude's *Tender Buttons* (1914), they excited a number of young writers who were hoping to struggle free from the constraints of nineteenth-century diction. Among these was the American novelist Sherwood Anderson, who says of his discovery of her prose: 'It excited me as one might grow excited in going out into a new and wonderful country where everything is strange.'

After the publication of *Tender Buttons*, the *New York Times* dubbed Gertrude a 'Cubist of Letters', and she was delighted by this growing fame, telling Mabel Dodge: 'I get awfully excited about the gloire.' Meanwhile she was enthusiastic about the Cubist movement in painting. It had virtually begun at 27 rue de Fleurus, for she and Leo had hung Picasso's drawings for *Les Demoiselles d'Avignon*, the movement's first important achievement. Indeed, Picasso may have painted the picture in jealous reaction to Gertrude's admiration for Matisse, since he said it was intended to present 'venal realities' rather than the 'bourgeois idyll' of Matisse's *Bonheur de Vivre*. But though Gertrude greatly admired *Les Demoiselles*, Leo thought it 'a horrible mess', and said he had only bought Picasso's 'Negroid things' in 'hopes of something better'. He and Picasso began to quarrel about Cubism. Gertrude says of this: 'I was alone at this time in understanding him [Picasso], perhaps because I was expressing the same thing in literature.'

*

By 1914, Gertrude had become a fixture of Parisian cultural life, a necessary port of call for visitors from England and the USA. She writes of her Saturday evening salons:

Roger Fry . . . brought Clive Bell . . . Very soon there were throngs of Englishmen, Augustus John and Lamb . . . Wyndham Lewis . . . a great many young Oxford men . . . Lady Cunard brought her daughter Nancy, then a little girl, and very solemnly bade her never forget this visit . . . There was Lady Ottoline Morrell looking like a marvellous feminine version of Disraeli . . . And everybody came and nobody made any difference. Gertrude Stein sat peacefully in a chair.

One American visitor from this period, Joseph Stella, has left a sardonic account of Saturday night in the rue de Fleurus:

Somehow in a little side street in Montparnasse there was a family that had acquired some early work of Matisse and Picasso. The lady of the house was an immense woman carcass, austerely dressed in black. Enthroned on a sofa in the middle of the room where the pictures were hanging, with the forceful solemnity of a sibylla, she was examining pitiless all newcomers, assuming a high and distant pose.

Yet she could be strikingly generous. An American architect-turned-painter, Manierre Dawson, was introduced to her one Saturday, and when she gathered he could not stay in Paris because his money was running out, she asked to see a painting he had with him, and offered 200 francs for it. It was his first ever sale.

Leo, still in arms against Cubism, had once attempted to dismantle the Saturday evenings when Gertrude and Alice were away in London. He wrote to her: 'A lot of Hungarians, Turks, Armenians & other Jews came here Saturday to celebrate your birthday but I told them it was the wrong day & beside there was no one at home.' The Saturday salon was reinstated on Gertrude's return, but a split appeared between brother and sister. Leo was irritated not just by her championship of Cubism (which he called 'tommyrot') and her word-portraits ('damned nonsense') but also by her all-too-apparent thirst for 'gloire'. The only feature of her life to which he had no apparent objection was Alice; he said her presence had been a 'godsend' since it allowed him and Gertrude to differ without explosions. He kept away from the Saturday evenings ('I would rather harbor three devils in my insides, than talk about art') and hinted that he would soon leave Paris for the Mediterranean. Gertrude's response was to write of the change in their relationship: 'Slowly and in a way it was not astonishing but slowly I was knowing that I was a genius and it was happening and I did not say anything . . . This thing of being a genius, there is no reason for it, there is no reason that it should be you and should not have been him . . .' Leo's moving-out from the rue de Fleurus, when it finally happened, was much like a divorce, with acrimonious notes being exchanged about money and the ownership of particular pictures, and he and Gertrude often not on speaking terms; Gertrude sent Alice a note: 'Your brother-in-law is still mad.'

Despite Leo's disclaimer, it seems likely that a deep-seated jealousy of Alice, and of Gertrude's settled relationship with her, was what really drove him out; conceivably he became an opponent of Cubism because it was an emblem of Gertrude's and Alice's world. He went to live for a time in Florence, spent the First World War in the USA, and then returned to Paris, but he and Gertrude had no subsequent communication with each other. Soon after the Armistice, she and Alice were passing along the Boulevard St Germain when they noticed a man doffing his hat to them. Gertrude bowed solemnly in reply. It was Leo. They never met again.

*

Friends wondered at Alice's impassivity; Mabel Dodge, asking her the source of her eternal calm, received the reply: 'My feeling for Gertrude.' Her facial expression became almost hangdog as the years passed, while Gertrude grew ever more self-confident. Yet Alice had a certain steely will with which she could successfully oppose Gertrude. When she sensed that Gertrude and Mabel Dodge were flirting with each other, she brought about a permanent rift between them; Mabel refers bitterly to Alice's 'successful effort in turning Gertrude from me'. In 1922 Ernest Hemingway and his wife found Alice far more forbidding than Gertrude: 'We liked Miss Stein and her friend, although the friend was frightening.' Robert McAlmon's wife, the writer Bryher, observes that everyone called Gertrude by her first name from the outset, but only the most intimate were permitted to address Alice as anything other than Miss Toklas.

Gertrude and Alice spent much of the First World War working for the American Fund for French Wounded, Gertrude learning to drive a Ford truck purchased with funds she had raised; in it they distributed supplies to hospitals. Her attempts to park the vehicle caused the only arguments ever publicly observed between her and Alice.

In the truck, which they christened 'Auntie' after an aunt of Gertrude's who 'always behaved admirably in emergencies and behaved fairly well most times if she was properly flattered', they toured much of France on official and semi-official missions, Gertrude readily cranking the heavy engine when it stalled (which was often). She greatly disliked maps, preferring to voyage into the unknown. 'We had a few adventures,' she writes (in the persona of Alice) in the *Autobiography*, 'we were caught in the snow and I was sure that we were on the wrong road and wanted to turn back. Wrong or right, said Gertrude Stein, we are going on . . .'

2

The Amazon entertains

Settling in Paris during the same period as Gertrude Stein was a woman whose biographer has called her 'unquestionably the leading lesbian of her time'.

Natalie Clifford Barney was born in Dayton, Ohio, in 1876, into a family whose extensive fortune came from the Dayton Railroad Car Works. Her interest in things French derived partly from a French-born great-aunt who had lived in Baltimore most of her life but absolutely refused to speak English. Natalie's mother, an amateur painter, took her to Paris for some years, where she attended a boarding school and learned perfect eighteenth-century French. The school was a little hotbed of feminine flirtation, and Natalie left it with an intense interest in her own sex.

During a later visit to Paris, in her early twenties, she fell in love with a celebrated courtesan, 'Liane de Pougy' (Anne-Marie Chassaigne), on whom she paid a call dressed as a Renaissance page-boy. Liane after-wards described their affair in a novel, *Idylle Sapphique* (1901), which tells how their first embraces took place in her own Louis Quinze bathroom. During another love affair, with the writer Renée Vivien, Natalie had herself delivered to her beloved in her nightgown, with her long golden hair undone, concealed in an enormous box of lilies.

She wrote poems in French and English about her affairs:

> How write the beat of love, the very throb
> The rhythm of our veins' deep eloquence?
> How fix that darkness-rending final sob,
> That perfect swoon of each united sense?

Her father caught her reading a love-letter from Liane, brought the affair to a close, and tried to marry Natalie off to various young men, including Lord Alfred Douglas, then fortune-hunting in the USA. When she published a book of verse-portraits of her *inamorata* in French, *Quelques Portraits-Sonnets des femmes* (1900), Mr Barney bought up the entire edition and destroyed it. But in 1902, when she was twenty-six, he died, leaving her $2½ million. She immediately set up home in Paris and began to live as she liked.*

In 1928 a young member of Natalie's circle, the American poet and novelist Djuna Barnes, wrote and had printed privately a chapbook in mock-Elizabethan style, complete with woodcuts, entitled *Ladies Almanack*. It satirises Natalie's love affairs and life-style, introducing her to the reader as 'as fine a Wench as ever wet Bed, she who was called Evangeline Musset and who was in her Heart one Grand Red Cross for the Pursuance, the Relief and the Distraction of Girls'. Evangeline causes her father much anxiety by becoming associated with 'the Duchess Clitoressa of Natescourt' (an allusion to Natalie's affair with Lily, Duchesse de Clermont-Tonnerre), and when he reproves her she

answered him High enough, 'Thou, good Governor, wast expecting a Son when you lay atop of your Choosing, why then be so mortal wounded when you perceive that you have your Wish? am I not doing after your very Desire, and is it not the more commendable, seeing that I do it without the Tools for the Trade, and yet nothing complain?

By the time 'Dame Musset' becomes 'a witty and learned Fifty', she is

wide famed for her Genius at bring up by Hand, and so noted and esteemed for her Slips of the Tongue that it finally brought her into the Hall of Fame, where she stood by a Statue of Venus as calm as you pleased, or leaned upon a lachrymal Urn with a small Sponge for such as Wept in her own Time and stood in Need of it.

The book is full of private jokes about Natalie's conquests, and gives some glimpses of her bedroom manner: 'It's a Hook, Girl, not a Button, you should know your Dress better.' Eventually 'Dame Musset' is canonised a saint, and at her death her tongue miraculously escapes combustion on the funeral pyre.

Natalie herself greatly enjoyed the joke; her own copy of *Ladies Almanack* is generously annotated.

*

She lived for a while near the Bois de Boulogne, in a little house with a garden. Colette describes an afternoon there, with the Barney 'set' staging a masque, during which Mata Hari appeared on a jewel-encrusted white horse. In 1909 Natalie moved to the Left Bank, taking

*One might suppose that she chose Paris because lesbianism was easier to practise in safety there than in the USA. But there do not seem to have been any prosecutions for lesbianism at this period in the USA, and the case of the poet Amy Lowell, who in 1914 openly set up home in New England with an actress, whom she addressed by a masculine name and to whom she wrote love poems, indicates that such ménages were tolerated there.

up residence in an elegant *pavillon* in the garden of 20 rue Jacob, near the Boulevard St Germain. One Friday in October that year, she gave the first salon in her new house, and almost every Friday from that time onwards, for more than half a century, she was 'at home' from tea-time to friends and guests.

The Friday salon may have been a little in imitation of Gertrude Stein's Saturday nights – Natalie Barney knew Gertrude, though no real friendship sprang up until the late 1930s when they became near neighbours. More obviously, the salon was modelled on receptions given by the French aristocracy. Today an undistinguished shopping street, in 1909 the rue Jacob still retained some of the style it had possessed in the seventeenth and eighteenth centuries, when it was the main thoroughfare of the Faubourg St Germain, the fashionable quarter for the nobility. Not that Natalie attempted to imitate aristocratic style; she filled the interior of her *pavillon* with miscellaneous and mostly undistinguished furniture and bric-à-brac, and allowed what one visitor called an 'eighteenth century patina of dust' to accumulate. Another visitor said it was so damp that oysters grew under the dining-room chairs. Natalie's friend Radclyffe Hall writes in *The Well of Loneliness* (in which Natalie appears as Valérie Seymour) of the 'large and rather splendid disorder' of the house:

There was something blissfully unkempt about it, as though its mistress were too much engrossed in other affairs to control its behaviour. Nothing was quite where it ought to have been, and much was where it ought not to have been, while over the whole lay a faint layer of dust – even over the spacious salon. The odour of somebody's Oriental scent was mingling with the odour of tuberoses in a sixteenth-century chalice. On a divan, whose truly regal proportions occupied the best part of a shadowy alcove, lay a box of Fuller's peppermint creams and a lute, but the strings of the lute were broken.

As for the exterior,

The courtyard was sunny and surrounded by walls. On the right . . . some iron gates led into the spacious, untidy garden, and woefully neglected though this garden had been, the trees that it still possessed were fine ones. A marble fountain long since choked with weeds, stood in the centre of what had been a lawn. In the farthest corner of the garden some hand had erected a semicircular temple.

This temple was said to have been a trysting place of the eighteenth-century actress Adrienne Lecouvreur, though in fact it only dated back to the early nineteenth century. An inscription on its pediment dedicated it *à l'amitié*, to friendship.

Natalie's Friday salon was held in the two drawing rooms on the ground floor of the *pavillon*. Tea was served, and what one habituée called 'little cucumber sandwiches like damp handkerchiefs'. Radclyffe

Hall describes Natalie receiving her guests 'dressed all in white, and a large white fox skin was clasped round her slender and shapely shoulders. For the rest she had masses of thick fair hair, which was busily ridding itself of its hairpins'. Another guest writes that she 'looked like a Mother Superior or an abbess' but 'laughed with great dignity'. By the end of the 1920s, says the same person, she had filled out 'and began to look like Benjamin Franklin'.

In warm weather, guests were encouraged to stroll in the garden. Natalie's friend and one-time lover Dolly Wilde (Oscar's niece) was once heard to say, on the subject of statuary, 'Oh, Natalie, you forgot to put the hermaphrodite in the bushes.'

The salon was frequented by French intellectuals as well as expatriates, and something of its atmosphere is caught by the *pensées* which Natalie began to write soon after moving to the rue Jacob:

The Romantics appropriated all the big words, leaving us only the little ones.

To those who ask, 'Have you read my book?', I reply, 'I have not yet read Homer.'

Twenty paces from me she was already preparing her face for a smile.

Truman Capote, who attended the salon in its final years, describes it as 'always very proper – talk about this concert or that concert, or so-and-so's paintings, or "Alice has a fabulous new recipe for eggs".' The only shocking thing Capote remembered was when Carl Van Vechten, the elderly American novelist, who had made himself the leading authority on Gertrude Stein, 'came to tea and peed on the sofa by mistake'.

Capote says that 'until you got into conversation with her', Miss Barney 'seemed like a very refined lady from Shaker Heights'. He notes that though the salon was 'not limited to lesbians', certainly 'all the more presentable dykes in town were on hand . . . Many of them were friends of Proust who had been characters in *Remembrances of Things Past* . . . Miss Barney would say to me very specifically that she wanted me to meet somebody because that person was so-and-so in Proust.' It is said that Proust himself had wished to meet her, to learn all about lesbianism. After many failures of nerve, he finally managed to get himself to 20 rue Jacob in the middle of the night (his invariable time for activity), but he lacked the courage to ask the right questions, and passed the visit in prattling about duchesses.

Proust knew of Natalie because by that time Remy de Gourmont had immortalised her as *l'Amazone*. De Gourmont had been the leading critic of the Symbolist movement, a co-founder of the *Mercure de France*; his books included *Physique de l'amour: essai sur l'instinct sexuel* (1904), which praises promiscuity and mocks monogamy. However, de Gourmont himself lived as a recluse, largely because he suffered from lupus, a severely disfiguring skin disease. He occupied a sixth-floor attic not far from rue Jacob, and though he would usually only receive close friends, Natalie was introduced to him by a French literary acquaintance. She immediately decided to take de Gourmont out of himself. He found her enchanting, and they began a lively friendship, during which he wrote love letters to her. She responded affectionately though not romantically. By December 1911 he had begun work on his *Lettres à l'Amazone*, for publication in the *Mercure*, the title being inspired by a sight of Natalie in riding costume on her way home from the Bois de Boulogne.

But it was a rather one-sided relationship, and after a while Natalie virtually dropped the old man. She was proud of the *Amazone* title, but she has little to say about him in her autobiography, *Souvenirs Indiscret*, and her abandonment of him may have contributed to his death in 1915.

*

When war broke out in 1914, Natalie Barney stayed on in the rue Jacob, behaved as if the war did not exist, continued her love affairs, and went on holding her Friday salon. During the war she became involved with Romaine Brooks, an American portrait painter who had settled in Paris. Though uncompromisingly masculine in appearance – as opposed to Natalie's feminine looks – Romaine was bisexual, and had had affairs with Lord Alfred Douglas, the Princesse de Polignac (née Singer), and Gabriele d'Annunzio. Djuna Barnes's 'Dame Musset' says of her that she 'dresses like a Coachman of the period of Pecksniff', and in a self-portrait she is wearing what appears to be an eighteenth-century coachman's hat and is carrying a whip. She and Natalie were lovers for a while, thereafter companions. Romaine's splendid paintings of their circle include one of Radclyffe Hall's lover, Una, Lady Troubridge, dressed in a wing collar and frock coat and wearing a monocle – a form of costume that became identified with 20 rue Jacob. (Truman Capote describes the Romaine Brooks paintings as 'all the famous dykes from 1880 to 1935 or thereabouts . . . wonderful'.)

Not everyone appreciated Natalie's contribution to Left-Bank life. The American journalist Morrill Cody judged her Fridays and Gertrude Stein's Saturdays as equally tiresome events. Being invited to either, he says, was 'considered quite an honor and part of one's education, but was really quite a bore'. On the other hand Ezra Pound, who began to correspond with Natalie shortly before the First World War, when he was translating one of Remy de Gourmont's novels for the *Egoist* in London, classed her as one of those people who get a great deal out of life, 'perhaps more than was in it'. And, like Gertrude Stein, she was expert at introductions. As Truman Capote observes, 'she was one of those people who is always trying to bring other people together'.

3

Sylvia and Company

Like Gertrude Stein and Natalie Barney, Sylvia Beach was introduced to Parisian life during childhood. She was the daughter of a Presbyterian minister from Bridgeton, New Jersey, who brought his family to Paris in 1902 for a three-year ministry to American students in the Latin Quarter. He held his Sunday evening services in a big studio in Montparnasse, and declared that the students, who had been misrepresented as 'unconscionable Bohemians', were really 'soberminded' and lived lives of 'privation and unselfish devotion to work'. Not surprisingly Sylvia, then aged fifteen, found that in her father's company it was impossible to get 'anywhere near the living Paris'.

After this, the Reverend Sylvester Beach was called back to New Jersey, to a ministry at Princeton, where the family settled. But, says Sylvia, 'we often went to France for visits or longer stays, sometimes the whole family, sometimes just one or two of us. We had a veritable passion for France.' She managed her first adult trip there when she was twenty, in the company of her mother, and came again on her own four years later. She hoped for some sort of literary career, but nothing materialised, and in 1916, when she was twenty-nine, she decided to settle in Paris and try to get work as a *journaliste littéraire*, the profession she had optimistically given on her passport.

At first she lived with a sister who was a successful film actress in France. She did war work from 1914 to 1918, on the land with the Volontaires Agricoles, and became clear in her mind about the future. 'When the war is over,' she wrote to her mother, 'if I'm not old and buried by that time, I must have a bookstore, I must... I could make a nice little bookshop in New York go, working up a certain regular clientele. Good English and American books and a supply of French and others. I should love it (all but being in N.Y.).' One day in Paris in 1917, in search of a book, she went to the rue de l'Odéon, a quiet side-street which led up from the Boulevard St Germain to the Odéon theatre and contained a number of specialist bookshops. One of these, which bore the name A. Monnier, displayed American literature in its window, so Sylvia opened the door and peered inside. At a table sat a young woman, presumably A. Monnier herself.

As I hesitated at the door, she got up quickly ... drawing me into the shop, [and] greeted me with much warmth. This was surprising in France, where people are as a rule reserved with strangers ... As I stood near the open door, a high wind suddenly blew my Spanish hat off my head and into the middle of the street, and away it went bowling. A. Monnier rushed after it, going very fast for a person in such a long skirt ... Then we both burst out laughing.

Something like a love affair quickly began.

Adrienne Monnier was twenty-five years old, an enthusiast of American books who had read almost everything that had been translated into French, beginning with the works of Benjamin Franklin. She had opened her bookshop with money paid to her father as compensation for injury in a railway accident. To save expense she lived in a room behind the shop. She ran a lending library as part of the business. Plump, dark, and handsome at the time that Sylvia met her, she soon became very solid-looking; the poet William Carlos Williams says she seemed like a farm labourer standing up to her knees in heavy loam.

Sylvia herself was no beauty, but had a striking, determined appearance; she was only 5 feet 2 inches high, but her firm chin gave her an air of self-confidence. One day she aroused the admiration of local urchins when she dived into the Seine fully clothed to rescue her parrot, which had escaped and been swept away by the backwash from a barge.

After a few months she moved in with Adrienne. She enjoyed the lively atmosphere of the shop; French writers were always dropping in for conversation, some of them in army uniform straight from the front, and in the evenings they would sometimes give readings from their latest work to members of the lending library. 'Crowded into the little shop,' writes Sylvia, 'and almost on top of the reader at his table, we listened breathlessly' – to Jules Romains, Paul Valéry, André Gide. 'I believe that I was the only American to discover the rue de l'Odéon and participate in its exciting literary life at the time.'

By the summer of 1919 Sylvia had changed her mind about setting up her own bookstore in New York; she decided to establish it in London instead, to be nearer Adrienne. But when she went to London, Harold Monro – who ran the Poetry Bookshop and published the Georgians – said there was no British market for a shop specialising in French literature, which was what Sylvia had intended. So she went back to Paris and determined to operate there instead, selling American and English books. Adrienne found premises for her just around the corner from rue de l'Odéon, at 8 rue Dupuytren, and Sylvia began to ransack Paris bookstores for everything from Walt Whitman to *Beowulf*. She got a sister in New York to forward her the American literary 'little magazines', among them the *Little Review*, which was serialising James Joyce's *Ulysses*, already widely regarded as the most exciting book of its generation. Her mother mailed her large photographs of Edgar Allan Poe, Ralph Waldo Emerson, and other giants of American literature, for display in the shop. More important, Mrs Beach also sent $3,000 to pay the first six months' rent.

Sylvia chose to decorate the shop in a Greenwich Village rather than French manner. She laid white woollen rugs on the floor and hung beige sackcloth over the rather tattered walls. For her own costume as manager she chose a velvet smoking jacket. She had thought of calling the shop 'The Little Book Club', but one night the name 'Shakespeare and Company' came into her head, and seemed perfect. She commissioned a friend to paint a signboard depicting Shakespeare, and – despite Adrienne's disapproval of so un-Parisian a proceeding – had it hung at right angles to the shop front, like an English pub sign. On the shutters were painted the words 'Lending Library' and 'Bookhop' *(sic)*, an error that Sylvia did not hurry to correct, feeling it rather appropriate to so dotty an enterprise.

It was certainly a risky venture, for English-language books were already plentifully available in Paris. The sheer quantity of bookstores in the city astonished one American visitor, Sherwood Anderson: 'In Paris there are as many bookstores as there were saloons in Chicago before prohibition. Imagine the 1st ward in Chicago with every saloon of the old days turned into a bookstore. The Latin Quarter here is like that.' Sylvia's hope was that Adrienne's literary friends would give her a good start.

Sure enough from opening day, Monday 17 November 1919, they began to turn up at Shakespeare and Company; the first was Louis Aragon. But though there was no shortage of interest, actual sales were another matter. Few Frenchmen in 1919 could afford to buy new foreign books, with prices translated into francs at a very unfavourable rate of exchange. Nor could Sylvia's lending library pay for itself, not least because it was conducted according to what Adrienne called *le plan américain*, that is, no plan at all; at first Sylvia did not even bother to keep a record of borrowers' addresses. Fortunately her mother was willing to continue subsidising the enterprise with her savings.

*

Though the lending library failed to make money, it quickly acquired dozens of subscribers. Natalie Barney was among the first, though Sylvia noticed that she only took out works by writers who were expected at her Friday salon, sending a chauffeur to the shop a day or two in advance. Gertrude Stein and Alice Toklas made their first visit to Shakespeare and Company about six months after it had opened, Gertrude paying 50 francs for a year's subscription to the library. Sylvia was 'very joyful over my new customers'. Gertrude borrowed about seventy volumes during her first two years of membership, but Sylvia felt that really 'she took little interest ... in any but her own books'.

However, Gertrude did present Sylvia with a poem she said was designed to attract attention to the shop; entitled 'Rich and Poor in English' and subtitled 'Sylvia Beach', it made no reference to Shakespeare and Company by name, and seemed of rather dubious value as advertising copy. It began:

> Not a country not a door send them away to sit on the floor.
> Cakes. This is not the world. Can you remember...

Sylvia was encouraged to appear at the Saturday-night salons at 27 rue de Fleurus, and she began to bring American writers to meet Gertrude, since they were often too nervous to approach her direct: 'So the poor things would come to me, exactly as if I were a guide from one of the tourist agencies.' Her first significant introduction to Gertrude was an author who arrived in Paris in June 1921. 'One day,' writes Sylvia, 'I noticed an interesting-looking man lingering by a book in the window... *Winesburg, Ohio*, which had recently been published in the United States. Presently he came in and introduced himself as the author.'

Then in his late forties, Sherwood Anderson had made his name with *Winesburg, Ohio* and with *Poor White* (1920), a novel about the corrupting effects of industrialisation on a rural community. He explained to Sylvia that he had 'suddenly abandoned his home and a prosperous paint business, had simply walked away one morning, shaking off forever the fetters of respectability and the burden of security'. Leaving his family, he had gone to Chicago to become a writer.

He had arrived there soon after the so-called Chicago Renaissance in American literature had got under way, centred on the offices of the magazine *Poetry*, with Harriet Monroe editing and Ezra Pound in London stirring up expatriate poets to contribute. Anderson met the *Poetry* set, which included Carl Sandburg and Vachel Lindsay who were trying to write distinctively Mid-Western poetry, and he was introduced to Margaret Anderson, who was just starting the *Little Review* in Chicago. He had already written some fiction, which he now reworked under the influence of Gertrude Stein's word-portraits. For days he carried around a notebook in which he experimented with new combinations of words. 'The result,' he says, was 'a new familiarity with the words of my own vocabulary...I really fell in love with words, wanted to give each word I used every chance to show itself off at its best.'

In Paris, Anderson explained to Sylvia Beach what Gertrude Stein meant to him, and asked if she would introduce them. The meeting took place and was highly successful, Gertrude being delighted by the homage of Anderson, the first successful American writer to say she had influenced him. After the tea party he wrote down his impressions of her in his own version of her style: 'A strong woman with legs like stone pillars sitting in a room hung thick with Picassos...She laughs, she smokes cigarettes. She tells stories with an American shrewdness in getting the tang and the kick into the telling.'

His second wife Tennessee, who was there too, tried to take part in the conversation with Gertrude, but in vain. 'Alice held her off,' says Sylvia. 'I knew the rules and regulations about wives at Gertrude's... Alice had strict orders to keep them out of the way.'

*

As a mark of their approval of her, Sylvia was sometimes invited for drives in the open-top car Gertrude and Alice had purchased after the First World War, and had named Godiva (Gody for short). 'Gertrude showed me Gody's latest acquisition – headlights that could be turned on and off at will from inside the car and an electric cigarette lighter. Gertrude smoked continuously...When a tyre blew out, she did the mending. Very competently too, while Alice and I chatted by the roadside.'

Meanwhile, news of Shakespeare and Company spread in American literary circles, 'and it was the first thing the pilgrims looked up in Paris...Many of them looked upon [it] as their club. Often, they would inform me that they had given Shakespeare and Company as their address, and they hoped I didn't mind.'

PART TWO

Being Geniuses Together

1

Melancholy Jesus

Eight months after the opening of the shop, on a hot Sunday afternoon in July 1920, Adrienne took Sylvia to a reception at an apartment in a side-street off Avenue Foch, near the Bois de Boulogne. Sylvia did not want to go; she had never met the host, a poet called André Spire, and she feared it would be a rather daunting gathering of literary types whose gossip would mean nothing to her. But Adrienne insisted.

When she arrived, Sylvia was relieved to spot several familiar faces from the hallway. There was Jenny Serruys, Paris agent for one of the New York publishers, and Madame Ludmilla Bloch-Savitsky, who had taken out a subscription to the Shakespeare and Company library. Also, Sylvia could see Ezra Pound and his English wife Dorothy – her maiden name was Shakespear – who had recently come to inspect the shop; they were passing through Paris on their way back to London after an Italian holiday.

No sooner had Sylvia begun to feel at her ease than the host whispered in her ear: 'The Irish writer James Joyce is here.' Sylvia, who had read *A Portrait of the Artist as a Young Man* and had been following *Ulysses* in the *Little Review*, was greatly alarmed. 'I worshipped James Joyce, and on hearing the unexpected news that he was present, I was so frightened that I wanted to run away.' However, Spire told her it was the Pounds who had brought Joyce and his wife. 'I knew the Pounds, so I went in.'

In the drawing room, there indeed was Pound, stretched out in a big armchair. 'His costume – the velvet jacket and the open-road shirt – was that of the English aesthete . . . There was a touch of Whistler about him; his language, on the other hand, was Huckleberry Finn.'

Sylvia struck up a conversation with Dorothy, who immediately introduced her to Joyce's wife, Nora. Sylvia thought Mrs Joyce charming and entirely natural – she said she was relieved that they could speak English together, since she knew no French and could not understand a word that was being said. 'Now if it had been Italian!' she exclaimed. The Joyces had lived for years in Trieste, and the whole family spoke Italian, even among themselves at home. They had been there for most of Joyce's self-imposed sixteen-year exile from Dublin earlier; he made such money as he could by giving English lessons. When the family had moved temporarily to Zurich during the First World War they still went on speaking Italian *en famille* – Joyce said it was the easiest language on the voice.

André Spire announced that everyone should take their place for lunch. Sylvia identified Joyce, and noticed that he refused all offers of wine, turning down his glass and saying he did not want to touch a drop until the evening. Pound responded facetiously by lining up all the wine bottles opposite Joyce's place; he knew how much Joyce drank when he was not abstaining. Joyce seemed distressed by all the attention.

Soon, the usual sort of talk about publishers and authors was under way, most of it in French. Sylvia felt out of her depth, so as soon as everyone got up from their places she escaped to a little back room, which was lined with books. But Joyce had had the same thought. He hated the false sophistication of literary salons. When someone took him to Natalie Barney's one Friday, he happened to observe that he 'couldn't bear Racine and Corneille'. Miss Barney responded icily: 'Don't you think that sort of remark shows something about the person who says it?' Joyce spent the rest of that evening trying to pretend he was not there.

Now, Sylvia found him drooping in a corner between two book-cases. 'Trembling, I asked: "Is this the great James Joyce?"

'"James Joyce," he replied.'

'We shook hands; that is, he put his limp, boneless hand in my tough little paw.'

She observed that he was

of medium height, thin, slightly stooped, graceful . . . His hands . . . were very narrow. On the middle and third fingers of the left hand, he wore rings, the stones in heavy settings. His eyes, a deep blue . . . were extremely beautiful. I noticed, however, that the right eye had a slightly abnormal look and that the right lens of his glasses was thicker than the left . . . On his chin was a sort of goatee . . . I thought he must have been very handsome as a young man.

He was now thirty-nine. Sylvia goes on:

His enunciation was exceptionally clear. His pronunciation of words such as "book" (bōo-k) and "look" (lōo-k) and those beginning with "th" was Irish . . . Otherwise there was nothing to distinguish his English from that of the Englishman. He expressed himself quite simply but, as I observed, with a care for the words and the sounds – partly . . . I believe, because he had spent so many years teaching English.'

She asked him about his recent adventures moving from Trieste. At Pound's recommendation he was going to try living in Paris. He hated travelling, but 'Mr Pound', as Joyce always called him, had done everything possible: arranged lodgings, found folding beds for the children, looked for a French translator. Mr Pound, said Joyce, was insistent that Paris would be a good deal cheaper than Trieste, and that the French and the expatriates could easily be persuaded to take an interest in Joyce's work.

Joyce then enquired: 'What do you do?' So Sylvia told him about the shop. Taking a small notebook out of his pocket and holding it very close to his eyes, he wrote down the name and address. 'He said he would come to see me.'

★

He did, the very next day. Sylvia was in the shop when 'Joyce came walking up my steep little street wearing a dark blue serge suit, a black felt hat on the back of his head, and, on his narrow feet, not so very white sneakers. He was twirling a cane... "Stephen Dedalus," I thought, "still has his ashplant."'

He stepped into Shakespeare and Company, peering at the photographs of writers, and sat down in the armchair beside Sylvia's desk. He explained to her that he had three problems: 'Finding a roof to put over the heads of four people; feeding and clothing them; and finishing *Ulysses*.' The first was the most pressing. Madame Bloch-Savitsky had lent them her apartment, but the lease expired in two weeks. As for money, would Sylvia look out for pupils who might want English lessons? He assured her he had a great deal of experience working for the Berlitz in Trieste, and he had given private lessons too. He could also teach German and Latin, even French. Would she send people to 'Professor Joyce'?

She asked about *Ulysses*: was he progressing all right? He answered: 'I am.' (She observes: 'An Irishman never says a plain "yes".') He was five episodes from the end. But several issues of the *Little Review* had already been confiscated by the US Post Office because passages in the novel were judged obscene; it looked as if complete suppression could not be far off. Joyce said it was all very alarming. He told Sylvia that he would keep her informed about it. Before he left the shop he joined the lending library.

He became a regular at the bookshop, and could often be found sitting by the desk, talking to Americans who drifted in. 'He obviously enjoyed the company of my compatriots,' writes Sylvia. 'He confided to me that he liked us and our language.' Sometimes she would find him waiting for her at the bookshop, listening attentively to a long tale her concierge was telling him. '"Melancholy Jesus," Adrienne and I used to call him.'

Sylvia introduced him to Sherwood Anderson, whose vacation in Paris was nearing its close. Anderson wrote of Joyce in his journal as 'a long, somewhat gloomy, handsome man with beautiful hands'. And of his works: 'Among all modern writers his lot has perhaps been the hardest and it may well be that his *Ulysses* is the most important book that will be published in this generation.'

In the informal atmosphere of Shakespeare and Company, Joyce alone was formal, 'excessively so', writes Sylvia. The French authors who sat around in the shop would address her and Adrienne by their first names, but Joyce seemed to be trying to set a good example with his 'Miss Monnier' and 'Miss Beach'. No one dared to call him anything but 'Mr Joyce'.

It appeared that he was sustaining himself and his family by borrowing from anyone who would lend. After a few weeks he received £2,000 as a gift from Harriet Shaw Weaver, his publisher in London, who had been contributing anonymously to his support for some time. With this, he took a flat on the Boulevard Raspail.

Soon after he had settled there, late in 1920, the expected prosecution against the *Little Review* for serialising *Ulysses* was launched by the New York Society for the Suppression of Vice. The case came to court the following February, and resulted in a conviction and fine for the editors, Margaret Anderson and Jane Heap; a prison sentence was staved off only because it was understood that no further episodes of Joyce's book would be printed in the magazine. Joyce came to tell Sylvia the news. He said to her: 'My book will never come out now.'

It occurred to her that something might be done. She asked: 'Would you let Shakespeare and Company have the honor of bringing out your *Ulysses*?'

Joyce, naturally, accepted the offer immediately and joyfully. Sylvia had absolutely no experience of printing or publishing, but Adrienne had been using a Dijon printer called Darantière to produce a series of reprints for her, and he now agreed to take on *Ulysses*, even though Sylvia warned him that there could be no question of paying his bill till the whole job was finished and the subscriptions could be collected. Adrienne gave her approval to the project.

At the beginning of April 1921, Joyce signed an agreement that Sylvia should order an edition of 1,000 copies of the book from Darantière; he would receive the very generous royalty of two-thirds of the net profits when it came out. He, Sylvia and Adrienne set off from the shop to celebrate. Joyce was in high spirits; he remarked that the concierge's son, who was playing on the steps, would one day be 'a reader of *Ulysses*'.

2

The fastest man on a typewriter

Sylvia dashed off an excited letter to her mother: 'Mother dear it's more of a success every day and soon you may hear of us as regular Publishers and of the most important book of the age...I'm going to publish "Ulysses" of James Joyce in October.' The French authorities were not likely to concern themselves about a literary work in English, even though an American court had judged it obscene, but the *Paris Tribune* (the European edition of the *Chicago Tribune*) speculated that if she published *Ulysses*, Sylvia Beach 'will not be allowed to return to America'.

Galley proofs of the early chapters started to arrive from Dijon, whereupon Joyce set to work on revisions so extensive (and expensive for Sylvia) that the book began to increase drastically in length, and the publication date had to be pushed back. Meanwhile, Sylvia and her friends collected subscriptions from anyone who came within reach, and Shakespeare and Company took on a girl to cope with the extra work. This young woman had a boyfriend studying at medical school in Paris, a Cambodian prince, and in honour of Joyce's work he changed his name to Ulysses.

In the midst of this, Sylvia moved the shop around the corner to rue de l'Odéon, Adrienne having found that the antique dealer at no. 12, opposite her own premises, was disposing of the lease. It was at this new shop, at Christmas 1921, that Sylvia noticed a young man standing in a corner, glancing through the magazines and looking at the adventure stories of Captain Marryat. She describes him as 'a tall, dark young fellow with a small mustache'.

Sylvia began to talk to him, trying to draw him out in her usual friendly way. She discovered that he did not have enough money in his pocket to join the lending library, so she told him he could pay the deposit when he liked, and meanwhile he could borrow as many books as he wanted. She wrote him out a member's card.

It was only now that she discovered that he had a letter of introduction to her from Sherwood Anderson, who was back in Chicago. He had been too shy to present it. 'I am writing this,' said the letter, to make you acquainted with my friend Ernest Hemingway, who with Mrs Hemingway is going to Paris to live, and will ask him to drop it in the mails when he arrives there.

Mr Hemingway is an American writer instinctively in touch with everything worth while going on here and I know you will find both Mr and Mrs Hemingway delightful people to know.

Sylvia asked the young man more about himself. All shyness now overcome, he explained that he had 'spent two years in a military hospital getting back the use of his leg'. What had happened to it? 'He had got wounded in the knee, fighting in Italy.' Would Sylvia care to see the wound? 'Of course I would. So business at Shakespeare and Company was suspended while he removed his shoe and sock.'

Ernest Miller Hemingway had only spent two months in hospital, not two years, and he had been a Red Cross orderly, not a soldier. Almost nothing Sylvia says he told her that day was true. Very likely she remembered everything wrongly, since her memoirs (in which she describes their talk) were written nearly forty years after the first conversation with Hemingway. Yet she showed him the text before publishing the book, so everything in it seems to have had his approval; and the things she quotes him as saying that day in 1921 are exactly the sort of stories he did tell about himself, to anyone who would listen.

She says he went on to explain that 'before he was out of high school' his father 'had died suddenly and in tragic circumstances leaving him a gun as sole legacy'. At this time, Dr Clarence E. Hemingway, MD, was very much alive and living in Oak Park, Illinois; he did eventually shoot himself, but not until 1928. Sylvia says Hemingway told her that his father's death had left him 'the head of the family' so that 'he had to leave school and begin making a living. He earned his first money in a boxing match, but, from what I gathered, didn't linger in this career. He spoke rather bitterly of his boyhood.'

This is complete invention; for a start, he had never supported his family. Certainly his parents did not get on – the father suffered terrible depressions and the mother seems to have had a lesbian affair – and Oak Park, Illinois, where his father practised medicine, was a stuffily respectable 'village' on the edge of Chicago; but a lot of Hemingway's time was spent at a family lakeside cottage in Michigan, where he learnt to fish, hunt, make shelters and build camp fires, and enjoy the wild. As to boxing, certainly he had taken up the sport while in high school, and thereafter would tell tales of having sparred with famous men of the ring, alleging that the poor vision in his left eye was due to their dirty tactics; but there is no evidence that he ever boxed against professionals in his youth, while the bad eyesight was inherited – other members of the family suffered from it. However, there was no stopping the boxing stories. This is another version, told by Hemingway to a Montparnasse barman, Jimmie Charters:

One Christmas his father presented him with a course of fifteen lessons at the local gym. The managers, who operated the business as a racket, insisted on payment in advance for all the lessons. When the candidate presented himself for the first workout, the instructors so beat, mauled and manhandled him that he rarely returned a second time. But Hemingway, as soon as he could stand up again comfortably, returned for more.

The sport that he really mastered in childhood, the skill that kept him going after he left school, was the telling of tall tales. At the age of five he was claiming to have stopped a runaway horse single-handed, and in his earliest recorded letter he describes making 'the largest catch of trout that has ever been made' in a certain stretch of water. A minor incident in his adolescence, when he got into trouble for shooting a heron, was elaborated by him into an account of how a couple of game wardens had pursued him all over Michigan; he had been lucky, he said, not to be sent to reform school.

'He didn't tell me much about his life after he left school,' says Sylvia. 'He earned his living at various jobs, including newspaper work, I believe, then went over to Canada and enlisted in the armed forces. He was so young he had to fake his age to be accepted.' Again, this is largely invention. Hemingway's father wanted him to have a university education, but his son, impatient for a taste of city life, went off to live with an uncle in Kansas City, where he was allowed to do some cub reporting on one of the daily newspapers. He aspired to be like another journalist on the paper, whom he described as being able to

carry four stories in his head and go to the telephone and take a fifth and then write all five at full speed to catch an edition ... If any other man was getting more money he quit or had his pay raised. He never spoke to the other reporters unless he had been drinking. He was tall and thick and had long arms and big hands. He was the fastest man on a typewriter I ever knew.

When America entered the war in 1917, the eighteen-year-old Ernest Hemingway did not go to Canada nor enlist – he was judged unfit for active service on account of his eyesight – but it is perfectly true that he was determined to go to war. 'I can't let a show like this go on without getting into it,' he wrote to his family. 'I'll make it to Europe.' He enrolled in the Red Cross and soon found himself in Paris. The Germans were just then bombarding the capital with their long-range gun, Big Bertha, and the delighted Hemingway and a friend rushed about the city in taxis in the hope of seeing the shells actually fall. Then they went to Italy and worked in an ambulance unit, but Hemingway was soon grumbling: 'There's nothing here but scenery and too damn much of that.' He decided to 'find where the war is'.

He managed to get posted to a canteen near the front line in the Piave district, and a few days before his nineteenth birthday he was up at the front itself – where he had no right to be – distributing chocolate and cigarettes in a forward observation post, when he was hit by shrapnel from an enemy shell. The most plausible account of what happened next comes in his novel *A Farewell to Arms* (1929), where the American lieutenant Frederic Henry, serving with an ambulance corps, undergoes just such an experience:

I tried to breathe but my breath would not come ... I tried to move but I could not move ... I heard close to me someone saying, 'Mama mia! Oh, mama mia!' I pulled and twisted and got my legs loose finally and turned around and touched him ... His legs were towards me and I saw in the dark and the light that they were both smashed above the knee ... [He] was quiet now ... I made sure he was dead ... My legs felt warm and wet and my shoes were wet and warm inside. I knew that I was hit and leaned over and put my hand on my knee. My knee wasn't there. My hand went in and my knee was down on my shin. I wiped my hand on my shirt and ... I looked at my leg and was very afraid. Oh, God, I said, get me out of here. I knew, however, that there had been three others ... Someone took hold of me under the arms and somebody else lifted my legs.

'There are three others,' I said. 'One is dead ...'
'Hold onto my neck, Tenente [Lieutenant]. Are you badly hit?'
'In the leg ...'
A shell fell close and they both dropped to the ground and dropped me ...
'You sons of bitches,' I said.
'I am sorry, Tenente,' Manera said. 'We won't drop you again.'

Hemingway was sent to the Red Cross hospital at Milan, and at once stories began to circulate of his bravery. A friend who visited him in hospital wrote to the Hemingway parents:

The concussion of the explosion knocked him unconscious and buried him in earth. There was an Italian [who] ... was killed instantly, while another ... had both his legs blown off. A third Italian was badly wounded and this one Ernest, after he had regained consciousness, picked up on his back and carried to the first aid dugout. He says he did not remember how he got there, nor that he carried the man, until the next day, when an Italian officer told him all about it and said that it had been voted to give him a valor medal for the act.

He was indeed awarded the Medaglia d'Argento al Valore (Silver Medal for Valour), but the official citation made no mention of his carrying a wounded man. Its description of his behaviour is more like that of Frederic in *A Farewell to Arms*; it states:

Gravely wounded by numerous pieces of shrapnel from an enemy shell, with an admirable spirit of brotherhood, before taking care of himself, he rendered generous assistance to the Italian soldiers more seriously wounded by the same explosion and did not allow himself to be carried elsewhere until after they had been evacuated.

And in the novel, Frederic even denies that he performed this small piece of heroism:

'Didn't you carry anybody on your back? Giordini says you carried several people on your back but the medical major at the first aid post declared it is impossible. He has to sign the proposition for the citation.'
  'I didn't carry anybody. I couldn't move.'
  'That doesn't matter,' said Rinaldi...'I think we can get you the silver. Didn't you refuse to be medically aided before the others?'
  'Not very firmly.'

The real-life Hemingway was not so modest. Though others may have invented the carrying-a-man story, he was glad to give it credence. A letter to his parents from hospital in July 1918 alleged that he had '227 wounds', including 'bullets' in both knees, and a month later he was telling them the story about carrying the wounded man:

I...got my wounded into the dug out...The Italian I had with me bled all over my coat and my pants looked like somebody had made currant jelly in them...They couldn't figure out how I had walked 150 yards with a load with knees shot through and my right shoe punctured two big places. Also over 200 flesh wounds. 'Oh,' says I, 'My Captain, it is of nothing. In America they all do it!'*

A British officer who met Hemingway soon after he was discharged from hospital was given the impression that he had been wounded 'leading Arditi troops on Monte Grappa'.
  As soon as he could manage it, Hemingway put together a hero's uniform for himself – a Sam Browne belt, an Italian officer's cape, a brown tunic with a 'wound stripe' on the sleeve, elegant calf-length military boots – and began a romance with the hospital's most glamorous nurse. He was filmed for an American newsreel sitting in a wheelchair with her at his side. She wrote to him as 'My hero', and he observed: 'It does give you an awfully satisfactory feeling to be wounded.' She was an American, eight years older – it was still only a few weeks since he had turned nineteen – and she did not sleep with him; afterwards she said that they had both been 'very innocent'.

---

* Astonishingly, the carrying-a-man story has been accepted without question by most of Hemingway's biographers, though Michael Reynolds exposes it in *The Young Hemingway* (1986).

However, Hemingway was soon telling tales of amatory exploits. Shortly before returning to the USA he set off to join a friend for a holiday in Sicily, but alleged that he never got there because *en route* the proprietress of a small hotel had hidden all his clothes and detained him in her bedroom for a week. In another version, he claimed that her irate soldier husband had challenged him to a duel.

He got back to New York in January 1919, and was treated as a hero. A reporter recorded admiringly that there were '227 wounds' on his legs, and said he had 'defied the shrapnel of the Central Powers' more than 'any other man, in or out of uniform'. This journalist was also given the impression that he had spent the weeks leading up to the Armistice fighting in the vicinity of Monte Grappa. Considering that from Hemingway's native Oak Park alone, some 2,500 young men had gone to the war, and fifty-six of them had been killed on active service, it was a feat to attract such attention.

He returned to Oak Park and paraded his uniform: a photograph shows him on the sidewalk in his officer's cape and boots, leaning on a cane. He told the local War Memorial Committee that he had been a first lieutenant in the Italian Army and had fought in three major battles. Later, in a 1924 short story, 'Soldier's Home', he wrote candidly about his behaviour during these months. He explains that he had found that 'to be listened to at all he had to lie', because 'his town had heard too many atrocity stories to be thrilled by actualities'. His lies 'were quite unimportant lies and consisted in attributing to himself things other men had seen, done or heard of, and stating as facts certain apocryphal incidents familiar to all soldiers'. The truth was that he had hardly experienced the war at all.

He had a signet ring set with a piece of shrapnel from his leg, and showed it to the kids of Oak Park. He wrote daily to his nurse, but she wrote back from Italy that she had fallen in love with a handsome Neapolitan. Hemingway claimed that when he heard this he 'set out to cauterize her memory and I burnt it out with a course of booze and other women and now it's gone'. In fact at the age of nineteen he scarcely drank – Prohibition was in any case coming into force – and he seems to have had no sexual experience yet beyond 'petting'. He had, however, developed a terror of homosexuality; he writes in *A Moveable Feast* of his feelings about it as a teenager:

I knew it was why you carried a knife and would use it when you were in the company of tramps when you were a boy ... When you were a boy and moved in the company of men, you had to be prepared to kill a man, know how to do it and really know that you would do it in order not to be interfered with ... If you knew you would kill, other people sensed it very quickly and you were let alone.

He also spoke of 'the old man with beautiful manners and a great name' who had visited him in hospital in Italy, 'and then one day I would have to tell the nurse never to let that man into the room again'.

*

While convalescing at his parents' home he began writing short stories, sending them to the *Saturday Evening Post* and the other popular papers. There was no question of trying to be a serious author; at nineteen, he simply wanted to make a name for himself and a lot of money. Also, the stories allowed him to live out his fantasies without fear of being called a liar.

One of the pieces he wrote a little before his twentieth birthday, 'The Mercenaries', describes an American army officer, Perry Graves, getting involved with the wife of the Italian ace pilot, Il Lupo, of whom the narrator says: 'Any school boy can tell the number of his victories and the story of his combat with Baron Von Hauser, the great Austrian pilot. How he brought Von Hauser back alive to the Italian lines, his gun jammed, his observer dead in the cockpit.' It is the usual boys' adventure stuff. Graves is found by Il Lupo having breakfast with his wife, and Il Lupo challenges him to a duel: 'You won't fight me. You dirty dog, I'll cut you down!' Graves takes over the narration:

If he killed me at that three foot range with his gun I would take him with me. He knew it too, and he started to sweat. That was the only sign. Big drops of sweat on his forehead... 'Una!' said the waiter. I watched the Lupo's hand. 'Dua!' and his hand shot up. He'd broken under the strain and was going to fire and try and get me before the signal. My old gat belched out and a big forty-five bullet tore his out of his hand as it went off. You see, he hadn't never heard of shooting from the hip... I shoved my gun into the holster and got my musette bag and started for the door, but stopped at the table and drank my coffee standing. It was cold, but I like my coffee in the morning.

The *Saturday Evening Post* expressed no interest, and another magazine advised Hemingway to try writing from real experience instead. But at nineteen he did not want to. He had been trying to turn his own life into the stuff of a thriller or a dime novel, so he had no wish to be truthful in his writing. Quite apart from this, he had read scarcely any good modern fiction and knew almost nothing worth imitating other than Jack London's *The Call of the Wild* (1903).

He was also labouring to get out from under a considerable family repression. When his mother discovered that he had been assigned Jack London's novel in his freshman year at high school, she went before the School Board to protest that 'no Christian gentleman should read such a book'. His father, meanwhile, was quoted in a local newspaper on the necessity of the adolescent 'choosing active Christian associates' and avoiding all temptations, 'since each step in self-control lends additional strength and beauty to the character'.

*

After a while, Hemingway drifted to Toronto and found a sinecure as companion to the son of a wealthy family. He began to hang about the office of the weekly *Toronto Star*, trying to impress people with stories of his experiences as a Kansas City newsman and his war heroics. Eventually they agreed to print some pieces by him, mostly feature articles about prizefighters, bootleggers, and suchlike. A little later, during 1920, he shifted to Chicago, still wearing his Italian officer's cape, and found a job of sorts editing a journal for the Co-operative Society of America. A friend gave him a room rent-free in an apartment while he waited for something better to come along.

Among the crowd that hung about in the apartment was Elizabeth Hadley Richardson, aged twenty-nine, eight years Hemingway's senior. Her father had shot himself when she was a child, and she had inherited a substantial sum of money, invested in a trust fund from which she drew an income. Hadley, as she called herself, was good-looking in a rather masculine way; a friend describes her as 'rather on the square side, vigorously muscular...a natural-born "hiker"'. (This is the type to which Hemingway was attracted throughout his life; for example, Maria in *For Whom the Bell Tolls* (1940), the most passionately described of all his heroines, has cropped hair and looks like a boy.)

By 1921, Chicago was nearing the end of its much-vaunted literary renaissance. Vachel Lindsay and Carl Sandburg were still producing new work there, but other Chicago successes, Ring Lardner among them, had gone East. The *Little Review* had moved to New York, as had another more heavyweight Chicago literary journal, the *Dial*, and *Poetry* had gone into a decline. However, Sherwood Anderson was still there, at the height of his fame, and Hemingway was befriended by him.

Anderson's Gertrude-Stein-influenced style and his facility for writing about tough but credible people certainly impressed Hemingway when he read Anderson's *Winesburg, Ohio* – a set of stories about small town life. He was more affected, though, by Anderson's paternalistic advice about how to succeed in the literary life. After getting to know Anderson he began to realise that there were other ways of being a writer besides churning out sensational stuff for the magazines. Anderson introduced him to the work of Mark Twain and Edgar Allan Poe and made him leaf through *Poetry* and the *Dial*. He met Carl Sandburg and began to write his own Chicago-style free verse. It was unremarkable – 'Cover my eyes with your pinions / Dark bird of

night...' – and both *Poetry* and the *Dial* rejected it, but it was a step
forward from Il Lupo.

Hemingway had also discovered the novels of Joseph Conrad, which
showed him that high adventure and fine writing could be combined. In
the few weeks in which he and Sherwood Anderson saw each other
early in 1921, Anderson reinforced this and persuaded him that slick
popular fiction was bound to be junk, because the characters had to
do and say things that no human being had ever really done or
said. Anderson believed that the modernist movement in literature –
especially Gertrude Stein – was not just high art, but really did hold
opportunities for fame and commercial success.

But though the prospect of being a serious writer appealed to
Hemingway, there seemed to be no material on which he could work,
and the short stories he wrote in Chicago were almost as juvenile as his
earlier attempts. One of them, 'The Current', written in June 1921 just
before his twenty-second birthday, is narrated by Stuyvesant Byng, a
man at whom women invariably look 'with more than approbation'.
Byng proposes to Dorothy Hadley, whose hair is 'the raw gold color of
old country burnished copper kettles, and it held all the firelight and
occasionally flashed a little of it back' (Hadley Richardson was a
redhead). She laughs 'tinklingly, like the chiming of one of those
Chinese wind bells', and tells Stuyvesant

'You're inconstant... You play a good game of polo. But you never would
stick to it. One year you were runner-up at the National Open. The next year
you didn't enter. You play lots better polo than at least two internationalists
that I know... But you're not a sticker, Stuy.'... She stroked his arm again.

She goes on: 'Pick something out and make an absolute, unqualified
success of it... And then you can come and ask me again.' He answers:
'By Gad... I'll do it.' Following the advice of his 'best pal', he becomes
a professional boxer, under the name of 'Slam Byng, the Hoboken
Horror'. In the ring he learns 'what it was to take punishment and to be
hit hard and often', and eventually comes up against the notorious Ape
McGibbons – 'either of his hands carried the deadly knockout poison'.
Dorothy takes a ringside seat for their fight; Byng is nearly beaten by
the Ape, but feels that 'there was a current somewhere. He must go
with the current. That was all that mattered, the steady current. The
current that made things move.' (The Gertrude-Stein influence, filtered
through Anderson, is evident, though Hemingway is already imposing
his own cadences on it.) At the last moment Byng 'crashed on the Ape's
jaw with the force of a pile driver', and after the knockout Dorothy
rushes up to him: '"Oh Stuy!" she sobbed. "You're so homely and
beautiful with your smashed bloody face."'

Hadley Richardson thought the story 'the most wonderfully keen and superbly done thing'. Underneath the crass writing there is certainly a good idea for a plot, but one more suited to P. G. Wodehouse than an apprentice Conrad.

*

Hemingway and Hadley were married in September 1921. Shortly afterwards, Sherwood Anderson came back from the Paris trip on which Sylvia Beach had introduced him to Gertrude Stein, and told Hemingway that Paris was *the* place for serious writers. The financial exchange rate was amazingly favourable, and there was a good cheap hotel in the rue Jacob, right in the middle of everything. Hemingway, who had wanted to get back to Europe ever since the war, needed no further persuasion.

He decided that Hadley had enough money to keep them both above poverty level, and he persuaded the *Toronto Star* to agree to take some European reports from him. They sailed for France soon before Christmas 1921, armed with several letters of introduction from Anderson. Arriving in Paris, they followed his advice and took a room in the Hôtel Jacob. 'Well here we are,' Hemingway wrote to Anderson. 'And we sit outside the Dôme Café, opposite the Rotonde that's being redecorated, warmed up against one of those charcoal braziers… Anyway we're terrible glad we're here.'

3

No fat, no adjectives, no adverbs

Hemingway told Sylvia Beach he had a job as 'sports correspondent' for the *Toronto Star*, and he took her and Adrienne Monnier to a boxing match in Montmartre, commentating on the boxers' tactics with professional expertise. But he had no such job; the *Star* had merely agreed to take anything he sent them. His time was entirely his own, and with Hadley paying the bills he wanted to concentrate on learning to write really well. In *A Moveable Feast* he recalls how he would tell himself: 'All you have to do is write one true sentence. Write the truest sentence that you know.' Sherwood Anderson and the rejection slips from the *Saturday Evening Post* had finally persuaded him to get away from sensationalism.

Anderson's French translator Lewis Galantière found the Hemingways an apartment on the Left Bank, at 74 rue du Cardinal Lemoine, and they moved in at the beginning of January 1922. It was in the district where Rodolphe lives in *Scènes de la Bohème*. Hemingway called it the 'best part' of the Latin Quarter, but it was about ten blocks from the St Germain–St Michel area and on the extreme eastern edge of the *Quartier*. Rue du Cardinal Lemoine was a dark, windswept, narrow street running steeply down from the slightly sinister Place de la Contrescarpe towards the river, which could not be seen from it. There was an unpleasantly smelly workmen's café in the square, and a cheap *bal musette* (dance hall) stood just below the apartment. Hemingway was irritated by the noise of the accordion.

He called the apartment 'a high grade place', but it was very Spartan. There was no hot water, and he and Hadley had to use a communal 'squatter' toilet on the stairs, which emptied into a downstairs cesspool that could be smelt all through the building. Hemingway remembered that Sherwood Anderson in Chicago had rented a hotel room for his writing, away from domestic life, so he followed suit and took a garret in a shabby hotel in the rue Mouffetard, just beyond the Place de la Contrescarpe. (He alleged, on inaccurate evidence, that it was 'the hotel where Verlaine had died'.) On days when the garret proved too cold to be endured – it was a particularly bone-chilling January – he migrated to the bustling centre of the Latin Quarter, to 'a good café that I knew on the Place St-Michel'.

Here, 'I hung up my old waterproof on the coat rack to dry and put my worn and weathered felt hat on the rack above the bench and ordered a *café au lait*'. (This is the old Hemingway writing in the 1950s about the young Hemingway, in *A Moveable Feast*.) 'The waiter brought it and I took out a notebook from the pocket of the coat and a pencil and started to write. I was writing about up in Michigan . . .'

He had begun a short story called 'Up in Michigan' a few months earlier. It was about a young waitress's feelings for a blacksmith, and its style was derived from Sherwood Anderson, hence from Gertrude Stein:

Liz liked Jim very much. She liked it and the way he walked over from the shop and often went to the kitchen door to watch for him to start down the road. She liked it about his moustache. She liked it about how white his teeth were when he smiled. She liked it very much that he didn't look like a blacksmith. She liked it how much D. J. Smith and Mrs Smith liked Jim. One day she found that she liked it the way the hair was black on his arms and how white they were above the tanned line when he washed up in the washbasin outside the house. Liking that made her feel funny.

Gertrude Stein had used the 'insistence' technique non-naturalistically, choosing for repetition words that seemed irrelevant or unimportant, but Hemingway was identifying the element of 'insistence' in real speech, the fact that people repeat the same word rather than search for a synonym. This substantiates his claim that he was trying to achieve 'one true sentence' – but only this, for in every other respect 'Up in Michigan' is thoroughly artificial and non-naturalistic. An incantatory manner has replaced the wham-bam narrative style of the Stuyvesant Byng and Il Lupo stories, and a carefully contrived syntax is being developed, on the principle of 'unpacking' the sentence's meaning piece by piece rather than compressing its ideas or fitting them together.* Meanwhile the subject matter remains the same as in the juvenilia – the worship of he-man masculinity:

The boards were hard. Jim had her dress up and was trying to do something to her. She was frightened but she wanted it. She had to have it but it frightened her.

'You mustn't do it, Jim. You mustn't.'

'I got to. I'm going to. You know we got to.'

'No we haven't, Jim. Oh, it's so big and it hurts so. You can't. Oh, Jim. Jim. Oh.'

* I owe this observation, and much of what I have to say about Hemingway's style, to some very shrewd suggestions by Ian Smith.

In the café on the Place St Michel, with the students and tourists of the Latin Quarter wandering around him, Hemingway 'was writing about up in Michigan and since it was a wild, cold, blowing day it was that sort of day in the story . . . In the story the boys were drinking and this made me thirsty and I ordered a rum St James. This tasted wonderful on the cold day and I kept on writing . . .' Later, after he had drunk more rum, 'the story was writing itself and I was having a hard time keeping up with it'. (It required far more effort than this suggests; his notebooks from this period are full of false starts and deletions.) Some days, rather than go out to the café, he would light a fire in the hotel room. 'I had a bottle of kirsch . . . and I took a drink of kirsch when I would get towards the end of a story or towards the end of the day's work.' Alcohol was very cheap, thanks to the exchange rate. 'I get rum for 14 francs a bottle,' he wrote to friends in Prohibition-ridden America. 'I'm drinking Rum St James now with rare success.' He also tried out 'an Absinthe, they call it by another name, but it is the Genuwind'.*

★

One of Sherwood Anderson's letters of introduction was to Gertrude Stein. It took Hemingway two months to pluck up courage to deliver it to 27 rue de Fleurus, but eventually he managed it, and an invitation came for him and Hadley to call.

Gertrude Stein writes: 'I remember very well the impression I had of Hemingway that first afternoon. He was an extraordinarily good-looking young man . . . rather foreign-looking, with passionately interested, rather than interesting eyes.' For his part, Hemingway found Gertrude and Alice 'very cordial and friendly', and he and Hadley 'loved the big studio with the great paintings . . . and it was warm and comfortable and they gave you good things to eat and tea and natural distilled liqueurs made from purple plums, yellow plums or wild raspberries'.

Gertrude did most of the talking. Hemingway, despite having his tongue loosened a little by the liqueurs, was very shy. He listened while

---

*It wasn't; it was Pernod, which had been marketed when the genuine absinthe was banned in France in 1915. Absinthe was flavoured with wormwood (*Artemisia absinthium*), and this herb came to be considered the cause of the mental afflictions and paralysis which were supposedly caused by the drink, though the high alcohol content (68 per cent) was more probably responsible. True absinthe was served in an aperitif glass accompanied by a lump of sugar in a perforated spoon through which iced water was dripped to dilute it. John Glassco, who drank it in Luxembourg in 1928, said that its effect was 'as gentle and insidious as a drug: in five minutes the world was bathed in a fine emotional haze unlike anything resulting from other forms of alcohol'. On the other hand Nina Hamnett said it was 'horrible . . . reminded me of cough drops'.

It is tempting to speculate whether Hemingway developed his characteristic style by writing when he was mildly drunk. Certainly it comes particularly alive when the reader is in that state himself.

she 'talked all the time and at first it was about people and places'. She spoke of Sherwood Anderson, and he was amused that she had nothing to say about Anderson's writing; she spoke only of his 'great, beautiful, warm, Italian eyes'. Then the subject of Joyce and *Ulysses* came up, and Hemingway asked her opinion. She would say nothing about *Ulysses* itself, but made some caustic observations about Joyce's constant demands for money: 'The damned Irish, they have to moan about something or other, but you never heard of an Irishman starving.'

Sylvia Beach explains that Gertrude 'was disappointed in me when I published *Ulysses*; she even came with Alice to my bookshop to announce that they had transferred their membership to the American Library on the Right Bank. I was sorry, of course, to lose two customers all of a sudden, but one mustn't coerce them.' Since *The Making of Americans*, which Gertrude regarded as her own modernist masterpiece, had yet to find a publisher, her jealousy of Joyce was understandable. Hemingway formed the impression that a visitor to rue de Fleurus who brought up Joyce's name with any frequency would not be invited back.

Hadley had the worst of the tea party since she was only allowed to talk to Alice, who poured the tea and liqueurs, worked away at a piece of needlepoint, and, says Hemingway, 'made one conversation and listened to two and often interrupted the one she was not making'. But it was Hadley who had the courage to press a return invitation on Gertrude and Alice.

So the two ladies took a taxi up the hill to the top of rue du Cardinal Lemoine, went in past the dance hall, and climbed the stairs above the cesspool. Gertrude comments only slightly sardonically in *The Autobiography of Alice B. Toklas* that Hemingway 'has always a very good instinct for finding apartments in strange but pleasing localities'.

Hadley served refreshments, and Hemingway diffidently showed Gertrude some of his writing. She looked at the poems he had recently written and said she rather liked them; she called them 'direct, Kiplingesque'. She also glanced through a novel he had begun, and this time she was discouraging. 'There is a great deal of description in this,' she told him, 'and not particularly good description. Begin over again and concentrate.' He also fetched from a drawer the manuscript of 'Up in Michigan'. She thought this was much better than the novel – it was, after all, an imitation of her own style – but she was displeased by the sex scene, or at least she thought he would never be able to publish it: 'It is like a picture that a painter paints and then cannot hang it.'

Gertrude and Alice went home, and Hemingway wrote to Sherwood Anderson that his letter of introduction had borne fruit; he did not mention the criticisms: 'Gertrude Stein and me are just like brothers and we see a lot of her.'

*

There still remained one of Anderson's letters to send out, to Ezra Pound. Anderson had explained to Hemingway that Pound was influential: he had been responsible for much of the early success of *Poetry*. But Hemingway was suspicious of what he had heard. Eventually he sent off the letter, and received an invitation to the Pounds' studio at 70 *bis* rue Notre Dame des Champs, a side-street much favoured by painters, near the Dôme café in Montparnasse.

They had settled in Paris the previous spring, Pound having written off London as 'waterlogged'. Until Christmas he and Dorothy had been living in a hotel, and though they now had the studio it was sparsely furnished; Hemingway noted that it was 'as poor as Gertrude Stein's studio was rich'. Pound had made most of the furniture himself with a hammer and nails, and the tea table was a packing-case with a cloth spread over it. But there were paintings by a Japanese protégé of Pound's, and also pictures by Dorothy, who painted in the Vorticist style of the Wyndham Lewis group.

Tea was served in the English manner. Hadley, who came too, thought that even 'low-voiced words seemed a little presumptuous' during the tea-ceremony, and was overawed by Dorothy's very British reserve. But Pound swallowed cup after cup, sprawling in one of his vast, canvas-bottomed, home-made chairs and pontificating noisily on one subject after another while Hemingway listened rather resentfully. He was irritated by Pound's absurd clothes, a stage bohemian outfit including beret and painter's smock that seemed to be based on Whistler's Latin Quarter garb of half a century earlier. He was every bit the poseur Hemingway had expected.

Yet there were several similarities between them. Like Hemingway, Pound had fled from a conventional 'village' on the edge of a big American city (in his case Philadelphia), and from the restraints of a strictly Christian home. Also, again like Hemingway, he was apt to make grandiose claims for himself, which the facts did not altogether support.

Fourteen years Hemingway's senior, he had fled to Europe at the age of twenty-two and had arrived in London in 1908 with a small book of privately printed poems, florid imitations of the troubadours, Browning, and the Celtic Twilight. On this slender literary base he had quickly erected a considerable reputation, achieved largely through his vivid appearance and brashly self-confident public manner. *Punch* was soon caricaturing him as the most comic creature on the literary scene since Oscar Wilde.

Just as Hemingway had sought out Sherwood Anderson and Gertrude Stein, so in 1908 Pound had sat at the feet of W. B. Yeats and Ford Madox Ford. Sensing that a poetic revolution was in the air, without having much idea what form it should take, in 1912 he had invented what he called the Imagist school of poetry, appointing himself its leader. Such acolytes as 'H.D.' (Hilda Doolittle), Richard Aldington, and Amy Lowell were soon writing *vers libre* under his instruction, dutifully pruning away all but the barest statements of images, and allowing him to blue-pencil out their more florid phrases. At the same time he became a long-distance huckster for *Poetry* in Chicago, and found for its editor, Harriet Monroe, such unknown poets as D. H. Lawrence, Robert Frost, and William Carlos Williams. But he was strikingly jealous when Miss Monroe began to discover some first-rate talent on her own doorstep, in the form of Vachel Lindsay, Carl Sandburg, and other members of the 'Chicago School', and he showed his resentment quite openly. He next devoted all his showman's energy to the promotion of the then unknown James Joyce, whom he discovered in 1913, when Joyce was languishing in Trieste unable to get *A Portrait of the Artist as a Young Man* into print. Pound found publishers for it, and persuaded the *Little Review* to serialise *Ulysses* four years later as soon as Joyce had begun to write it. But when everyone else started to take up Joyce – as was now happening in Paris – Pound backed away, and became almost as resentful about the fuss over *Ulysses* at Shakespeare and Company as was Gertrude Stein. He and Gertrude, though, were openly hostile to each other: she dismissed him tartly as a 'village explainer', and he dubbed her 'an old tub of guts'.

His next one-man discovery after Joyce had been T. S. Eliot, whose 'The Love Song of J. Alfred Prufrock' he had persuaded *Poetry* to print after he had met Eliot in London in 1914. Since then, he and Eliot had worked closely together at the development of a strict technique for modern poetry, and when Hemingway called on him early in 1922 Pound was in the final stages of 'editing' *The Waste Land* for Eliot, pruning it from a sprawling collection of poems into a terse modernist sequence. He was also, with the aid of Natalie Barney, about to launch a scheme to rescue Eliot from his job in Lloyds Bank in London and finance his becoming a full-time writer. In the midst of all these activities, Pound had somehow found time to translate ancient Chinese poetry – or rather, brilliantly rewrite the translations by Ernest Fenollosa; produce a madcap modern version of the elegies of Sextus Propertius; write a gnomic verse farewell to London, *Hugh Selwyn Mauberley* (1920); turn out pseudonymous weekly art and music reviews for a London journal; and begin what he called an 'endless poem' that was appearing from his desk canto by canto. On arrival in Paris in the spring of 1921 he also began to compose an opera.

Nevertheless he was rather bored, and was on the look-out for a new protégé. Joyce, Eliot, and his other discoveries had little need of him now – he had always been almost as much of a nuisance to them as a help, with his constant and sometimes banal trumpetings of their work – and his cantos occupied him only in a rather desultory fashion, as he 'bottled' random characters from European and American history. He had settled experimentally in Paris in search of some action, the kind of excitement he had known in his early days in London, and Hemingway was exactly the kind of person he had hoped to find.

Pound himself had a lot of Hemingway's swagger. He liked to imply that women flocked after him, but sometimes it seemed that he really cared very little for the opposite sex. Much more sincere was his hero-worship of such masculine figures as Wyndham Lewis, another of his protégés. He took to 'Hem', as he called him, largely because Hemingway was a tough guy, or liked to behave as one.

A few days after the tea party in rue Notre Dame des Champs, Hemingway handed Lewis Galantière a satirical piece he had just written about Pound's pretentious bohemianism. He intended to offer it to the *Little Review*, but Galantière said that there was no point in offending such an influential person as Pound, and advised him to tear it up. Hemingway did so, and by 9 March 1922 the relationship with Pound had warmed up considerably. That day Hemingway wrote to Sherwood Anderson that 'Pound took six of my poems and sent them with a letter to Thayer'. Scofield Thayer of the *Dial* paid better than any other American editor with whom Pound was in touch; on the other hand he by no means always took Pound's advice, and now he rejected Hemingway's poems. Pound also sent a Hemingway story to the *Little Review*; it fared no better, but he had at least shown himself willing to help. Also, he displayed interest when Hemingway said he was an experienced boxer.

For all his Whistlerian way of dressing, Pound liked physical sports. He regarded himself, scarcely with justice, as a skilled fencer and tennis player, and the thought of pugilism appealed to his aggressive nature. 'I've been teaching Pound to box,' Hemingway reported to Anderson in the same letter of 9 March, but added that it had met with 'little success' since Pound had 'the general grace of the crayfish'. However, 'it's pretty sporting of him to risk his dignity'. One day Wyndham Lewis walked into Pound's studio without knocking, and found them at it; he was impressed by Hemingway's 'dazzling white' torso, and calls him 'tall, handsome, and serene'; Pound was attempting 'a hectic assault' at the other's 'dazzling solar plexus', but this was repelled 'without undue exertion' and Pound 'fell back upon his settee'.

Hemingway remembered the occasion vividly:

Wyndham Lewis wore a wide black hat [he writes in *A Moveable Feast*], and was dressed like somebody out of *La Bohème*. He had a face that reminded me of a frog...He watched superciliously while I slipped Ezra's left leads or blocked them with an open right glove. I wanted to stop but Lewis insisted we go on, and I could see that...he was...hoping to see Ezra hurt.

They all had a drink, and Hemingway studied Lewis more closely. 'I do not think I had ever seen a nastier-looking man.' He decided that

Lewis's eyes were 'those of an unsuccessful rapist'. Actually, Lewis was a thoroughly successful womaniser; he had scattered illegitimate children all over the place, having learnt his trade in the Latin Quarter while studying painting there in the early 1900s.

Hemingway told Gertrude Stein that he could not stand Lewis. She agreed, and said she called him The Measuring Worm, because 'he comes over from London and he sees a good picture and takes a pencil out of his pocket and you watch him measuring it on the pencil with his thumb. Then he goes back to London and it doesn't come out right. He's missed what it's all about.' This was nonsense, but then Gertrude had probably seen very little of Lewis's Vorticist painting.

Pound told Hemingway about his scheme to rescue Eliot from slavery in Lloyds Bank, and encouraged him to come to Natalie Barney's Friday salon where the plan was being formulated. Miss Barney had given the scheme the high-flown name 'Bel Esprit'. Hemingway was wary of salons – 'I figured very early that they were excellent places for me to stay away from' – but he could not help seeing the funny side of Pound's scheme, all the funnier since Pound would keep sidestepping into his obsession with Social Credit, an obscure economic theory devised by one Major C. H. Douglas. Hemingway had not yet read a word of Eliot's poetry, and he pretended to confuse him with Major Douglas. He began to refer to Eliot as 'the Major', and fantasised about his being released from the bank and given the temple in Miss Barney's garden to live in, and 'maybe I could go with Ezra when we would drop in to crown him with laurel.' Bel Esprit soon foundered, having hugely embarrassed Eliot. Hemingway gathered some subscriptions for it, but then lost them all at a racetrack. However, he continued to show his writing to Pound; as it steadily improved, Pound said it showed 'the touch of the chisel.' In 1933 Hemingway claimed that he had learned more about 'how to write and how not to write' from Pound than from anyone else. Possibly Pound applied his editorial pencil to Hemingway's drafts much in the way he had to *The Waste Land*; certainly he made the biggest technical advances of his career during the months when he was seeing Pound frequently. On the other hand, Pound claimed to have little feeling for prose, and the influence most clearly visible in Hemingway's writing was, of course, that of Gertrude Stein.

'He and Gertrude Stein used to walk together and talk together a great deal,' she writes in *The Autobiography of Alice B. Toklas*, and Hemingway records that he was welcome to come to 27 rue de Fleurus 'any time after five'. She always gave him *eau-de-vie*, 'insisting on refilling my glass', and they looked at the pictures and talked. She pointed out the Matisse *Femme au Chapeau* as the picture beneath which she had sat while writing *Three Lives*, and talked to him about Cézanne. Hemingway decided that he 'wanted to write like Cézanne painted. Cézanne started with all the tricks. Then he broke the whole thing down and built the real thing.'

Sometimes he met Gertrude walking her dog in the Jardin du Luxembourg. He soon lost most of his wariness with her, and began to enjoy her company in a relaxed way that few other people had managed. He perceived that beneath the formidable exterior lay a great sense of humour and an almost peasant shrewdness. She told him how she and Leo had amassed their art collection. 'You can either buy clothes or pictures,' she said. 'It's simple. No one who is not very rich can do both.' Looking at the 'strange, steerage clothes' she wore, Hemingway could well believe it.

He let slip to her his fear of homosexuals, and she responded with spirit: 'You know nothing about any of this really, Hemingway . . . The act male homosexuals commit is ugly and repugnant and afterwards they are disgusted with themselves. They drink and take drugs, to palliate this, but they are disgusted with the act and they are always changing partners and cannot be really happy . . . In women it is the opposite. They do nothing that they are disgusted by and nothing that is repulsive and afterwards they are happy and they can lead happy lives together.'

*

Hemingway began to send regular pieces to the *Toronto Star*, writing about anything on which he could glean information: Swiss tourism (after a short trip he and Hadley had made to the Alps), the depreciation of the German mark (a favourite topic among Americans travelling around Europe), tuna fishing, the election of a new Pope, and the politics of France. Besides bringing in money it was good practice; but Gertrude did not approve. 'One day,' she writes in the *Autobiography*, 'she said to him, look here, you say you and your wife have a little money between you. Is it enough to live on if you live quietly. Yes, he said. Well, she said, then do it. If you keep on doing the newspaper work you will never see things, you will only see words and that will not do, that is of course if you intend to be a writer.'

This was intellectual snobbery, and he wisely ignored it. He told her he undoubtedly intended to be a writer, but he let himself be drawn more and more into newspaper work – it allowed him to travel, to gain the varied experience he so badly needed. In April 1922, he went to Genoa to cover an international economic conference. The following month, visiting Milan with Hadley, he interviewed Mussolini. During a Black Forest holiday in August 1922 he reported on unrest in Weimar Germany; he also went to Constantinople to cover the war between Greece and Turkey, catching malaria in the process; interviewed Clemenceau at his seaside retreat (the old man attacked Canada for not having done her part in the First World War, and the editor in Toronto thought the story too hot to print); and covered the Lausanne Peace Conference, convened to settle the Graeco-Turkish conflict. On these trips he made friends with such seasoned newspapermen as Lincoln Steffens, celebrated exponent of the 'muckraking' school, and Bill Bird, a thin American who ran the European office of Consolidated Press in Paris and practised high-quality printing as a hobby. These and other old hands taught Hemingway 'cablese'; Steffens describes him joyously exclaiming: 'Stef, look at this cable: no fat, no adjectives, no adverbs... It's great. It's a new language.'

In the intervals between these trips, affected by what he had seen and learnt during them, he worked away at his prose style, recording in his notebooks some distillations of Paris:

I have seen the one-legged street walker who works the Boulevard Madeleine between the Rue Cambon and Bernheim Jeune's limping along the pavement through the crowd on a rainy night with a beefy red-faced Episcopal clergyman holding an umbrella over her.

I have watched the police charge the crowd with swords as they milled back into Paris through the Porte Maillot on the first of May and seen the frightened proud look on the white beaten-up face of the sixteen-year-old kid who looked like a prep school quarter back and had just shot two policemen.

I have stood on the crowded back platform of a seven o'clock Batignolles bus as it lurched along the wet lamp lit street while men who were going home to supper never looked up from their newspapers as we passed Notre Dame grey and dripping in the rain...

These might seem like exercises in modernism, but their subject matter was traditional to the point of romanticism – the hypocrisy of American puritanism, teenage heroism, the beauty of Paris. He tried the same thing in free verse, and though this time Harriet Monroe at *Poetry* agreed to print some of the results, the experiment suggested that he was not a modernist at all:

> Yesterday's *Tribune* is gone
> Along with youth
> And the canoe that went to pieces on the beach
> The year of the big storm
> When the hotel burned down
> At Seney, Michigan.

Hemingway began to feel that Gertrude Stein was rather dangerous as a model. He judged her *Three Lives* 'intelligible to anyone', and the 'Melanctha' story in it 'very good', but he despaired of *The Making of Americans* (she had let him see the vast manuscript), saying it 'began magnificently, went on very well for a long way with great stretches of great brilliance and then went on endlessly in repetitions that a more conscientious and less lazy writer would have put in the waste basket'. He felt that her reputation as a writer was largely due to her obvious achievement as an art collector, and suspected that 'critics who met her and saw her pictures took on trust writing of hers that they could not understand because of their enthusiasm for her as a person'. He saw that she was incorrigibly lazy, that while she longed for publication and *gloire*, she 'disliked the drudgery of revision and the obligation to make her writing intelligible'.

He had only picked up certain verbal tricks from her – the elimination of complex sentence structures, the unembarrassed repetition of the same word rather than the use of synonyms, the description of a scene or person 'cubistically' by setting down first one facet and then the other. His developing style owed just as much to his work as a journalist. Long ago, when he had been a cub reporter in Kansas City, he had been drilled into the use of 'short snappy sentences, clarity, and immediacy', and now he felt that these were 'the best rules I ever learned'. In fact Gertrude Stein eventually acquired as much from him as he had from her. By the time she came to write *The Autobiography of Alice B. Toklas* in the early 1930s, she had picked up several of his tricks, and the book is as lively as a Hemingway novel.

She tried to guide his reading. He had now discovered D. H. Lawrence and Aldous Huxley, but she was disapproving; she dismissed Lawrence as 'pathetic and preposterous' and said he wrote like 'a sick man'. Why did Hemingway bother to read Huxley – 'Can't you see he is dead?' She recommended, of all things, thrillers by Marie Belloc Lowndes. In turn, Hemingway suggested she read Simenon, but discovered that she 'did not like to read French'. He began to realise that she only had good words for writers who had praised her own work. The sole exception was Ronald Firbank; she was greatly amused by his high-camp fantasies with their sexual ambiguities.

Talking to Sylvia Beach, Hemingway showed a mild curiosity about Joyce. He mentioned that he had seen him eating with his family at a smart restaurant, Michaud's, peering through his thick glasses at the menu, all of them talking Italian to each other. But usually he paid no attention to Joyce, whose experiments and achievements did not seem relevant to what he was trying to do himself. Places like Michaud's were usually beyond his own pocket, not least because he was gambling away a lot of Hadley's money at the Paris racetracks. As for the stories he was writing, although they were now far better than anything he had completed before he came to Paris, 'every one I sent out came back'.

*

In December 1922, when he had been in Paris for a year, there was a disaster. Hadley, on her way to join him at Lausanne, decided to take all his typescripts with her so that he could work on them. Rashly, she packed both top copies and carbons. While her back was turned at the Gare de Lyon the suitcase containing them was stolen.

When she arrived and told Hemingway the news, he simply could not believe her. He took the next train back to Paris to see if the carbons, at least, were not still in the apartment. They were not; all that had survived was a story called 'My Old Man', set at a Paris racetrack, which was out with an editor, and 'Up in Michigan', which was in a different drawer from the rest. Among other losses was the novel at which he had been working for months.

'I suppose you heard about the loss of my Juvenilia?' Hemingway wrote to Pound in mid-January 1923. 'You, naturally, would say "Good" etc. But don't say it to me. I ain't yet reached that mood, 3 years on the damn stuff.' Sure enough, Pound wrote back that the loss was an 'act of Gawd', and Hemingway should write it all out again from memory, which was 'the best critic'. (Privately, Pound said that Hadley must be jealous of Hemingway's writings, and had lost the manuscripts deliberately.)

In *A Moveable Feast*, Hemingway claims that the loss affected him deeply, and says that though he quickly put a brave face on it he was only doing this for Hadley's sake. However, the January 1923 letter to Pound shows that he had already started reconstruction: 'Am now working on new stuff.'

Pound had a plan for him. In mid-November 1922, a couple of weeks before the loss of the manuscripts, Hemingway had written to Harriet Monroe at *Poetry* explaining that 'the Three Mountains Press here, Ezra Pound editing, is bringing out a book of my stuff shortly and I want to use the poems you have if you will give me permission to republish them'. Three Mountains Press was the small printing business run by Hemingway's journalist friend Bill Bird, using a hand press 'of about Benjamin Franklin vintage' on the Île St Louis. Bird had gone to Pound asking if he had any cantos that could be printed; instead, Pound came up with a plan for a series to be called 'The Inquest' because it was intended to show the state of prose after the publication of *Ulysses*, which Pound claimed had killed off nineteenth-century writing. He enlisted Ford Madox Ford, William Carlos Williams, and several other contributors, including young Hemingway – indeed he probably dreamt up the series in order to get Hemingway into print. But Hemingway had almost nothing to put in the book. When Bird issued a prospectus for the series, he had to describe one item as simply 'Blank, by Ernest M. Hemingway'.

4
McAlimony

Hadley now discovered that she was pregnant. Hemingway was not exactly overjoyed; Gertrude Stein says that when she next saw him, he spent hours plucking up courage to tell her and Alice, then said gloomily: 'I am too young to be a father.' Gertrude and Alice 'consoled him as best we could and sent him on his way'.

He and Hadley had been invited by Pound to go down to Rapallo, on the Italian coast near Genoa, to join him and Dorothy on a walking tour in the steps of Sigismondo Malatesta, a fifteenth-century Italian despot whom Pound was going to write about in the Cantos. Hemingway had never heard of Sigismondo, and the thought of a walking tour in February, even in Italy, was not attractive; but he and Hadley went. Rapallo disappointed them – it was just a seaside resort – and as soon as they got there the Pounds vanished on some expedition of their own, saying they would be back in a couple of weeks.

Hemingway sat around gloomily in the hotel. Among the other people staying there was an amiable Princetonian named Mike Strater, with whom he had fought a round in Pound's Paris studio. He wanted to box with him again, but Strater had sprained his ankle, and the only fun he could offer was painting Hemingway's and Hadley's portraits. Every day Hemingway would ask how the ankle was getting on – he said he had stopped making love to Hadley in order to save his energies for the fight.

He wrote to Gertrude that he had got two new stories done: 'I've thought a lot about the things you said ... Am working hard about creating and keep my mind going about it all the time.' He was greatly encouraged when an American called Edward O'Brien, who was staying in a monastery near Rapallo, accepted one of the two stories that had survived the theft of the suitcase, 'My Old Man', for an anthology he was editing, *The Best Short Stories of 1923*. Hemingway wrote to Sylvia Beach: 'Don't say anything about it or he might change his mind.'

Hemingway described another visitor to Rapallo in a note to Pound: 'McAlmon came and stayed a long time. I read all his new stuff. Some 16–18 stories a novel or so. He wrote seven or nine new stories while at Rapallo.'

Robert McAlmon was, says William Carlos Williams, 'a coldly intense young man, with hard blue eyes'. Another friend describes 'his lean mouth closed like a wallet, his eye like iron'. John Glassco, a young Canadian who first met him in Paris in 1928, was immediately refreshed by McAlmon's rudeness and 'total absence of attitude or artifice.' Glassco goes on: 'He admired no writing of any kind, either ancient or modern; all government was a farce; all people were fools or snobs. He spoke of his friends with utter contempt... but all with such an absence of conviction that one could not take him seriously.'

Hemingway's chief reaction to McAlmon during this first encounter at Rapallo was admiration of his literary productivity. 'If I was in the tipster business,' he wrote to Pound, 'I would whisper into the shell like ear of a friend, "go and make a small bet on McAlmon while you can still get a long price."' McAlmon had a volume of short stories in print. True, he had published it at his own expense, but people spoke well of it. He had also written a novel about 'arty' life in Greenwich Village, *Post-Adolescence*, and there was a volume of poems, *Explorations*, issued by the *Egoist* in London, who were Joyce's British publishers. Now he said he was at work on a long family novel set in the Dakotas; he would mention casually that he had knocked off 150,000 words during the last few months. Glassco describes him pounding ceaselessly at the typewriter keys: 'It must be a wonderful thing, I thought, to be able to write so fast.' Since Hemingway was still struggling to shape individual sentences he was understandably impressed.

In Paris, McAlmon was an habitué of the Dôme and other Montparnasse cafés, where he was popular with almost everyone. Somehow, says Sylvia Beach, 'he dominated whatever group he was in. Whatever café or bar McAlmon patronised at the moment was the one where you saw everybody.' This was largely because, unlike most of the expatriates, McAlmon had plenty of money. 'The drinks were always on him,' writes Sylvia, 'and alas! often in him.' Though a teetotaller herself, she was sometimes prepared to venture into Montparnasse night-life in his company; she says he made it 'quite bearable'.

Everyone, she says, was 'looking forward to his contribution to the writing of the twenties'. If nothing remarkable had emerged yet, it was probably because his friends were always distracting him. 'He would tell me,' says Sylvia, 'he was leaving for the south of France, to look up some place where he could get right away from people and do some work.' Then she would get a telegram: 'Found right place and quiet room.' Soon, somebody would tell her they had seen McAlmon down there: 'His room is above the bistro and they all meet at this bistro.'

*

Robert McAlmon's father was an Ulster Protestant from County Armagh, and all his life McAlmon wore the grim intolerant visage of an

Ulsterman confronting a naughty world. The father had emigrated first to Canada, where he married a Scottish Canadian, and then to the USA. He became a nomadic Presbyterian minister, and McAlmon (who was three years older than Hemingway) spent most of his childhood in a succession of small towns and villages in South Dakota. Later the family moved to Minneapolis, then to California; McAlmon found high school boring, and drifted uninterestedly to university. He hoped that the First World War would take him to Europe, but never got further than an airfield in San Diego. After demobilisation in 1919 he took a variety of jobs, working for an aviation magazine, doing some manual labouring, and picking up cash as a movie extra. Eventually he took off for Chicago, where Harriet Monroe had printed a few poems by him in *Poetry*, but he found nothing there to excite him, so he went on to New York and Greenwich Village, where he earned a dollar an hour posing in the nude for drawing classes.

In *Post-Adolescence*, McAlmon describes life as an art school model:

There were no students yet at the studio when he arrived, but he undressed anyway . . . He sat on the model stand. The looking glass faced him, reflecting his body. What was he posing for? None of the students would ever sketch or sculpture him well enough for it to matter. Nice lines he had, after all, there around the belly particularly. It was nice being slender, but his belly might be getting a little too paunchy. He'd have to stand straighter, draw it up, take some exercises. Hated a paunchy belly. He ran his lips along his arms, his hands up and down his legs. Legs are graceful things; slender, deerlike, and how fine the skin is on the side of the foot, frogbelly fine with ethereal tiny pores and pearly white. That's the nicest skin on the body. He wondered if he could touch it with his mouth, and strained to do so, but was unsuccessful. He supposed a contortionist could. Wished there was a young girl in here with him, and undressed, but she'd have to be young and slender. He was tired of older women, too sophisticated, and not buoyant enough; wanted one with exuberance, not shy but capricious – what to hell anyway, always looking forward to a climax . . .
Students began to come in . . .

At a studio party in Greenwich Village, McAlmon met William Carlos Williams, a doctor from New Jersey who had been a college friend of Ezra Pound. Williams had taken much longer than Pound to make a reputation as a poet, partly because he scorned – or claimed to scorn – the professional literary life, and he also refused to become an expatriate like Pound. McAlmon's bored intolerance and his disdain for the Village appealed to Williams, and during 1920 the two of them started their own 'little magazine'. They named it *Contact* because it was supposed to exemplify 'the essential contact between words and the locality that breeds them', though Djuna Barnes said it did not seem to have much contact with anyone or anything. To support himself and the magazine, McAlmon worked in an advertising agency, trained polo ponies, and did landscape gardening on Long Island. He lived on a garbage boat on the Hudson.

One day Hilda Doolittle wrote to Williams, whom she had known since college days, that she would be passing through New York with a friend. She invited him to meet them for tea. Williams says he asked McAlmon: 'Wanna see the old gal?' (Hilda was by now in her mid-thirties.) McAlmon said yes. 'So one afternoon,' continues Williams, 'we decided to take in the show. Same old Hilda, all over the place looking as tall and skinny as usual. But she had with her a small, dark English girl with piercing, intense eyes...."Well, how did you like her?" I asked Bob when we came away. "Oh, she's all right, I guess," said Bob. "But that other one...she's something."'

Hilda thought her friend was 'something' too, for she was making plans to share her life with this girl, having given up men. After a youthful romance with Ezra Pound she had been married for a while to Richard Aldington, but her daughter Perdita (still a baby when McAlmon met her) had been fathered by a music critic named Cecil Gray. The dark girl was called Annie Winifred Ellerman; she was twenty-five – eighteen months McAlmon's senior – and the daughter of the British shipping magnate Sir John Ellerman. She wrote poems and fiction under the name of Bryher, taken from one of the Isles of Scilly.

About six months after this tea party, in February 1921, McAlmon and Bryher were married. It was strictly a business arrangement, or so both parties afterwards claimed, and Bryher describes it in these terms:

I had happened to meet a young American writer...who was full of en-thusiasm for modern writing. He wanted to go to Paris to meet Joyce but lacked the passage money. I put my problem before him and suggested that if we married my family would leave me alone. I would give him part of my allowance, he would join me for occasional visits to my parents, otherwise we would lead strictly separate lives.

Bryher's 'problem' was that her father tried to act the perpetual watch-dog over her life. It does not sound typical of McAlmon that he should have urgently desired to go to Paris to meet Joyce, but the prospect of a free trip to Europe and a handsome income cannot have been unappealing.

A few weeks after the wedding, McAlmon wrote to Williams:

The marriage is legal only, unromantic, and strictly an agreement. Bryher could not travel, and be away from home, unmarried...She thought I under-stood her mind, as I do somewhat, and faced me with the proposition...There are discomforts, but I don't give a damn. Bryher's a complexity, and needs help.

He added that his only regret was 'I don't like pretense'. He was uncomfortable at having to pass it off as a real marriage.

A few people supposed it to be a love match, but the general assumption was that McAlmon was after Bryher's money. Possibly he was also attracted by her lesbian inclinations; Williams says he once tried to kiss Sylvia Beach's beloved Adrienne Monnier in a taxi, whereupon she 'sank her teeth into his lips'. In his bitchy memoirs, John Glassco portrays McAlmon addressing him and his friend Graeme as 'sweetie-pie' and taking them to homosexual bars in Paris, but not making an overt pass at them. When drunk, says Glassco, he would sometimes claim to be bisexual. Probably he was as bored with sex as with everything else.

*

Before going to Paris, it was necessary for McAlmon to play the son-in-law, so he, Bryher, Hilda Doolittle, and Hilda's baby all set off for London. Early in 1921 the British capital struck McAlmon as 'sodden' – much the way Ezra Pound had described it a few weeks earlier when he left for Paris – and the atmosphere of the Ellerman home in Mayfair was oppressive. Sir John was a stickler for routine, but, says McAlmon, 'after two weeks of our presence in the household he looked a bit harried'. McAlmon made an ally of the butler so that nobody would be informed when he crept home late and awash.

Exploring London on his own, McAlmon ran across Wyndham Lewis, who emerged out of the shadows like an anarchist spy: 'His hat shaded his eyes and a faded blue scarf was in disarray about his neck. His overcoat looked seedy.' Lewis began to gossip about the intrigues of artistic London, but McAlmon only found this irritating, and when Lewis discovered that McAlmon had access to money he set about trying to ensure that none of his own enemies should receive any. Sitting in the Tour Eiffel restaurant in Percy Street, where the Vorticists had met in the heady days before the First World War, he warned McAlmon against rash remarks: 'Ssh,' he cautioned, gesturing over his shoulder with his thumb to an empty table behind, 'they're listening.' It was paranoid, but Pound had suffered from the same delusion, and there was something unpleasant about the London atmosphere.

T. S. Eliot was now in the ascendancy as the leading critic of the new generation; he had not yet started the *Criterion* nor become a publisher, but he had been editing the literary pages of the *Egoist* and reviewed for the more imposing journals. McAlmon did not care for Eliot's poetry – he calls it 'mouldy' and says it struck him as 'the perfect expression of a clerkly and liverish man's apprehension of life' – but the *Egoist* had published his own book of poems, and it seemed worth making contact with Eliot, if only out of curiosity.

Eliot was wary when McAlmon phoned for an appointment, but

when they met, says McAlmon, 'I was surprised to find him very
likeable indeed, with a quality ... of charm that few people possess',
though he looked 'tired and overworked' from his job in Lloyds Bank.
He warned McAlmon against the distractions of Paris; he had spent a
year there himself from 1910 to 1911, after finishing his undergraduate
studies at Harvard, and had liked it enough to consider 'giving up
English and trying to settle down and scrape along in Paris, and
gradually write French'. He had been to lectures at the Sorbonne and
heard Henri Bergson, but had made almost no friends and lived quietly
in his *pension*, watching the café celebrities from a distance. Most of
them, he felt, were 'futile and timewasting'.

After a few weeks, Bryher kept her promise and released McAlmon
to go off to Paris, giving him a considerable share of the large allowance
she received from her father. She set off for Switzerland with H.D.
using Shakespeare and Company as a forwarding address so that her
father would think she was with McAlmon. In Paris, McAlmon
introduced himself to Sylvia Beach and, like everyone else, used the
bookshop as a post office. 'I shared Bob McAlmon with the Dôme, the
Dingo, and other such places,' writes Sylvia, 'but his permanent address
was c/o Shakespeare and Company, and at least once a day he wandered
in.' McAlmon also looked up Pound. 'I mildly liked a poem or so of
his,' he says, but 'disliked his critical work generally'. Pound met him
for lunch and was 'very instructorial', though McAlmon formed the
impression that under all the brashness he was shy.

Harriet Shaw Weaver of the *Egoist* had given McAlmon a note of
introduction to Joyce. McAlmon did not care for *A Portrait of the
Artist as a Young Man*, calling it 'precious, full of noble attitudinizings,
and not very admirable in its soulful protestations', but the short stories
in Joyce's *Dubliners* attracted him, as did those passages of *Ulysses*
which had already appeared in the *Little Review*. McAlmon called at
the Joyces' apartment on Boulevard Raspail and was greeted by Nora.
'Although there was a legend that Joyce's eyes were weak,' he writes, 'it
was evident that he had used eyesight in choosing his wife. She was very
pretty, with a great deal of simple dignity and a reassuring manner.
Joyce finally appeared, having just got up from bed. Within a few
minutes it was obvious that he and I would get on.' McAlmon was soon
writing to William Carlos Williams: 'I believe I understand him better
than most people because of the Irish in me.'

They had dinner together that first night, and hit it off, though
McAlmon admits that they had little in common intellectually; Joyce
refused to understand that questions of theology did not disturb or
interest McAlmon, and never had. 'When I assured him that instead of
the usual "religious crises" in one's adolescent life I had studied logic
and metaphysics and remained agnostic, he did not listen. He would
talk about the fine points of religion.' Moreover, when Joyce began to

read aloud from *Ulysses*, McAlmon soon became bored by 'the high-minded struttings and the word prettifications and the Greek beauty part'.

McAlmon was the first male American Joyce had seen at length, and he was interested in his speech. 'He was constantly leaping upon phrases and bits of slang which came naturally from my American lips.' One night when 'a bit spiffed' he wept while explaining to McAlmon 'his love or infatuation for words, mere words'. However, what really appealed to Joyce about McAlmon was his money and his readiness to part with it. He got McAlmon to 'lend' him $150 a month to 'tide him over' until the completion of *Ulysses*. It was very likely Joyce who, when McAlmon's marriage was eventually dissolved (in the late 1920s) with a beneficial settlement from Sir John, dubbed him 'McAlimony'.

Joyce was ready enough to go out drinking with McAlmon, who invariably picked up the bill. 'Although he was working steadily on *Ulysses*,' says McAlmon, 'at least one night a week he was ready to stay out all night, and those nights he was never ready to go home.' One of their favourite haunts was a seedy establishment called the Gypsy Bar. 'The *patron* and the "girls" knew us well, and knew that we would drink freely and surely stay till four or five in the morning. The girls... collected at our table and indulged in their Burgundian and Rabelaisian humours.' Joyce, currently at work on Molly Bloom's soliloquy, listened attentively, says McAlmon, as 'Jeanette, a big draught horse of a girl from Dijon, pranced about like a mare in heat and restrained no remark or impulse which came to her'. (According to John Glassco, by 1928 the Gypsy had become a lesbian bar; he describes it as 'a little foul-smelling *bôite* on the Boulevard Edgar-Quinet, full of hardfaced young lesbians and desperate looking old women'.)

One night at the Gypsy, Joyce 'wept in his cups when telling of his forefathers. His father had parented a large family, and his grandfathers before him had been parents of families of from twelve to eighteen children. Joyce would sigh, and then pull himself together and swear that by the grace of God he was still a young man and he would have more children by the end.' Later, moved by the drink, the girls, and his own lachrymose reflections, he began to recite long passages of Dante in sonorous Italian, like a priest saying mass, with 'owl eyes' and a mesmerised expression; all this (says McAlmon) 'amid the clink of glasses, jazz music badly played by a French orchestra, the chatter and laughter of the whores'. Eventually Joyce and McAlmon made their way homeward; they had consumed a particularly wild assortment of drinks, and McAlmon leant against a lamp-post and threw up while Joyce watched him solicitously: 'Maybe they'll be saying I'm a bad example for you.'

McAlmon found him utterly unpredictable as a drinking companion.

'We went one night to the Brasserie Lutetia, and he ordered, as usual, that horrible natural champagne . . . We had but one glass when suddenly I saw a rat running down the stairs from the floor above. I exclaimed upon it. "Where, where?" he asked nervously. "That's bad luck."' Joyce had a whole range of superstitions, and a moment later he had fainted in terror. McAlmon quickly got him home.

When Joyce was laid low for several weeks with eye trouble, delaying the completion of *Ulysses*, McAlmon vowed never to take him out drinking again for fear of further damaging his health and the book. But that decision was useless: 'When Joyce wants to drink he will drink.' One night, accompanied by Joyce's friend Frank Budgen, they went to the Gypsy Bar. Budgen got drunk, decided that the girls were paying more attention to Joyce and McAlmon than to him, and rushed out into the night. Joyce thought that he had lost a valuable friend and sank into melancholy. He and McAlmon lingered in the Gypsy until five in the morning, when the *patron* finally told them to get out.

'Out we got, and ensconced ourselves in a small bistro on the Boulevard St Germain. We bought cigars . . . As we had decided to drink through the list of French drinks, Joyce began dropping cigars. At first I leaned to pick them up and return them to him. When I could no longer lean without falling on my face I took to lighting the cigars and handing them to him. He almost immediately dropped them, and I lighted cigar after cigar until they were all gone, and then we took to cigarettes. At ten in the morning we sat alone in the small bistro, the floor covered with some twenty cigars.'

The *patron* helped them into a taxi. Back at the Joyce apartment, Nora looked at them and began: 'Jim, you've been doin' this for twenty years, and now you've started McAlmon in the same say.' McAlmon crept back to his hotel room and fell into an alcoholic slumber – only to be woken by a telegram from Joyce summoning him round at once: 'I must not fail him. I must be in for tea at four-thirty.' He struggled back to Boulevard Raspail and discovered that Joyce had concocted some sort of cover-up story to explain why they had been out all night; McAlmon was required to back him up. He duly played his part, then crawled back to bed. 'It took me three months to get my health mildly into order after that night.'

*

Though he had mixed feelings about *Ulysses*, McAlmon helped Sylvia Beach to gather subscribers for the book. She describes how he would 'comb the night clubs' for prospective purchasers, persuading them to put their signatures – many of them 'slightly zigzag' – on the order forms. When the book was published many people were surprised to find they had signed up.

As composition drew to a close, Joyce began to worry about getting a typist for Molly Bloom's interior monologue. The 'Circe' episode, set in a brothel, had already caused enough trouble; Sylvia had found a series of typists for it but they had dropped out in quick succession, and the husband of one of them, a Mrs Harrison at the British Embassy, threw the manuscript in the fire when he saw what it contained. (Joyce managed to retrieve an earlier draft which had been sold to a patron in America.) Molly's sexual musings now made 'Circe' seem positively demure.

While drunk in Joyce's company one night, McAlmon rashly offered his own services as typist – 'Fifty pages, that's nothing' – and was accepted. The next day Joyce handed him the manuscript. Not only was it difficult to decipher, but it was accompanied by four notebooks containing additional passages; throughout the text were markings in red, yellow, blue and purple, referring to passages which must be inserted from each of these notebooks. For the first three pages McAlmon painstakingly observed instructions, though it meant retyping to get everything right. After that he decided: 'Molly might just as well think this or that a page or two later, or not at all . . .'

Joyce wanted the book to be published on his fortieth birthday, 2 February 1922. Darantière, the printer, just managed to get the first two copies to Paris early that morning, and Sylvia picked them up at the Gare de Lyon; before eight o'clock she was at Joyce's door to hand over one of them. 'Copy No. 2,' she writes, 'was for Shakespeare and Company, and I made the mistake of putting it on view in the window. The news spread rapidly in Montparnasse and outlying districts, and next day, before the bookshop was open, subscribers were lining up.' Thereafter Joyce could often be seen in the shop, helping to wrap parcels, 'lavishing glue on the labels, the floor, and his hair'. Sylvia and her helpers managed to get all the English and Irish copies dispatched and delivered before the authorities in those countries were aware of it, but it soon transpired that copies for American subscribers were being confiscated at the Port of New York. Replacements were shipped to Canada and smuggled across the border by a couple of sympathisers. Shakespeare and Company subsequently published and sold ten further printings between 1922 and 1932 (Joyce said that the numbering of the printings as 'Ulysses IV' and so on made it sound like the popes). Copies sold over the counter in rue de l'Odéon to Americans or English about to return home could be disguised, if the customer wished, as *Shakespeare's Complete Works* or *Merry Tales for Little Folk*.

Naturally the reputation of *Ulysses* as a banned book helped the sales; an Irish priest asked Sylvia: 'Any other spicy books?' Not only readers but writers began to visit the shop on the assumption that she was going to specialise in erotica. One day a small man with whiskers drove up in a barouche and pair, hired for the occasion to impress her, and introduced himself as Frank Harris. He undid a parcel 'and showed me a thing called *My Life and Loves*'. She sent him to a Paris publisher genuinely specialising in such things, Jack Kahane of Obelisk Press. On another visit to the shop, Harris asked for something exciting to read on the train, and Sylvia handed him a copy of *Little Women*. 'He jumped at the title.'

*

Although Joyce seemed unaware of or unconcerned by McAlmon's cavalier treatment of the Molly Bloom text, he afterwards wrote a short spoof of his typist's careless and hasty attitude to the job:

Did Fossett change those words? They was two. Doesn't matter. 'Gromwelling' I said and what? Oh, ah! Bisexcycle. That was the bunch. Hope he does, anyhow. O rats! It's just a fool thing, style. I just shoot it off like: If he ain't done it, where's the use? Guess I'm through with that bunch.
    (With apologies to Mr Robert McAlmon.)
    (Re-enter Hamlet.)

Joyce remarked to a mutual acquaintance: 'Maybe McAlmon has a *disorderly* sort of talent,' and suggested that McAlmon should call his book of short stories *A Hasty Bunch*. McAlmon, perhaps not perceiving the joke against him, used the title.
    A Hasty Bunch consists of 300 pages of stories and prose sketches, all of them written after McAlmon arrived in Paris – in a mere six weeks. He sent the manuscript to a printer in England, but received it back with this letter:

You have quite evidently mistaken the standing that our firm enjoys in the Printing World. We have been established over 60 years and do not remember ever being asked to place such literature before our workspeople before, and you can rest assured that we are not going to begin now.

McAlmon decided to get Darantière to print *A Hasty Bunch*, and to publish it himself.
    Ezra Pound had earlier grumbled at McAlmon's literary ambitions – 'another young one wanting me to make a poet out of him with nothing to work on' – but he expressed some admiration for *A Hasty Bunch*, writing of it in the *Dial* that McAlmon showed 'little skill' but had at least been determined to present the American small town 'in a hard and just light'. As for the style, 'McAlmon has written in the American spoken language'.
    Certainly McAlmon wrote as he spoke. While Hemingway was trying to achieve his 'true sentence' by cutting and polishing, refining and experimenting, McAlmon put down the first thing that came into his head and never revised. This lack of artifice extended to the

construction of the narratives. Indeed they were hardly constructed at all; Hemingway's friend Harold Loeb scarcely exaggerates when he says that McAlmon 'wrote indefatigably, without plots'. Unfortunately this did not prevent McAlmon from descending into the occasional purple passage:

The wheat fields were ripening, caressed to sleek maturity by the sun as a calf is licked by the tongue of its fond mother, and upon its bosom the sunlight poured and rippled so that across its gold expanse was continual gentle breathing.

This is from 'A Boy's Discovery', one of the stories which upset the English printer; it describes a group of boys puzzling over sex and persuading some girls to experiment with them. The most shy of the boys is deeply shocked, and soon afterwards contracts a fatal illness, but his sense of horror at sex is so lightly conveyed that the end of the story lacks bite. The small town atmosphere is conveyed, but rather limply, and the book has none of the strength of *Winesburg, Ohio*, which it resembles in form.

John Glassco writes of McAlmon's books:

I would have liked to admire them but it was impossible. There was neither invention nor subterfuge . . . The style and syntax revealed the genuine illiterate. I was soon to discover that Bob had in fact read absolutely nothing . . . He formed his critical opinions of books from reviews and personal contacts and his blanket condemnation of almost everything was mainly due to laziness and pique.

(In 1928 McAlmon told Morley Callaghan: 'I haven't read Joyce or Hemingway. I don't have to, I *know* them.')

But although he judges McAlmon no writer, Glassco admits that he had a knack for good titles, such as *Post-Adolescence* and *Being Geniuses Together*. Indeed, Glassco alleges that the content of the books scarcely mattered to him; they were so like each other that he was constantly switching whole chapters from one book to the other, and was even unsure whether he should exchange the titles themselves. 'When he asked me,' says Glassco, 'I was able to say it could make no difference – an opinion that delighted him.' For some years Glassco believed that if McAlmon would condescend to work hard at writing, his books could be very fine. 'I see now, of course, that if he had done so they would have been still worse.'

*

McAlmon spent the autumn and winter of 1922 in Italy, and was on his way back to Paris in February 1923 when he called in at Rapallo, vaguely expecting to see Ezra Pound, and found instead Mike Strater and Ernest Hemingway. He had never heard of Hemingway.

He liked Strater immediately, 'a direct young American'. Hemingway aroused more ambiguous feelings: 'He was a type outside my experience.' McAlmon particularly noted the 'small-boy, tough-guy swagger' put on for strangers. As Hemingway approached a café where McAlmon and others were sitting he would prance about, sparring at imaginary opponents, his lips moving as he called their bluff. McAlmon also guessed that his war reminiscences were largely sham. He guyed them in a short story, 'Three Generations of the Same', in which the narrator meets

Bob Goff, who was ornately groomed, with brilliantined hair smoothed carefully upon a head tending to fleshiness in the back. He worked his smile extensively to show even and tiny cut white teeth. He was smooth with the suavity begot of tailoring establishments, and barber-shop treatments.

'Bob, show Carl that skull of a German you got when you were at the battlefront,' Billy requested, wanting to make his friend appear impressive.

Goff took down a skull nonchalantly, saying, 'There – not a bad one. Of course I got more than one Hun, but I couldn't take a trunkload of skulls back with me, could I? But I've forgotten all that now – don't even know where my medals are.'

McAlmon liked Hemingway enough, however, to agree to go with him on a trip to Spain in May 1923, three months after they had first met. The idea was to see bullfighting at first hand – it was Hemingway's first experience of Spain and the country's national sport. They went by train from Paris, and during the journey they drew up opposite a goods wagon on which lay the maggot-eaten corpse of a dog. McAlmon wrinkled his nose and turned away, whereupon Hemingway began a lecture on the necessity of 'facing reality', holding forth about how he had seen decayed corpses of men stacked up during the First World War. As it happened, McAlmon, during his barge-dwelling days in New York Harbour, had seen his own share of dead dogs, cats, and men, floating on the tide. He left Hemingway in the compartment and went to the dining car to order whisky.

During the trip, Hemingway made some notes on McAlmon's personality:

27 years old ... ridden horses on farm as a boy. Took flask of brandy to his first bullfight – took several drinks at ring – when bull charged picador and hit horse ... gave sudden screeching intake of breath – took drink of brandy – repeated this on each encounter between bull and horse. Seemed to be in search of strong sensations. Doubted genuineness of my enthusiasm for bullfights. Declared it was a pose. He felt no enthusiasm and declared no one else could ... Amusements and occupation drinking, night life and gossip.

In turn, McAlmon noticed how, after this first experience of bullfighting, Hemingway substituted shadow-bullfighting for shadow-boxing, and went in for imaginary cape-work and sword-thrusts.

Sylvia Beach says that Joyce observed to her that it was a mistake Hemingway thinking himself such a tough fellow and McAlmon trying to pass himself off as the sensitive writer: it was the other way round.

*

McAlmon was told about Hemingway's loss of his manuscripts, and asked to see the two pieces that had survived. To these, Hemingway could now add another story, 'Out of Season', which portrayed himself and Hadley on holiday in the Dolomites having an argument while being taken trout-fishing by a drunken villager. Now that he had put his own short stories into print, McAlmon had decided to publish other writers under the name of Contact Editions, with Darantière as his printer and Shakespeare and Company as the mailing address. (Ford Madox Ford afterwards described the enterprise, not altogether unfairly, as 'a number of uglyish wads of printing called *Contact Books*'.) He announced that he wanted manuscripts that showed 'individuality, intelligence, talent, a live sense of literature, and...the colour and timbre of authenticity'. Despite his reservations about Hemingway, he presumably found evidence of these qualities in his writing, since the first prospectus (summer 1923) of Contact Editions advertised a forthcoming and titleless book of 'Short Stories by Ernest Hemingway'.

Publication by McAlmon was not necessarily an accolade; Ezra Pound once suggested that he had chosen to print the work of several 'geniuses' simply to show them up as fakes. But the other books in this first batch were respectable enough – the authors included Bryher, Mina Loy, and William Carlos Williams – and the only objection might be to a lack of a coherent programme for publication; Sylvia Beach says she never quite understood what the 'Contact movement' was all about.

When the book was announced, Hemingway still had only three short stories to his name, 'Up in Michigan', 'My Old Man', and 'Out of Season'. However, there were also his poems, already published in *Poetry*, so he told McAlmon the title would be *Three Stories and Ten Poems*.

Meanwhile, Pound and Bill Bird were still waiting for their own Hemingway book for the 'Inquest' series. Pound had recently persuaded the *Little Review* to publish some of Hemingway's 'true sentences', short exercises in prose realism like those he had written about Paris a few months earlier, and it was now agreed that Hemingway should put a set of these pieces together for the 'Inquest' book.

Darantière sent proofs of *Three Stories and Ten Poems* at the beginning of August 1923. Hemingway was excited by the look of it, though he worried that it was so slender, and decided to have it fattened with blank pages at each end. He announced proudly to an old Chicago room-mate, with no more than his usual degree of exaggeration, that the book was being published by 'the same gang that published *Ulysses*'.

5

Summer's just started

Hemingway wrote to a friend from Paris on 24 June 1923: 'Here summer's just started.' On Saturday night they had all been to five prize fights – himself, Hadley, Pound, Jane Heap of the *Little Review*, Mike Strater, and McAlmon. 'Swell fights. Warm weather started since yesterday.'

There was much more than prize fighting on offer to those with cultural appetites. Margaret Anderson, co-editor of the *Little Review*, describes Parisian artistic life as it was then flourishing:

The Swedish Ballet gave nightly galas in the Théâtre des Champs Elysées. Jean Cocteau's *Les Mariés de la Tour Eiffel* was given for the first time...Groups of insurgent artists prayed for scandal, hissing, booing...After a ballet Satie and Picabia appeared on the stage in a motor car to acknowledge applause. They received enough hisses to please any Parisian. Stravinsky gave his *Noces* with the Ballets Russes...[with] a new curtain by Picasso – two running women a hundred times larger than life. Picasso sat in Diaghilev's *loge*, determined to be seen without evening clothes. Braque threatened to hold up a performance – one of his greens had been tampered with...Satie was discovered in tears because his ballet (décor by Picasso) was applauded less than others...Man Ray was photographing pins and combs, sieves and shoe-trees. Fernand Léger was beginning his cubist cinema, Ballet Mécanique, with music by Antheil. The Boeuf-sur-le-Toit (named by Cocteau) had a negro saxophonist, and Milhaud and Jean Wiener were beginning their worship of American jazz...The Dadaists gave performances at the Théâtre Michel where the rioting was so successful that André Breton broke Tzara's arm.

Margaret Anderson is conflating several years, but her account gives the flavour of the times. Some of the events she mentions involved the Cubists, whose work had seemed so revolutionary before the First World War but who now appeared to the younger generation as somewhat 'establishment' figures. In 1917 Picasso had provided the décor for *Parade*, a ballet about a group of music-hall artistes, with music by Erik Satie; this had caused a storm at its première, but by 1923 it seemed slightly *passé* and (to Satie's distress) received little attention when it was revived. Picasso was now providing drop curtains for

Diaghilev's Ballets Russes during their Paris seasons (the two running women were seen not at Stravinsky's *Les Noces*, premièred in June 1923, but in *Le Train Bleu* (1924) with music by Darius Milhaud), and another Cubist, Georges Braque, was designing ballets for Diaghilev. By 1923 the 'revolutionary' mantle had passed to the Dadaists, whose aim was to attack the bourgeois element in art. The painter Francis Picabia, a Cubist-turned-Dadaist, provided Satie with a libretto and décor for a ballet entitled *Relâche*, premiered at the Théâtre des Champs-Élysées in 1924. Picabia describes this Dadaist entertainment as depicting

life as I like it; life without a morrow, the life of to-day, everything for to-day, nothing for yesterday, nothing for to-morrow. Motor headlights, pearl necklaces, the rounded and slender forms of women, publicity, music, motor-cars, men in evening dress, movement, noise, play, clear and transparent water, the pleasure of laughter, that is Relâche . . .

The Dadaists had already split into two warring factions. At the Théâtre Saint-Michel on 6 July 1923 they staged a 'manifestation' for which the American painter–photographer Man Ray had provided a three-minute film, *The Return to Reason*, but it came to pieces in the projector and plunged the auditorium into darkness, whereupon a fight began between André Breton, leader of one group, and his rival Tristan Tzara. As was usual at Dadaist events, the police had to be called.

On the fringe of the Dadaist group but commanding his own followers and audience was Jean Cocteau, who had been presenting 'revolutionary' material to the public before Dada had appeared in Paris – he was the librettist of Satie's *Parade* in 1917. When his entertainment *Les Mariés de la Tour Eiffel* was premièred at the Champs-Elysées theatre by the Swedish Ballet in June 1921, with music by the group of composers known as Les Six, the Dadaists tried to break up the performance by heckling, though the Cocteau work was itself 'insurgent': it depicted a farcical *petit-bourgeois* wedding party in a restaurant on the Eiffel Tower. The Cocteau group had its headquarters at a nightclub near the Madeleine, named Le Boeuf-sur-le-Toit after the ballet with libretto by Cocteau and music by Milhaud (one of Les Six) first performed in 1920. Milhaud and his musician friend Jean Wiener, often to be found at the piano at Le Boeuf along with an American saxophonist, were taking a close interest in jazz.

Man Ray was the only American to participate fully in these activities. Born Emanuel Rabinovitch in Philadelphia, he had established a New York Dada group with Marcel Duchamp before coming to Paris in 1921. Originally a painter, he was now making experiments in photography – his Rayographs, made in his Montparnasse hotel room, were images of miscellaneous objects placed on the photographic paper which was then exposed directly to the light. Ray's work inspired the 'Cubist cinema' of Fernand Léger, culminating in Léger's 1926 film *Ballet Mécanique* with music by George Antheil, a young American protégé of Ezra Pound whose score called for such curious instruments as aeroplane propellers.

Pound bridged the gap in his own way between American and French writers and artists in Paris. He had been coming to Paris regularly since before the First World War, had met survivors of the Symbolists and mingled with older French writers at Natalie Barney's salon. He now took a paternalistic interest in the activities of the Dadaists and the Cocteau group (he once reduced Cocteau to helpless giggles by performing his opera single-handed). But on the whole the American crowd went its own way. Many of its members spoke not a word of French, and while a few young American writers had studied French literature and did their best to discover what was going on in French cultural circles, they were the exception. Certainly Hemingway and McAlmon – to mention only two – took not the slightest interest in the events described by Margaret Anderson.

*

'The influx of expatriates,' writes McAlmon of the early 1920s, 'had begun before this, but now they hung out in Montparnasse at the Dôme and the Rotonde.' During his own first few months in Paris, McAlmon, like Hemingway, had tended to frequent cafés in the St Germain–St Michel area of the Left Bank, the centre of the Latin Quarter next to the Sorbonne. He was 'hardly aware of Montparnasse', and Sylvia Beach informed him it was 'ghastly'. But Sylvia, whose bookshop was just off the Boulevard St Germain, hardly ever went there; and by 1923 the group of cafés at the intersection of Boulevard du Montparnasse and Boulevard Raspail, just by the entrance to Métro station Vavin, had become the heartland of Left Bank artistic expatriate life. McAlmon was among many who shifted their headquarters there.

The 'mountain' from which Montparnasse originally took its name was simply a grass-covered heap of rubble from an old quarry on the edge of the city. During the seventeenth century, students from the Latin Quarter, who would come out there for some fresh air, sarcastically nicknamed the place Mount Parnassus. As the city expanded the stone-heap disappeared and the area became a pleasure quarter of cafés, cabarets, and dance halls. At the end of the nineteenth century writers and painters began to move there because Montmartre, their traditional home in the north of the city, was becoming increasingly tourist-ridden. Alfred Jarry and 'Douanier' Rousseau were among the first arrivals, and Amedeo Modigliani, Marc Chagall, and Guillaume Apollinaire – the man who coined the word 'Cubism' – soon followed.

By the outbreak of war in 1914, Apollinaire could say that Montparnasse had become 'for painters and poets what Montmartre was fifteen years ago'.

Marcel Duchamp, one of the pioneers of Dadaism, observes that the place felt 'superior' to Montmartre, Greenwich Village or Chelsea, because unlike them it was not populated largely by art students, but was full of established painters, and so seemed 'more mature'. One of the last significant arrivals was Picasso, who moved his studio down from Montmartre to a street overlooking the Montparnasse cemetery just before the First World War. But he made less impression on Montparnassians than did the usually penniless Modigliani, who could be found wandering around the café tables offering his work for sale. The English painter Nina Hamnett describes him carrying pictures in a roll of newspaper and calling mournfully: 'Je suis Modigliani, Juif, Jew.' His paintings cost 5 francs each. When he died of tubercular meningitis in 1920, says Hamnett, 'telegrams were sent to London to put up the prices of his pictures'.

For a while Montparnasse had also become a meeting place for political exiles. During the First World War, Trotsky had been seen there selling newspapers on the street and eating free of charge at a canteen run for starving artists by a Cubist painter, Marie Wassiliev. Lenin, too, lived in the quarter from 1909 to 1912 and could be found on the terrace of the Dôme. But by 1920 pride of place there was taken by a 'painters' table', with Georges Braque and André Derain among the regulars, and Matisse and Picasso occasionally dropping by. So well established was Montparnasse as the domicile of Parisian artists that the custom had grown up of referring to it casually as 'the Quarter', a title properly belonging to the true Latin Quarter.

The presence of the French painters and writers soon attracted Americans to Montparnasse, and the Americans attracted more Americans. In the early 1920s the plain little cafés and bistros began to disappear from Boulevard du Montparnasse and its side-streets, to be replaced by more ambitious establishments competing for the new arrivals' money. Harold Stearns, one of the American inhabitants of Montparnasse, recalls how as late as 1921 the Dôme itself was 'just an old fashioned corner *bistro*, with César still puttering around and never giving you the drinks you ordered', while on the other side of the street the Rotonde was 'small and dirty and historical (Trotsky used to go there in the old days)'; the Dingo was 'a tiny workmen's café', and the others did not exist. Jimmie Charters, who came to Montparnasse to work as a barman, similarly describes how 'the year before I went to the Dingo it had been but a small *bistro*, a regular workman's café, without even a name, or at least no name that anyone remembers'. Then around 1923 the Dingo, at 10 rue Delambre, just round the corner from the Dôme, was taken over by a Frenchman who named it, redecorated it, and installed a cocktail bar and an English interpreter. The American crowd discovered it and soon there was rarely a free table. The proprietor, with his big moustaches and goatee, was immediately christened Old Man Dingo. 'He spoke not one word of English,' says Jimmie Charters, 'and 90 per cent of his clients spoke no French. He was making money faster than he had ever dreamed.'

In *A Moveable Feast*, Hemingway describes the sudden Americanisation of the old Closerie des Lilas, a couple of hundred yards up the road from the Dôme, which until the 1920s had remained virtually unchanged since the days of Mürger – its name came from the lilac bushes that decorated it: 'They're changing the management,' [Evan] Shipman said. 'The new owners want to have a different clientele that will spend some money and they are going to put in an American bar. The waiters are going to be in white jackets, Hem, and they have been ordered to be ready to shave off their moustaches.' During 1923 the Rotonde, opposite the Dôme, and, like it, taking its name from the rotunda on its roof, took over the café next door, redecorated itself, installed a jazz band upstairs, and tripled the price of drinks. The next year the Dôme had its walls repapered in Jazz-Age style. The model Kiki complained: 'It is too bad the little wine-shops where one used to be able to get so nice a meal have all disappeared.'

Places became fashionable overnight, and not just in Montparnasse. In Hemingway's *The Sun Also Rises*, Jake Barnes and Bill Gorton eat at 'Madame Lecomte's restaurant' on the Île St Louis:* 'It was crowded with Americans and we had to stand up and wait for a place. Someone had put it in the American Women's Club list as a quaint restaurant on the Paris quais as yet untouched by Americans, so we had to wait forty-five minutes for a table.' In Montparnasse only the Café Sélect, almost next door to the Rotonde, remained comparatively unspoilt. Though adorned in the latest manner it was in the charge of old-style proprietors, described here by John Glassco:

Madame Sélect . . . had a high colour, shrewd eyes, and a bosom like a shelf; she wore little black fingerless mittens that kept her hands warm without preventing her from counting the francs and centimes. Monsieur Sélect, who made the Welsh rarebits on a little stove behind the bar, had long melancholy moustaches like Flaubert's.

The chief attraction of the Sélect, however, was that it stayed open all night.

For many Americans, Paris meant a welcome escape from Prohibition, which had been in force throughout the USA since a year after the Armistice. In his memoirs, *Being Geniuses Together*, McAlmon harps like a boastful schoolboy on the number of drinks he and his friends

---

* Probably the restaurant on the Quai de Bourbon now named Au Pont Marie.

consumed, and Hemingway often writes in similar terms when describing his Paris life to friends back home: 'I morted a fiasco of wine at lunch ... and I drank a cup full of 3 star Hennessy to see me homeward.' Some of the French drinks were as dubious as the stuff the bootleggers were selling in New York and Chicago. Jimmie Charters says that one bar where he worked sold a good deal of mint julep, made from so-called 'Green River Bourbon' that had been left behind during the war by the US Army. It eventually turned out to be neat alcohol with added flavouring. Other examples were encountered of what Jimmie calls 'the bootlegger's Miracle of Cana'.

Jimmie Charters himself was a principal feature of the Quarter. He turns up in most published reminiscences of Montparnasse at this era and features in several novels. He was a Liverpool-Irish prize fighter, an ex-professional flyweight, who had come to Paris in June 1921 to learn French in the hope of qualifying for a head waiter's job back home. His first Paris job was at the Hôtel Meurice in the rue de Rivoli – much favoured by rich Americans – and after working in other establishments he landed up in 1924 at the Dingo in Montparnasse. 'It seemed a bit off the beaten track, but I liked the idea of working with English and Americans.' He later moved to the Falstaff, a bar in rue du Montparnasse decorated in what was supposed to be the style of an English pub, and his customers came with him. John Glassco caught him in his Falstaff days:

The Falstaff gained a special charm from the contrast between its rather stuffy oak panelling and padded seats and the haphazard way it was run by the bartender Jimmie Charters ... and the waiter Joe Hildesheim, who came from Brooklyn and was known as Joe the Bum. The Falstaff was owned jointly by two Belgian gentlemen who also shared a mistress, a very plump handsome grey-eyed woman called Madame Mitaine. The three of them sat quietly in the ingle of the fireplace every evening and did not interfere in any way, being content to count the cash when the bar closed ... Jimmie and Joe ran the place on the principle that about every tenth drink should be on the house, so that regular clients, and still more the casual visitors, were constantly being surprised by a whispered intimation that there was nothing to pay.

In his novel *The Façade* (1927), the English writer Douglas Goldring describes how his hero Rex, a veteran of Montparnasse, returns there from an absence to find that Jimmie is not in his usual bar, and will not rest until he has found the establishment where

... dressed in a spotless white coat and polishing a glass, stood the diminutive figure of the most popular barman in the Quarter. Having discovered Jimmie, Rex was now quite certain that he would meet during the evening all of his friends and acquaintances who happened to be in Paris.

'Hullo, James', he cried.

Jimmie's face became wreathed in smiles as he put down his glass and held out his hand.

Goldring writes of Jimmie's 'fertile imagination' at creating 'every form of poisonous drink', and particularly mentions Jimmie's 'knockout' which was

never composed until half an hour or so before closing-time. Its composition varied with the inspiration of the moment . . . 'I had to give up serving them at the "President Wilson".' Jimmie once admitted. 'People started climbing up lamp-posts and knocking down policemen and revolving like teetotums between the Dôme and the Rotonde. It gave us quite a bad name.'

Jimmie also observes, in Goldring's novel, that Americans 'don't seem somehow to enjoy themselves in a bar until they've punched someone in the jaw and smashed the place up'. Bar fights among Americans were certainly common in Montparnasse. A friend of Hemingway's, Mike Ward, told Hemingway one day that he had been in a certain bar where he had heard 'two men talking about you. I couldn't hear what they were saying, but I kept hearing the name Ernest Hemingway. So I went over to them and I said, "Are you friends of Ernest Hemingway?" And they said, "No." So I socked them both!'
Jimmie himself liked a fight. McAlmon describes how 'when liquored up he was apt to remember his fighting days, and insist upon "protecting" friends he drank with. Sometimes his protection resulted in a night in jail for both Jimmie and his friends.' On his very first night in Paris, Jimmie had picked an inebriated fight with a street-corner fire alarm, resulting in three weeks in the Santé prison. Samuel Putnam, another Montparnasse habitué, recalls Jimmie using his fists to keep order in his own bar: 'I can see Jimmie . . . reaching across the bar, gentle like, to put an obstreperous customer to sleep . . . then, one hand on the bar and he's across, picking the guy up, dusting him off and sending him home in a taxi – *and* paying his fare! That was Jimmie. I often wonder how he made any money.' Hemingway describes gentler treatment from Jimmie: 'I can hear him saying, "You should go home, sir. Shall I get a taxi?"' According to McAlmon, Jimmie would even use his fists on himself: 'When his blood pressure was too high from overeating and drinking, Jimmie had a habit of going to his room, banging his own nose so that it would bleed, and thereby reducing his blood pressure.'
Jimmie did not know absolutely everybody in the Quarter; he was under the impression, when dictating his memoirs in the early 1930s, that 'Mr Joyce . . . leads a very retired life and never visits bars . . . [but only] attends quiet little gatherings now and then when the intellectuals foregather'. But he saw plenty of Hemingway; he describes how Hemingway 'came to my bar frequently and we would have long

conversations about boxing or he would tell me about bull fighting...
On my night off we often went to boxing matches together... Sometimes he would start sparring in the bar and almost knock someone
over.'

In his memoirs, Jimmie describes a cross-section of lesser-known
Montparnassians. There was Captain Walker, a 'pseudo-English officer
with a game leg', who claimed to have sailed a destroyer across the
Atlantic in record time in 1917 to tell President Wilson to declare war at
once; Captain Walker said that the President was 'forced to agree, and
declared war that same day'. There was Panama Al Brown, the black
American boxer and 'ankle dancer'; Jimmie recalls his notable imper-
sonation of a short man dancing with a tall woman. There was an
American named Leaming who claimed to have been a monk in Russia
and said he had come to Paris for a rest from 'monking'; and there was

old Mitrony, the Roumanian with a grey beard, poor as a beggar but extremely
erudite. He carried a quantity of books and papers under his arm... and said he
was writing a history of the Jews, though no one ever saw him write anything.
At night he slept on chairs in the chauffeurs' restaurant near the Gare
Montparnasse. Every week or so he would disappear, and then a rumour went
around that he was dead... He spoke ten languages fluently and I sometimes
called him in to interpret for me.

Jimmie also recalls

Joe Goodman, the song writer, author of 'Rose of Washington Square' and
'Second-hand Rose'... with his lawyer, Finnety. Goodman could not survive
more than a few minutes without his lawyer. It was a joke in the Quarter to try
and separate Joe from Finnety. They both lived at the Hôtel Lutetia, and Joe,
who spoke not a word of French, could use the telephone, when he was out
somewhere, to reach Finnety at the hotel with great ease. Joe... would say
'Cigar carrot cat carrot wheat'. The number of the hotel was *Ségur quarante-
quatre quarante-huit.* He always got the number without difficulty.

And there was Captain Vail, who 'purchased second-hand airplanes,
fixed them up so they would fly (once anyway) and sold them. He
would deliver them himself, which was proof that they were airworthy.
Vail was one of the heaviest brandy drinkers I have ever known. "You
haven't been anywhere until you've had the D.T.'s," he used to say.
"Those are real travels!"'

Marcel Duchamp points out that 'colourful but non-productive
characters' like these often 'contributed to the success of the creative
group' in Montparnasse. Though non-workers themselves, they provided an entertaining backdrop for those writers and artists who really
were doing something, and not infrequently became 'material' for
paintings and novels. As McAlmon puts it, 'Bohemian centers [like

Montparnasse] present in concentrated form their share of human types and manifestations.' Those who complained about lazy Montparnassians, about bar-flys and café hangers-on who did no work, were missing an essential point about the place.

In *The Façade*, Jimmie Charters sums up the drop-outs of the Quarter: '"I think the people who come here regularly, sir, have, as you might say, given up everything. This is the end, so to speak." Jimmie beamed, his small round eyes twinkled. "They have a lot of fun, though, when they get to that stage."'

*

In his memoirs, Jimmie says: 'One of my best friends among the writers is Bob McAlmon.' John Glassco observes that 'McAlmon's own capacity for alcohol was astounding', and says that during the half-hour of their first meeting McAlmon 'drank half a dozen double whiskies with no apparent effect'. This capacity to remain comparatively sober while making the rounds of the bars meant that McAlmon was one of the more observant chroniclers of the Quarter's night-life.

By the summer of 1923 he had been in Paris for a little over two years, Hemingway for eighteen months. This was the first year after the war, says McAlmon, that 'foreigners began again to congregate numerously in Paris'. The steamship companies had started to introduce cheap transatlantic fares, and the American community, already well established, was being further swelled almost daily by new arrivals who had docked at Le Havre and caught the train to the capital. When Ezra Pound first came to Paris before the war he had been introduced to an elderly marquise who had never before met an American. By 1923 this seemed an impossibility. Pound reported to Ford Madox Ford that Americans were arriving 'like leaves in autumn', and said the place was beginning to seem like Eighth Avenue, New York.

On the night of 13 July 1923, France began its annual three-day celebration of the fall of the Bastille, and this year, says McAlmon, Montparnasse 'extended the gala days to a three months' period'. Jimmie Charters says it was quite normal for parties in the Quarter to go on for three days without sleep or rest, so naturally an official festival like Bastille Day became the excuse for prolonged saturnalia. 'Enough of afterwar recklessness and enough of dawning hopefulness were about,' writes McAlmon, 'for dissipations to have a mass velocity.' This 13 July, McAlmon himself had just returned to Paris from the Forest of Rambouillet, 'where I had been for two months writing on a two-decker novel. I felt entitled to a letdown...The idea of Paris in drunken festival and me not one of the drunkest there, was austere.'

Montparnasse night-life would begin at around five thirty, the hour at which a few habitués would start to drift on to the terrace of the

Dôme, seat themselves at separate tables, and order a drink and sip it slowly while glancing at the paper or a book. Laurence Vail, a regular in the place, writes of this time of day: 'The first hour in Paris and I am hopefully searching the *terrasses* for a drinking companion, a boon Pernod pal.' There was also the Rotonde or the Sélect, or even the Coupole, a little way down Boulevard du Montparnasse, but by general consent the Dôme was the expatriates' headquarters. The novelist Sinclair Lewis, who spent some months in Paris in 1924 to 1925, writes that 'among the other advantages of the Dôme, it is on a corner charmingly resembling Sixth Avenue at Eighth Street, and all the waiters understand Americanese, so that it is possible for the patrons to be highly expatriate without benefit of Berlitz'.

This Bastille evening McAlmon had half arranged to meet an American painter friend, Kenneth Adams, at the Dôme, but when he arrived there could see no sign of him. However, 'it was impossible not to hear Florence Martin as soon as I entered the Quarter. She was at the Dôme bar, electing herself Dowager of the Dôme, Queen of Montmartre and Montparnasse . . . Queen Bee of drinkers.'

Florence Martin was a New York chorus girl who had been sent to Paris for voice training. 'But,' says Jimmie Charters, 'she did little studying and finally stopped entirely. The fascination of the Dôme *terrasse* in the daytime and the Dingo at night were too much for her.' Hemingway describes her as 'a splendid sort of two-hundred-pound meteoric glad girl . . . the only really gay person during the time I frequented the Quarter'.

McAlmon portrays her as 'a dashing bit of colour, of the Rubens type. Her orange hair was piled neatly above her clear, baby-smooth skin. It was easy to believe that the Flossie of some years back, when some pounds lighter, had been one of the more dazzling of Ziegfeld's show-girls.' Jimmie calls her 'pretty and very jolly' and says she was 'not too selfish in her pleasures . . . Many a chap, temporarily down and out, was helped financially by Flossie, though she had no large sums at her disposal.'

At one stage in her Paris career Joe Zelli, the Montmartre night-club king, gave Flossie a so-called 'job', paying her simply to be in his club every night since her mere presence and exuberant gaiety would attract a crowd. 'I have been told,' says McAlmon, 'Zelli did the biggest business of his career during the six months Flossie stayed at his club!'

Laurence Vail says she would regularly begin her day at 6 p.m. with a 'breakfast' of potatoes and gin, and would thereafter quickly reach top form. McAlmon singles her out as one of the few people with whom Joyce could not cope: 'He had difficulty in believing that such a person really existed.' The Bastille celebrations always found her at her most exuberant; one July she was seen, says Jimmie, sitting next to the trombonist on the bandstand outside the Coupole. 'Every time the trombonist took his instrument from his lips Flossie kissed him!'

Seeing her at the Dôme at the beginning of his evening, McAlmon realised that 'she was sure to be sounding off for the next twenty-four hours'. Already she had in tow a somewhat dismayed young Frenchman, who was muttering *'Quelle type!'* The *patron* of the Dôme shrugged and smiled: 'Mais alors, c'est Mlle Flora. Elle est jeune. Toujours gaie.' To which, says McAlmon, Flossie – who did not speak French – responded 'Koochy, koochy' and tickled the *patron* under the chin.

McAlmon had no sooner greeted her in his usual laconic fashion than they were joined by Sylvia Gough, 'slender and beautiful in a fawnlike way'. The daughter of a diamond millionaire, she had been married to the son of a general, and also to an American sculptor; like Flossie she had appeared in the Ziegfeld Follies. Her sons, whom she never saw, were at Eton; Augustus John and one of the Rothschilds had been cited as co-respondents in her divorces. This evening she was 'depressed over newspaper publicity', and she complained languidly to McAlmon, 'delicately weary, with aristocratic and oh, so worldly ennui'. McAlmon bought her several drinks. 'Life began to stir in her,' he writes. '"Bob, you are the most adorable...the most generous darling...He's the only man who doesn't try to come to bed with me every time we get drunk together." "*Merde!*" Flossie exploded.' (It was her only word of French.) '"Lay off your crap of being the gushing lady! We're all bitches together."' Harold Loeb says that Flossie claimed to be a virgin, but 'no authentic data on the subject' had been collected.

McAlmon decided that buying Flossie and Sylvia drinks was too expensive a pastime for so early in the evening, so in an unobserved moment he slipped away to the Stryx, a new Swedish restaurant in a side-street near the Dôme, already popular for more 'intimate' sessions. 'At the Stryx, I found Ezra Pound talking to an English girl, and describing America as it never was...Ezra was not drinking.' (He rarely drank.) Also, 'Florianne was sitting at a table with Yvonne Georges and Kiki.'

Yvonne Georges was a famous Belgian cabaret singer who performed at the Boeuf-sur-le-Toit; she had an Eton crop and immense melancholy eyes. Her companion Florianne liked to behave as the 'French queen' of Montparnasse just as Flossie Martin thought of herself as the 'American queen'; of Spanish blood, she invariably came and went in taxis, being supported by a champagne manufacturer who, says McAlmon, 'gave her thirty thousand francs a month'. She could afford the luxury of the Right Bank but 'preferred the casual camaraderie of the Quarter'. Her penchant for taxis was shared by a British girl whom Jimmie Charters calls simply 'Peggy', who would 'ride all over town in a taxi without a sou in her pocket to pay the fare'. No sooner had she arrived in a bar than the door would burst open and the driver would shout for his money: '"Pay?" she said. "Pay? You frogs! We paid in 1914. You have been paid many times. We paid with our lads and our money!"'

Florianne's other companion at the Stryx, the celebrated Kiki, was the truly regal figure of Montparnasse, mascot and figurehead of the Quarter. Hemingway writes of her: 'For about ten years she was about as close as people get nowadays to being a Queen.' At the Dôme she presided over a central table on the terrace, which had a 'reserved' sign and was known as 'Kiki's table'. Hemingway compared her memoirs, published in the early 1930s, to Defoe's *Moll Flanders*; Samuel Putnam, who edited and translated them, said he was reminded of *Fanny Hill*.

Kiki was born Alice Prin, in Burgundy in 1901, and was brought up in poverty. At the age of twelve she was sent to Paris where she sold flowers, and began to pose for a sculptor, eventually moving in with a pimp. By the age of sixteen she would 'go by the Dôme or the Rotonde and look in to see if I could spot any artists . . . young painters that I went home with, to spend most of my nights in posing and singing'. When that failed she could get 'two francs for showing my bosom' to old men behind the Gare Montparnasse. 'Sometimes I got five francs. I have a terrific bosom.'

Jimmie Charters says she was particularly fond of American seamen. 'I do not suppose there is a single sailor on the U.S.S. *Pittsburgh* who has not toasted Kiki. Once I saw her on the Dôme *terrasse* with thirty sailors and not another girl.'

'Little by little,' writes Kiki of her own life, 'I made my way into artistic circles.' Eventually she took up with 'an American who makes the nicest photographs . . . He speaks just enough French to make himself understood; he photographs folks in the hotel room where we live . . . We hang out with a crowd called Dadaists and some called Surréalistes – for my part, I don't see much difference between them!' The photographer was Man Ray. William Carlos Williams describes a photographic session with him during a visit to Paris:

Man Ray had said that he would like to take my photo. It seemed a good idea . . . Man Ray posed me. I kept my eyes wide open. He asked me particularly to close them a little and I, not knowing, did as he told me to, not realizing the sentimental effect that would be created. (I opened them, though, later when I got his bill.)

Kiki appears in Ray's 1922 photograph 'Kiki de Montparnasse', in which she is nude and holds one hand modestly over her crotch; also in his famous 'Violon d'Ingres' (1924), in which the *f* holes from a violin are superimposed on her bare back. Bryher, visiting Man Ray's studio, was being shown some pictures 'when a door in the gallery opened and I looked up to find Kiki, literally a "nude descending the staircase", attired in a couple of soap bubbles and a wisp of towel, tied where she did not need it, round her neck'.

During her years with Man Ray, Kiki became not merely his model but his visual creation. 'Man Ray had designed Kiki's face for her,' writes Kay Boyle, 'and painted it on with his own hand. He would begin by shaving her eyebrows off . . . and then putting other eyebrows back, in any colour he might have selected for her mask that day, sometimes as fine as a thread and sometimes as thick as your finger, and at any angle he chose. Her heavy eyelids might be done in copper one day and in royal blue another, or else in silver or jade.' John Glassco describes how 'her eyelashes were tipped with at least a teaspoonful of mascara', and her cheeks were 'plaster-white' with 'a single beauty spot . . . placed . . . with consummate art, just under one eye'. Laurence Vail writes: 'You should have seen Kiki in her first coats of paint.'

Frederic Kohner, who wrote a life of her, describes his first drunken sight of Kiki singing at the Jockey Club in Montparnasse one night in the early 1920s when he was a new arrival from Austria:

Neither the years nor my state of inebriation at the time can erase my first impression of her. She wore a simple black dress; her hair was pitch dark and cut with bangs low on the forehead. She had a full mouth, white teeth, and amber-coloured, green-speckled eyes with long, curved eyelashes. Her brows tilted upward to enhance fine, dauntlessly candid eyes. Her figure was on the plump side, not conforming to the then prevailing ideal of the flapper. But it was Kiki's face that one could never forget: a face beyond childhood, yet this side of belonging to a woman.

John Glassco, more cruelly, says that her face in full profile 'had the lineal purity of a stuffed salmon'. Kohner goes on:

When complete stillness had settled over the room she began to sing in a raspy voice:

> '*Les filles de camaret se disent toutes vierges*
> *Les filles de camaret se disent toutes vierges*
> *Mais quand elles sont dans mon lit*
> *Elles preferent tenir ma vis*
> *Q'un cierge – qu'un cierge – qu'un cierge.*'

I understood only a few of the words, but Kiki came to the aid of the uninitiated. She reached for a candle and pointed it, with exaggerated daintiness, at the centre of her thighs. The audience went wild. Without blinking an eyelid she continued:

> '*Mon mari s'en est allé a la pêche en Espagne*
> *Mon mari s'en est allé a la pêche en Espagne*
> *Il m'a laissé sans un sou*
> *Mais avec mon p'tit trou*
> *J'en gagne – j'en gagne – j'en gagne.*

The applause was uproarious. Now, for the first time, Kiki smiled. Then she snatched a hat from one of the customers and went around collecting money.

*

At the Stryx this Bastille night, McAlmon decided not to involve himself with Kiki and her companions. Instead he 'stood at the bar with Rita. She always delighted me.' Rita was a French girl, the kept mistress of a detective who allowed her a lot of freedom. McAlmon says she was 'chummy' with 'the less successful *poules*' (prostitutes), many of whom she virtually supported. Jimmie Charters records that she later took up with an Argentine, and one day shot him and then killed herself.

The Stryx 'orchestra' was by now playing out in the street, and Florianne 'was doing an Eastern dance, writhing her long-waisted hipless body'. ('Florianne . . . does the naughty-naughty dances that go over so big,' writes Kiki.) Somebody was playing a honky-tonk piano on the pavement, and outside other cafés the street orchestras were grinding out their music.

This was the hour of the evening that brought the tourists to Montparnasse – 'Americans in checked shirts,' writes Frederick Kohner, 'Scandinavians in sweaters and heavy boots, playboys in tuxedos, women in men's clothes, dipsomaniacs, dope fiends, schizophrenics, Hindu mystics; it seemed that the whole world had contributed its most extraordinary specimens, its most promising artisans to that incredible conflux at Métro Vavin.' John Glassco complains that the Dingo and the Stryx 'were too full of alcoholics and Scandinavians respectively', and Morley Callaghan mentions some Icelanders who were forever propping up the Stryx bar.

This July evening, the true Quarterites could be seen too. Across the street from the Stryx, says McAlmon, was a long open-air table at which 'the older, staider and productive members of the community' were collecting. 'Jane Heap was there with Mina Loy . . . and Kathleen [Kitty] Cannell . . . Bob Coates, Malcolm Cowley, Harold Loeb and Jim Butler were wandering about before deciding where to have the next drink.'

Jane Heap, co-editor of the *Little Review*, looked entirely like a man and behaved as one. McAlmon describes her conversational style as 'breezy, travelling-salesman-of-the-world tosh', and says her 'strong white teeth' were inherited from Lapp ancestors, 'and well they could gnaw into chunks of whale or seal blubber'. She and her fellow editor Margaret Anderson had recently arrived in Paris with the intention of running the *Little Review* there, but Anderson had fallen in love with a Paris beauty, the singer Georgette Leblanc, and Heap soon returned in dudgeon to New York to edit the magazine single-handed.

Mina Loy was an American by adoption. Born in London, she had trained as an artist in Paris at the turn of the century and had married an English painter, by whom she bore a strikingly beautiful daughter, Joella. The marriage broke up and she went to New York, where she met and married Arthur Cravan, nephew of Oscar Wilde and professional bohemian. Cravan opened a boxing school, prospected for silver, wrote poetry, and disappeared in the desert less than a year after the wedding, leaving Mina with their daughter Jemima. Mina took both her girls to Paris and supported them by making lampshades, which she sold in a shop rented for her by the heiress Peggy Guggenheim. She dressed strikingly. 'Her hats were very like her lampshades,' says Sylvia Beach, 'or perhaps it was the lampshades that were like the hats.' To McAlmon she looked 'as beautiful as a perfect-featured English beauty can look'.

She occasionally published poems in the little magazines. Most of her friends thought them excessively cerebral, but they admired her 'Brancusi's Golden Bird', printed in the *Dial* in 1922 opposite a photograph of the sculpture it described. She also wrote a neat little poem about Gertrude Stein:

> Curie
> of the laboratory
> of vocabulary
> she crushed
> the tonnage
> of consciousness
> congealed to phrases
> to extract
> a radium of the word.

William Carlos Williams says that the line from her poems that everyone remembered was 'Pig Cupid, his rosy snout rooting erotic garbage'.

At the Stryx, says McAlmon, she was talking 'her cerebral fantasies'. Near her at the open-air table, Kitty Cannell contributed 'gaiety, dazzle, a sparkling blondness'. Now in her early thirties, Kitty was currently engaged in divorcing a minor poet, Skipwith Cannell, and in having an affair with Harold Loeb. Later she supported herself in Paris by writing ballet and fashion reviews for the American papers. William Carlos Williams describes 'Kitty Cannell in her squirrel coat and yellow skull cap, which made the French, man and woman, turn in the street and stare seeing a woman, approaching six feet, so accoutred'.

Of the men in the Stryx group, Bob Coates and Malcolm Cowley were graduates of Yale and Harvard, both in Europe – like so many others of their age and background – in the hope of making themselves into writers. Harold Loeb, who came from a wealthy New York banking family and had abandoned business for literature, was running one of the expatriate literary magazines, *Broom*. Jim Butler was the son of an American painter who had married Monet's daughter.

By now, McAlmon had drunk himself into 'a most hilarious frame of mind', and his account of the evening becomes rather blurred; but he recalls, rather later at the Stryx, running across Harriet Monroe. Rather a fish out of water in Montparnasse, the spinster editor of *Poetry* had come over from Chicago to inspect the expatriate scene. McAlmon says she 'proved to me her matured wisdom by letting me buy her some fine old Madeira, served in huge bowl-like glasses of crystal clearness'. She began to lecture him about how he should come back to America and not waste his life in Europe. McAlmon answered that 'I was in Paris for its intellectual atmosphere'. His 'drunken consciousness' told him privately that 'discussion of that sort is useless'.

Miss Monroe had not crossed the Atlantic for many years, and consequently had never met some of her most celebrated contributors to *Poetry*. McAlmon records that someone remarked that Ezra Pound was outside. 'With an eager cry, Miss Monroe arose. "Ezra, I must meet Ezra! Will he be the way I imagined?"' A few minutes later she returned, 'eager and happy'. Margaret Anderson, herself meeting Pound for the first time in Paris this year, had been less impressed: 'It will be more interesting to know him when he has grown up.'

Deciding he had better put some food on top of all that he had drunk, McAlmon ordered a meal at the open-air table, where by this time 'fourteen of us were drinking or eating'. At last his painter friend Kenneth Adams rolled up, moaning about having to go back to America because he was running out of money. Adams soon drifted away again into the crowd, and somebody suggested going to a *bal musette*, or maybe seeing what was happening in other parts of Paris, but McAlmon refused to budge out of the Quarter. What was the point, he asked, when 'things are good just where one is'? Similarly Kiki says she would always refuse attempts 'to turn me aside from the path of duty and take me to Montmartre . . . I refused to be a deserter.'

McAlmon drifted back across the street towards the Dôme, where he 'met an excited group of Americans, headed by Peggy and Laurence Vail. It appeared that Malcolm Cowley had taken a sock at the *patron* of the Rotonde and the cops had arrested him.'

Laurence Vail, born in Paris, had been brought up by his American mother to 'live like a Frenchman but think like an American'. He was married to Peggy Guggenheim, had just published his first novel, and was noted for drunken outbursts of temper – Jimmie Charters describes him hurling bottles across a bar at some Frenchmen he thought were laughing at him: 'One man just missed being killed . . . and the dent in the wall can still be seen.'

Seven years younger than her husband, Peggy Guggenheim was, in her own words, the granddaughter of the 'Mr Guggenheim the peddler' who had bought up 'most of the copper mines of the world'. She had had a lonely, isolated childhood, and as soon as she came of age and inherited her fortune had thrown herself into bohemian literary circles in New York, working at a radical bookshop near Grand Central that her cousin Harold Loeb was then running: 'I became a clerk . . . doing various boring jobs. I was permitted downstairs only at noon, when I had to replace the people who went to lunch, at which time I sold books.' In the shop she met Laurence Vail: 'He had lived all his life in France and he had a French accent and rolled his r's. He was like a wild creature.' Peggy at this time 'was worried about my virginity. I was twenty-three and I found it burdensome. All my boy friends were disposed to marry me, but they were so respectable they would not rape me. I had a collection of photographs of frescos I had seen at Pompeii. They depicted people making love in various positions, and of course I was very curious and wanted to try them all out myself. It soon occurred to me that I could make use of Laurence for this purpose.' He acquiesced – 'I think Laurence had a pretty tough time because I demanded everything I had seen depicted in the Pompeian frescos' – and she married him in Paris, though neither of them was serious about it. They were soon having spectacular fights; Peggy found herself being knocked down in the streets, and for a grand finale Laurence 'would rub jam in my hair'. She says her money gave her a certain superiority over him, but to revenge himself 'he told me that I was fortunate to be accepted in Bohemia and that, since all I had to offer was my money, I should lend it to the brilliant people I met and whom I was allowed to frequent'.

McAlmon, catching up with the Vails and their friends, was told about Malcolm Cowley's fight with the Rotonde *patron*. They said that the café proprietor was a known swine; he had 'asked ladies not to smoke cigarettes or appear hatless on the terrace of his café. He also wished to make his place a rendezvous for sightseers, and comfortably incomed bourgeoisie.' Someone added that during the First World War he had informed on Trotsky. After hitting him, Cowley had been led off by two gendarmes, so everyone, says McAlmon, 'flocked to the police station and swore that the *patron* had started the fight. We knew he disliked Americans, although he had become rich through them, and that he was a sour-faced, scurvy swine.'

Losing interest in this fracas, and not bothering to discover whether Cowley would have to remain in jail, McAlmon observed to himself that the night 'was not yet over'. Forgetting his resolution to stay in the Quarter, and not altogether certain how he had got there, a little later he 'found myself at Bricktop's in Montmartre'.

*

John Glassco was taken up to Montmartre by McAlmon on a similarly festive night:

We found another open taxi... and drove along the wide bright boulevards... until we arrived in the blaze of lights of the spider-web of tourist traps, clip-joints and dives around the Place Pigalle... with the pimps slouching at every corner, the touts outside the boîtes yelling at the passing groups of soldiers and tourists, and every now and then a passing busload of middle-aged American women peeping out from the sectioned windows... 'God, what a wonderful smell this quarter has!' [McAlmon] said. 'Just like a county fair back home. It's got a special quality, too, so phony you can hardly believe it. The triumph of the fake, the old come-on, the swindle – it's marvellous, it's just like life.'

Bricktop's had a speakeasy door, leather-padded, with peepholes. ' "Why, Mistah Bob!" cried a big Negro in a scarlet-and-gold uniform who threw open the door at once. "Come in, Mistah Bob! And how you feelin'? Bricktop baby! Come! Here's the big spendin' man himself!" ' Bricktop was a black American singer named Ada Smith who came from Chicago and took her sobriquet from her dyed orange hair. Glassco describes how she ran up and embraced McAlmon,

twittering, 'Bob, honey, so *good* to see you! Just so *good*. You and you young friends want to sit at the bar, huh? Hey you, Houston, get off that stool and give some room to the clients, you hear me? Get behind that bar where you belong!

A small grinning black man in a white jacket slipped under the bar and came up on the other side.

'First round is on the house, Houston,' said Bricktop. 'Anything the boys desire, except champagne.'

We had three of Houston's specials. This was a long drink of such potency that the first sip seemed to blow the top of my head off.

Bricktop's club was very popular with Quarterites; it stayed open until the last customer had gone; Bricktop knew everyone's name, and her singing of the latest Cole Porter numbers was always exquisite. On Bastille Night 1923, McAlmon noticed quite a few Montparnasse faces in the club: 'Flossie Martin, Sylvia Gough, a young man she called California, Nina Hamnett, Man Ray and Kiki were there.'

Nina Hamnett, seasoned bohemian and veteran of the Bloomsbury and Vorticist circles in London before the First World War, was chiefly noted in the Quarter for her singing of the 'original version' of the ballad 'Rollicking Bill the Sailor', in which the hero becomes 'Bollocky Bill'. McAlmon says that she 'knew everybody and everything, and never let facts ruin a story'. The daughter of a regular army officer, she would tell how she had first sat for the sculptor Henri Gaudier-Brzeska – another of Ezra Pound's pre-war protégés – who had carved a fine torso of her. He was the first person who had persuaded her to model in the nude; when he had finished the preliminary drawings, he told her that it was her turn, and took off all his own clothes, 'and made me draw, and I had to'. Then he said: 'Now we will have some tea.'

She had lost her virginity with the same enthusiasm as had Peggy Guggenheim, in a room near Fitzroy Square where Rimbaud and Verlaine had once stayed, and she said this merited a blue plaque on the wall as much as they did. She first came to Paris just before Jacob Epstein's memorial to Oscar Wilde had been erected in Père Lachaise cemetery, causing a scandal with its prominent genitals. The authorities covered it with a tarpaulin, so every afternoon Epstein, Constantin Brancusi, and Nina would go to Père Lachaise and snatch it off.

Nina recalled the *quatorze Juillet* celebrations of pre-First World War Montparnasse as something of a golden age, simpler in its pleasures than the Bastille nights of the 1920s:

I went to the Avenue du Maine and bought a pair of French workmen's peg-top trousers. I borrowed a blue jersey and a corduroy coat from Modigliani and a check cap. I also bought a large butcher's knife made of cardboard and silver paper at the Bon Marché... I dressed myself up and went out alone. I met Modigliani at the corner of the rue Delambre and the Boulevard Montparnasse. He did not recognise me and when I produced the knife he ran away. I went to the Rotonde, and the waiters did not know me, and to a fair outside the Closerie des Lilas. I returned to the Rotonde and we danced in the streets all night and kept it up for three days... After a time Modigliani decided to undress... Everyone knew exactly when he was going to undress, as he usually attempted to after a certain hour. We seized him... and sat him down.

It is a little surprising that McAlmon ran across her in Bricktop's. She scarcely ever set foot in Montmartre – 'I did not like the atmosphere... or the people' – though she would describe how, long ago, she had visited the Moulin Rouge and watched 'elderly ladies in long skirts doing the can-can'; they looked like the very dancers Toulouse-Lautrec had painted, 'grown considerably older'.

According to Jimmie Charters, Nina knew everyone. 'It became rather a joke at the Dingo, for the telephone would ring constantly for Nina, and the waiter would announce in a loud voice that the Prince of something or the Count of something else wished to speak to Miss Hamnett.' She was greatly admired by Joyce – he 'said I was one of the few vital women that he had ever met. I don't know if that is true, but I have very big lungs and can make a great deal of noise if encouraged.'

At Bricktop's, continues McAlmon, 'we didn't ask each other's names', and on this July evening in 1923 'I sat for an hour at Beatrice Lillie's table, and didn't know it until Brick told me who she was, after she had gone'. The club had an all-black jazz band, and McAlmon listened while Buddy the trap-drummer played and sang Cole Porter's

'I'm In Love'. The piano-player was 'a high-yellow boy who played classical music as well as jazz. He complained mildly to me that if he were of my race he'd be a famous concert pianist, but as it was he didn't have a chance.'

Jimmie Charters says that one day at the Dingo, a Negro came to see the cook and went in through the bar, whereupon most of the American clients got up and walked out in protest. At French-owned nightclubs, black American musicians were commonly found, but some places with American proprietors preferred to have white bands or pianists. At the Jockey in Montparnasse could be found Les Copeland, an old-time pianist and singer from the Gold Rush saloons of the West, who, says Jimmie, had 'hoboed his way through every State in the Union... riding the rods', and 'always had about him that aura of "see what the boys in the back room will have"'. He claimed to have known the original Frankie and Johnnie, and was deeply contemptuous of the rising tide of jazz, complaining that 'all a performer was required to do today was to play the ukelele in three lessons and boop-oop-a-doop through the adenoids'.

College orchestras from Yale and Harvard soon began to appear in Montparnasse, introducing the Charleston. Frederic Kohner describes the arrival of this dance at the Jockey, with Kiki and her partner giving a 'furious performance' in the midst of an admiring circle.

On his visit to Bricktop's with McAlmon, John Glassco listened as Bricktop herself began her act:

Her voice, small but beautifully true, tracing a vague pattern between song and speech, fitting itself to the sprung rhythms of a piano played by an old and dilapidated Negro, seemed to compose all by itself a sentiment at once nostalgic and fleeting... The melody, something banal by Berlin or Porter, was transformed and carried into a region where the heard became the overheard.

The polite ripple of applause seemed suddenly to infuriate McAlmon. 'These bastards don't know what it's all about. Balls, balls!' he yelled. 'Ladies and gentlemen, did you know you were dead?' Someone began to laugh with embarrassment, and McAlmon got up and bowed gracefully at the audience. 'You, my friends, have the luck to be listening to an old-fashioned sot. And if there are any Canadians among you' – this was a dig at Glassco, who came from Montreal – 'let me say that I hate all Canadians, only not quite so much as yanks and limeys. Down with the maple leaf! Bugger the American eagle!'

Bricktop slid up to McAlmon, and Glassco heard her mutter: 'Now, Bob. Please, Bob, you keep this clean.' But there was no stopping him. He downed a fresh drink and stood up again: 'I'm going to sing! This is an aria from my Chinese opera.' He raised his arms, opened his mouth wide, and began what Glassco calls a hideous, wordless toneless screaming. The effect was both absurd and painful; a dead silence fell over the room. Reeling against his stool, his head raised to the ceiling like a dog, yowling, he suddenly seemed to be no longer a drunken nuisance but a man who had gone mad; he was, I thought, actually either out of his mind or trying to become so. Suddenly he turned white, staggered, looked around wildly, and fell back into the arms of the big dinner-coated Negro who had appeared at the bar. 'Gentlemen, you give me a hand with Mistah Bob, huh?' said the bouncer jovially.

Even then it was not the alcohol to which McAlmon had succumbed. Bricktop had slipped 'a little quietener', a Mickey Finn, into his drink.

*

On Bastille Day 1923 by 7 a.m. most of the other customers at Bricktop's had gone home, but McAlmon was still there, lingering with Nina Hamnett, Sylvia Gough, and Flossie Martin. Black musicians came in from other orchestras about town, and two tap dancers stood at the bar arguing about technique. Presently the young black pianist who had talked to McAlmon, Leon Crutcher, left the bar and McAlmon saw him outside talking to a French girl. Bricktop looked worried. 'She said the French girl was ruining a good man, the best pianist she'd ever had.' She told McAlmon she wanted to close the place, 'so a throng of us went on to the Capitol for food'.

At the Capitol there was a brawl going on between a waiter and a crippled Englishman with a swordstick. McAlmon made to throw a champagne bottle at the Englishman, but Sylvia 'held my arms down'. He and the others had just finished their steaks when 'Bricktop came into the place, a grim, frightened look on her face. She was carrying a huge bouquet of flowers. "Knock on wood," she said hoarsely. "Crutcher's shot dead. The best musician in Paris ... He was fighting with that French chippy outside my place ... They went home and she threatened to shoot him if he cut up with other women. He asked her how about with other men, and when she pointed a gun at him he dared her to shoot. She shot..."' There were a number of other Negro musicians from Zelli's and the Palermo eating in the Capitol, and when they heard what had happened they began to look anxious, for several had white mistresses, and, says McAlmon, 'they agreed among themselves that the French girl would not be sentenced'.

McAlmon paid the bill and decided to head off by himself for Les Halles, the central markets, 'hoping to run into somebody I knew or to pick up some strangers'. Sure enough he encountered Hilaire Hiler and his friend Wynn Holcomb. Hiler, a painter, had redecorated and taken over the running of the Jockey Club, just down the street from the Dôme, on the corner of Boulevard du Montparnasse and rue Campagne Première. Kiki describes the club – named after its former owner

'Jockey' Miller – as 'the rage, the one big-time attraction of the Quarter'. Frederic Kohner writes that 'the most remarkable thing... was its compactness. I had never seen so many human beings packed into such a minuscule area. There were long tables placed against the wall... and over a miniature floor space, dancers seemed to have achieved a plastic unity. A thick cloud of smoke and amiability hung over the scene.'

Hiler himself sometimes played the piano in the club, accompanying Kiki's torch songs; she calls him 'some player', and describes him as 'a guy who doesn't show his hand. He puts on a far-away look to help him get by, and hides behind his big ears.' Jimmie Charters says he looked rather like Oscar Wilde; McAlmon calls him 'a handsome frog: dark and sorrowful, with brooding eyes, a big mouth'.

Jimmie tells the story of Hiler finding that Finnety, the inseparable lawyer of Goodman the songwriter, was trying to poison himself in the washroom at the Jockey. Hiler got a stomach pump, saved him, and told him not to do it again. Finnety said he was suffering from a terrible bone disease and had to kill himself. 'Well,' said Hiler, 'the next time go somewhere else.' Finnety asked where. Hiler answered thoughtfully: 'The Dôme is my big rival, you know.' The next day Finnety was found dead in the washroom of the Dôme.

Running into Hiler and his friend on his way to Les Halles, McAlmon stopped with them at a bistro. 'We were all drinking cognac when Kenneth Adams discovered us, and he too was intent upon going to the markets. Hilaire and Wynn had other plans, so we separated.'

Les Halles was the traditional place to end an all-night binge, with a bowl of onion soup at one of the market cafés. 'It was a mistily glistening morning,' writes McAlmon, 'the dazzle seemed to splinter before our befuddled eyes. We knew we were too late for the great show of meats, vegetables, and flowers, but as we walked we spoke... of how Brueghel painted fishes, game, meats, and common, low-down people... At every bistro we stopped to have another cognac... "What's a guy to say?" Kenneth was saying again. He had constipation of the vocabulary... "What's a guy to say?" "Just that, or nothing. Damn the sayers and the knowers. They are lousy bastards generally." "Yep, they don't drink. They keep early hours. *Early to bed and early to rise, And you never meet the regular guys.* Hell, Ben Franklin was an old pirate. A whorehound. But he drank. He was a regular guy."'

The market workers were busy cleaning up the debris and closing their stalls. McAlmon and Adams bought a mass of flowers from an old woman, because she 'was very good-natured and said she wanted to get rid of her stock'. They thought of taking a taxi and presenting the flowers to some lady-friend, but then they encountered three further old women sitting on sacks, and Adams gave all his flowers to one of them who had no teeth. 'The women laughed heartily and complimented us for being young and happy and *si beau*. They insisted that we each accept bundles of their vegetables in return . . . So we left carrying radishes, carrots, and onions, and they also were a problem to dispose of.' Nina Hamnett says people were always coming back to the Dôme from a drunken breakfast at Les Halles, laden with vegetables: 'One day someone arrived back with a sack of potatoes.'

Walking down the market street with their burden, McAlmon and Adams were hailed by a couple of *poules*. 'One of them had no middle to her nose; the other was quite passable-looking . . . We agreed to buy them coffee and croissants, while we had *soupe à l'oignon*.' The girls suggested McAlmon and Adams go home with them, 'and mentioned prices, beginning at thirty francs and coming down to five, since the gentlemen were so charming. We thanked them and suggested another morning, as this was a gala day and we had other appointments. Instead, would they accept the vegetables? They did, for the vegetables would make a soup. We bade them goodbye.'

It was past ten in the morning when McAlmon got back to the Dôme, whence he had set out about fourteen hours previously. A few elderly women were having their morning coffee, but most of the Quarterites were still in bed, if they had gone there at all. McAlmon and Adams ordered 'a cooling *demi-blonde*', but then McAlmon, making a trip to the washroom, discovered that Flossie Martin was asleep at one of the inside tables. 'I became wise and grabbed a taxi, knowing that Flossie would waken and descend upon us all, insisting upon drink and more drink.' Not that McAlmon had decided to go to bed. He told himself: 'There's a Paris full of people I have to have a drink with yet.'

*

'The quarter is sort of more a state of mind than a geographical area,' Hemingway writes in a passage rejected from the final text of *The Sun Also Rises*. 'Perfectly good Quarterites live outside the actual boundaries of Montparnasse.' This state of mind, he goes on,

is principally contempt. Those who work have the greatest contempt for those who don't. The loafers are leading their own lives and it is bad form to mention work. Young painters have contempt for old painters, and that works both ways too. There are contemptuous critics and contemptuous writers. Everybody seems to dislike everyone else. The only happy people are the drunks, and they, after flaming for a period of days or weeks, eventually become depressed. . . . The Scandinavians are the regular, hard-working residents.

T. S. Eliot, discussing the Paris bohemian life in a 1921 letter to McAlmon, judged it with similar harshness, declaring it to be 'such a strong stimulus' that it 'incites to rushing about and produces a pleasant illusion of great mental activity rather than the solid results of hard work'. Eliot concluded: 'If I came to Paris the first thing to do would be to cut myself off from it, and not depend upon it.' William Carlos Williams alleges that, when briefly in Paris in the mid-1920s, Eliot once appeared 'at the Dôme and other bars in top hat, cutaway, and striped trousers. It was intended as a gesture of contempt and received as just that.' McAlmon asks: 'Is Eliot afraid of the interchange of relationships, with their attractions and antagonisms and experiences?'

Rex, the poet hero of *The Façade*, takes the opposite attitude to Eliot and finds the Montparnasse life positively conducive to work:

The writing of poetry seems to demand a particular sort of freedom from the trammels of a conventional existence, and this freedom, whatever its detractors may say, the Quarter undoubtedly provides. Any eccentricity of mood, any whim, could be easily humoured. If he felt sleepy at ten and went to bed, only to wake up at two in the morning, nothing was easier than to dress, leave his hotel, and continue talking to friends whom he had last seen at the hour of the *apéritif*. If he had one of those sudden cravings for excess which seem to afflict nearly all poets at different periods of their creative lives, nothing was simpler than to gratify it.

John Glassco probably comes nearest to a fair judgement on the Quarter when he says that its life did not deserve to be treated merely as a distraction from or background to the serious business of work; it was an end in itself. And did the work really matter? After a few weeks in Montparnasse, Glassco

began to feel that if I could only get rid of my itch for writing I might be quite happy. What, after all, was the use of tormenting oneself by putting words on paper, endlessly arranging and re-arranging them, and then, having at last accepted their inherent failure to say more than one-quarter of what they were meant to, of typing fair copies and hawking the work around to one editor after another until they were printed and perhaps read, if at all, by a few dozen people all busy doing the same thing? One might end up like Bob McAlmon, screaming with frustration in a nightclub.

Perhaps the truly 'productive' and 'creative' Montparnassians were the people who did not bother to work at all, but trained themselves to be artists at pleasure-seeking.* Certainly the Quarter could easily become a total *raison d'être*, a complete way of life. 'Montparnasse!' writes Kiki. 'You get into it you don't know just how, but getting out again is not so easy! There are people who have got off by accident at the Vavin Métro station, and who have never left the district again, have stayed there all their lives.'

*The women – many of whom had no literary ambitions – seemed to manage this more easily than the men. Several people have observed that it was they who dominated the Quarter. William Carlos Williams, though only an occasional visitor there, noticed this: 'The men merely served as their counterfoils.'

Interlude: The oldest country in the world

The man who socked the Rotonde *patron* on the jaw, Malcolm Cowley, was, in McAlmon's eyes, just one of the crowd in Montparnasse that summer. With hindsight, Cowley stands out from the flock of expatriates, since he, almost alone among them, became profoundly interested in his generation's motives for this mass exile to Paris. He eventually wrote a book largely devoted to analysing them, *Exile's Return*, in which his punching of the café proprietor features at some length, since he regarded it as emblematic of what had happened to him since he arrived in Paris in 1921.

In general, though, Cowley prefers to theorise rather than reminisce. Even the opening of his narrative, describing childhood, portrays the typical experience of his generation – that born between 1891 and 1905 – rather than specifically recalling Cowley's own young days in Pennsylvania:

Somewhere the turn of a dirt road or the unexpected crest of a hill reveals your own childhood...The scattered comfortable houses, the flat cornfield along the creek, the hillside pastures where the whitetop bends in alternate waves of cream white and leaf green. The Schoharie Valley in August – or perhaps what we find is an Appalachian parade of mountains rank on rank...Perhaps our boyhood is a stream in northern Michigan...Perhaps we remember a fat farm in Wisconsin, or a Nebraska prairie, or a plantation house among the canebrakes. Wherever it lies, the country is our own...and retains our loyalty even when casting us into exile; we carry its image from city to city as our most essential baggage.

Malcolm Cowley was born in a farmhouse on the western slopes of the Alleghenies. Boyhood summers were spent there, but his father was a doctor in Pittsburgh, and he attended high school in the city. His school was, he says,

like two hundred other high schools west of the mountains. It was new, it was well equipped, it was average in size, having in those days about a thousand pupils. All sorts of people went there – I can remember the daughter of a millionaire coal operator, a future All-American halfback, a handsome Italian who later became a big-time mobster...The atmosphere of the school was prosperous and middle class. Everyone was friendly.

Most of the young Americans who arrived in Paris in the 1920s had been chiefly brought up, like Cowley, in cities and suburbs. If, like McAlmon, they came from rural areas of the USA, they had usually lived and worked in Chicago or New York before moving on to Europe. Their experience was symptomatic of what the whole American nation was going through, for by the early 1900s, for the first time in the history of the USA, the flow of population towards the cities was greater than that to the West. Even such Westward movement as continued was now largely urban in character – people were congregating in the new towns that had been spawned by mining operations or railheads – while in the East the exodus from the countryside was all too visible. The census returns clearly documented the shift to the city, while stories began to circulate of whole rural regions where buildings had been abandoned and were going to ruin. The wilderness was reclaiming farms carved out of it during the previous 250 years.

Writing in 1921, the American social historian Lewis Mumford observed that 'today more than one half the population of the United States lives in an environment which the jerry-builder, the real estate speculator, the paving contractor, and the industrialist have largely created'. This process, said Mumford, had been going on since the 1880s. Whole cities, such as Pittsburgh where Malcolm Cowley was educated, had jumped overnight from a somnolent provincialism into the midst of the machine era. Consequently they were quite destitute of those cultural traditions and institutions which a more slowly developing community accumulates. Even their physical layout – the strictly rectangular arrangement of streets – discouraged a cultural life, for every street was a potential thoroughfare or trading artery, and the tendency towards movement and commerce vastly outweighed the inclination towards the creation of a community with roots.

The move to the cities had been accompanied by the break-up of traditional family structures. John Dos Passos's novel *The 42nd Parallel* (1930), one of the most ambitious pieces of fiction written by a member of Cowley's generation, describes a set of characters moving inexorably to the American cities from small-town beginnings. In every case they lose touch accidentally or deliberately with parents and siblings, and obliterate most traces of their origins.

At his Pittsburgh high school, Malcolm Cowley aligned himself with the 'literary crowd', those boys who 'made good marks in English Composition, read books that weren't assigned for reading, were shy, noisy, ill dressed and helped to edit the school magazine'. Like all literary crowds in all schools at all times, 'we brooded ... we yearned ... we dreamed of escape ... We admired and hated ... these people competent for every situation, who drove their father's cars and led the cheers at football games and never wrote poems or questioned themselves.'

Perceptive and literary-minded adolescents in urban America during the early 1900s had particular reason to feel disillusioned with the society in which they were growing up. The cities were expanding relentlessly year by year, the streets were increasingly busy with automobiles, and middle-class life had become secure and unexciting. The grand American Dream of the perfect society was leading inexorably towards what Cowley calls 'an intolerable utopia of dull citizens, without crime or suffering or drama'. His generation, or those members of it with eyes and minds, could perceive that they were being carried all too smoothly 'towards a destination we should never have chosen for ourselves'.

Sherwood Anderson, contemplating the American Dream from a vantage point in Paris during his visit there in 1921, came to the same conclusion. He wrote in the notebook he kept during this vacation: 'We . . . have all been fed upon the notion that it is our individual duty to rise in the world. No doubt this philosophy has worked out with a certain splendor for a few individuals but on the other hand it may have much to do with our national weariness.'

The weariness was not exclusively American. English writers had experienced much the same malaise, the same despair at 'progress', half a century earlier. In the 1870s Matthew Arnold had complained of the destruction of individuality by urban life, and John Ruskin, William Morris, 'aesthetic' writers and artists such as Oscar Wilde and Aubrey Beardsley, the ruralists like Richard Jefferies and Edward Thomas, and even children's authors such as Charles Kingsley and Kenneth Grahame, had offered a variety of escape routes from the dehumanising industrial monster. In the USA the emergence of this anti-urban sentiment had been delayed; the movement to the cities had begun by the 1870s, but the vast immigration to the USA from Europe during that period and the immense possibilities of 'get-rich-quick' that city life offered to immigrants (demonstrated by such families as the Steins and the Guggenheims) had distracted attention from the more insidious consequences of urban growth. While Arnold was preaching against the horrors of city life in England, Americans were reading Horatio Alger's urban fairy tales of poor-boy-makes-good, and were remembering Benjamin Franklin's precepts about self-improvement through hard work. Not until American society began at last to settle into something like a fixed pattern at the beginning of the twentieth century could it take candid stock of itself.

Malcolm Cowley's generation, growing up just before and in the early years of the First World War, might – as other generations had done elsewhere at times of self-doubt – have turned for consolation and guidance to its country's great authors. But the USA had scarcely had time, in its relentless haste towards material goals, to produce more than a handful of great writers. In any case, Cowley and his friends were not encouraged to read them: in high school they were given an almost exclusively English literary diet.

It was not a diet they relished. 'The authors we were forced to read,' writes Cowley, 'and Shakespeare most of all, were unpleasant to our palate; they had the taste of chlorinated water.' Among all their assigned reading, Washington Irving offered the sole hint of what might be done with native American materials – his 'Legend of Sleepy Hollow' showed that an American valley could be 'as effectively clothed in romance as Ivanhoe's castle or the London of Henry Esmond'. There was also *Hiawatha*, but it was difficult to take that seriously; Hemingway was among many boys who wrote a parody in high-school days. Longfellow's Indian legends seemed as remote from daily experience as the Greek myths.

Cowley's teachers did not encourage him to make explorations in American literature. They gave the impression that the USA was beneath the level of great writing, that 'literature in general, and art and learning, were things existing at an infinite distance from our daily lives'. The term 'literature' meant *English* literature, largely of the nineteenth century, with the addition of the Scriptures and the classics. At Oak Park High School, Hemingway's required reading included English narrative poems from the ballads to *Sohrab and Rustum*, the Greek myths, and stories from the Bible. These were taught in the so-called Oxford Room, a mock-medieval affair of stained glass, high-backed chairs, and exposed beams, decorated with an incorrectly copied Greek inscription and a line from the *Canterbury Tales*: 'And gladly wolde he lerne and gladly teche.' In Hemingway's time the school plays included *Beau Brummell* and *Robin Hood*.

Even the pupils' own writing was infected with this English blight. At that time in American schools, says Cowley, 'a definite effort was being made to destroy all trace of local idiom or pronunciation and have us speak "correctly" – that is, in a standardized Amerenglish as colorless as Esperanto'. Some of the instructors had themselves only acquired this 'correct' speech through effort and practice, and they now set forth its rules with pedantry, 'as if they were teaching a dead language'.

This was all the more damaging since most outstanding writers that the USA had so far produced had been characterised by a strong regionalism. There had been a Knickerbocker School of early nineteenth-century satirical writers, gathered round Washington Irving in New York; a Transcendental School at the village of Concord, Massachusetts, in which the principal figures were Ralph Waldo Emerson, Henry David Thoreau, and Nathaniel Hawthorne; a Charleston School of mid-nineteenth-century South Carolina writers; a Hoosier School of novelists and poets producing accounts of rural life in Indiana; and others. The very best American writing, such as

Herman Melville's *Moby Dick* (1851) and the book that Hemingway regarded as the beginning of American literature, Mark Twain's *Huckleberry Finn* (1884), transcended regional differences and interest. Yet even writers with an apparently pan-American appeal like Walt Whitman and Edgar Allan Poe had been regarded by many of their readers as remote New Yorkers, virtually 'foreigners'. The literary movement that was going on in Hemingway's youth, the Chicago Renaissance, was distinctively Mid-Western.

But local characteristics were fast vanishing, and in some instances had entirely gone already. Lewis Mumford observed that by 1921 even small New England towns like Concord itself had become mere 'mummy-cases', empty shells, as agriculture moved to the wheat-growing West and the population shifted to the cities. He regarded this as especially tragic since it had taken the culture of New England 'more than three centuries before it had borne its Concord fruit'; what hope was there for the new urban society?

Another contributor to the symposium in which Mumford's essay appeared, Clarence Britten, took a similarly pessimistic line:

The vestigial remnants of what regional cultures we have had are rapidly being effaced by our unthinking standardization in every department of life. The railroad, the telephone and telegraph, the newspaper, the Ford, the movies, advertising – all have scarcely standardized themselves before they have set about standardizing everything within their reach ... In the Old South, Birmingham loves to call herself 'the Pittsburgh of the South' ... those once spontaneous fêtes of the plains, the 'Stampede' and the 'Round-Up', have been made so spurious that the natives abandon them for a moth-eaten Wild West Show made in the East; and in only a year or two even New Orleans' Mardi Gras will be indistinguishable from its counterfeits in St Louis and elsewhere.

But right or wrong, the repression of regional differences was what many Americans wanted. Harold Stearns, the editor of the symposium to which Mumford and Britten contributed, observed that the desire not to identify with a particular region was a natural extension of the immigrant's repudiation of his background in the Old World: 'We deliberately sought a new way of life, for in the circumstances under which we came into national being, breaking with the past was synonymous with casting off oppression.' The only significant difference that was still respected between twentieth-century Americans, declared Clarence Britten in his article, was money. Families 'may continue to hold their place only on the condition that they keep their money or get more ... no matter how quickly come by'.

So it was that when Malcolm Cowley and his contemporaries tried to write about their lives and their surroundings, they did not have the words in which to do so. They had been schooled into using 'a language not properly our own', a correct Victorian English, and there did not

seem any way in which this language could be used to describe the
environment they actually inhabited, a jerry-built society that was
energetically repudiating such culture as past generations had achieved.
Certainly Cowley's and Hemingway's high-school instructors believed
in Art and Literature, but they held up these concepts like dead objects in
a museum, artefacts of a remote people, which had nothing to do with
their pupils' daily experience. As F. Scott Fitzgerald says in *This Side of
Paradise* (1920), young Americans were coming to consciousness in 'a
culture rich in all arts and traditions, barren of all ideas'.

Hence Hemingway's enthusiasm for journalism, and for newspapermen. In journalism it was acceptable to write in a plain American style
resembling the language that was actually spoken. Yet even here there
were severe constrictions on individuality. 'Tell your whole story in the
first paragraph,' Hemingway was told by the Oak Park High School
instructor in journalism. 'Leave the least important things till the end.
The editor may have to cut your stuff.' And the urban reader, exhausted
and bored by his day in factory or office, may yawn and turn the page
before he gets to the last paragraph of what the journalist has written.

*

It was scarcely better at university. During his time at Harvard,
Malcolm Cowley found himself studying Goethe's *Dichtung und
Wahrheit* and Elizabethan drama while remaining entirely ignorant of
the place where Harvard itself stood. Why, he vaguely wondered as he
passed a Roman Catholic church on the way to morning classes, was
Cambridge so very Irish? Why were the houses near Boston Old North
Church an Italian quarter? Who had built the elegant mansions on
Beacon Hill? 'I didn't know; I was hurrying off to a section meeting in
European history and wondering whether I could give the dates of the
German peasant wars.'

Still the process of depersonalisation went on. A Jewish boy coming
to Harvard on a scholarship would leave behind not only the whole
tradition of rabbinical literature but also his memories of street gangs in
his Brooklyn childhood, and his family's struggle against poverty. He
had four years of leisure in which to discover himself, to write. 'But
what he would write in those four years,' says Cowley, 'were Keatsian
sonnets about English abbeys, which he had never seen, and nightingales
he had never heard.'

In Cowley's day Harvard was largely occupied with trying to copy
the 'aesthetic' style of Oxford in the 1890s. Undergraduates read the
Yellow Book, discussed Walter Pater and Beardsley, displayed crucifixes
in their bedroom and declared that they found the Church 'voluptuous'.
They posed as Decadent poets and wrote sonnets to a chorus girl,
addressing her as 'little painted poem of God'. E. E. Cummings, four

years older than Cowley, studying at Harvard immediately before the First World War, was enthralled by the sonnets of Dante Gabriel Rossetti and decided to follow his example and become a Pre-Raphaelite poet-painter. He wrote lines about 'prayer-pale stars that pass to drowsing-incensed hymns' and lakes 'enchapleted with lilies white'. At Princeton there was a similar fashion for Swinburnian verse. In *This Side of Paradise* Amory Blaine is introduced to *The Picture of Dorian Gray* and reads Ernest Dowson, Arthur Symons, and Keats. By 1915 E. E. Cummings was aware of Gertrude Stein, and quoted from her *Tender Buttons* in a Commencement exercise at Harvard – but only to raise a laugh, which it duly did. Similarly at Princeton people burlesqued the free-verse experimenters whose work was being published by Harriet Monroe. An undergraduate poet in *This Side of Paradise* writes a piece of *vers libre* which is simply a list of contributors to *Poetry*, and concludes by stating that had he not immortalised them in his own poem they would soon be forgotten. At Harvard, Cummings duly read his way through *Poetry* but thought that Carl Sandburg and Vachel Lindsay were too colloquial, and only admired Ezra Pound, especially liking 'The Return', a poem in thoroughly un-contemporary language about the classical gods and their tenuous relationship to the modern world.

In McAlmon's *Post-Adolescence*, characters at a Greenwich Village party discuss the low self-regard of American literature:

'Lackeyship to England . . . We fête all these English novelists and poets, who are second rate in their own country . . . '

'Rats,' Peter exploded . . . 'That's the attraction of the foreign thing, and doesn't at all mean we're lackeys to England intellectually. We have the energy at the present moment, and any country is ours to learn from if there's anything to learn.'

Harold Stearns, editor of the symposium about American life in the early 1920s, took the same line – that 'whatever else American civilization is, it is not Anglo-Saxon'. The pretence in the cultural sphere that 'we are still an English Colony' was only, said Stearns, believed by 'certain financial and social minorities', and had to be swept away if the USA was to achieve any genuine national self-consciousness.

The writers who were coming to maturity during the First World War knew this, but did not know what their generation could do about it. Already, says Malcolm Cowley, they had become like a summer growth of weeds, precociously unfolding new leaves while the roots 'slowly dried and became brittle'.

*

Ideologically the First World War scarcely interested them. It was not a matter of saving their own lands from an invader, merely an abstract struggle concerning world democracy and the rights of small nations, which, says Cowley, 'apparently had nothing to do with our daily lives at home'. But it did seem to offer first-hand experience. 'We were eager to get into action.'

Those who were too young to fight or too impatient to wait their turn enlisted, like Hemingway, in the Red Cross or one of the American ambulance services, which in effect meant serving in the French or Italian armies. It was largely an exercise in dressing up, of putting on the uniform of a foreign country. In Cowley's case the game went one stage further, since by the time he got to Paris the demand for ambulance personnel had slackened; he and others joined the French military transport, driving munitions trucks. So the front line came in sight: 'Here was death among the flowers, danger in spring . . . real . . . near at hand'.

E. E. Cummings, signing up with a Red Cross ambulance unit the day after the USA entered the war in April 1917, told his family: 'It will mean everything to me . . . to do something I want to, in a wholly new environment . . . I only hope I shall see some real service at the front.' Yet the drivers' and stretcher-bearers' experience was not entirely real. They were non-combatants, spectators around an arena in which 'real' soldiers were being killed. 'We were seeing a great show,' says Cowley, 'collecting souvenirs of death, like guests bringing back a piece of wedding cake or a crushed flower from the bride's bouquet.'

Cummings's experience was fairly typical. He and a friend reached Paris, where they were accidentally separated from their group of ambulance volunteers and enjoyed a splendid five-week holiday before officialdom caught up with them. Cummings went to the Ballets Russes and saw *Petrouchka* and a Satie ballet with sets by Picasso, bought the poetry of Remy de Gourmont and Paul Fort, and had an affair with a *poule* named Marie Louise. Coming from a Unitarian family at Harvard, he decided that Paris was a 'divine section of eternity'.

When he was finally assigned to an ambulance unit near the front line, Cummings found himself in a district where military activity was almost non-existent. He spent most of his working hours cleaning mud off vehicles and aligning himself with his friend William Slater Brown against the despotic section chief, an American who objected to their desire to fraternise with the French. Cummings and Brown soon got into trouble for writing letters expressing their willingness to join the French army but their reluctance on moral grounds to kill Germans, and for Brown's allegations in letters home that 'the French soldiers are all despondent and none of them believe that Germany will be defeated'. They were both arrested and interned in a transit prison camp in Normandy, from which Cummings was only retrieved by his family with considerable difficulty. The consequence was his first book, *The Enormous Room* (1922), a prose account of his experiences there. The

1 (a)   The medallion of
Benjamin Franklin sold in Paris
in 1777
(National Portrait Gallery,
London)

1 (b)   The Statue of Liberty under
construction in Paris in 1883
(from Brian N. Morton, *Americans in
Paris*)

2 (b) Romaine Brook's portrait of Una, Lady Troubridge – in the style of dress that came to be associated with Natalie Barney's salon

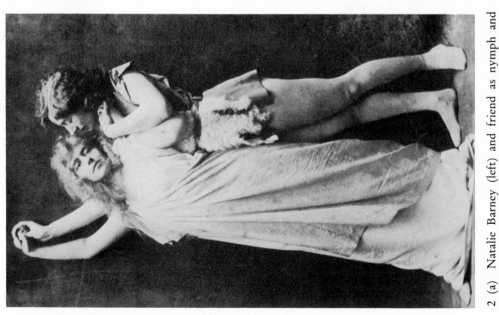

2 (a) Natalie Barney (left) and friend as nymph and shepherd

3   Alice B. Toklas and Gertrude Stein at home in the studio, 27 rue de Fleurus
(Princeton University Library)

4 (a)   Picasso's portrait of Gertrude Stein, completed in 1906 (Metropolitan Museum of Art, New York)

4 (b)   Gertrude Stein photographed by Man Ray in the early 1920s (Princeton University Library; copyright Juliet Man Ray)

5 (a)   (*above*) Sylvia Beach with
James Joyce in Shakespeare and
Company
(Princeton University Library)

5 (b)   Sherwood Anderson; a
photograph given to Sylvia Beach
(Princeton University Library)

6 (a)   Ernest Hemingway, photographed in Shakespeare and Company soon after he first went there in December 1921
(Princeton University Library)

6 (b)   Ernest Hemingway; a photograph given to Sylvia Beach
(Princeton University Library)

) Hemingway at home in Oak Park
919, still wearing his 'uniform'
n F. Kennedy Library)

b) (*below*) Ernest and Hadley
emingway (centre) in an Alpine refuge,
nter 1925–6
rinceton University Library)

KURS-HÜTTE. 1450 m.
DER
SKI-SCHULE SCHRUNS

To Sylvia Beach
from
Bob McAlmon

8 (a)　Robert McAlmon; a
photograph given to Sylvia Beach
(Princeton University Library)

8 (b)　Robert McAlmon; another
photograph from the files of
Shakespeare and Company
(Princeton University Library)

(a) Robert McAlmon and
James Joyce, drawn by Paul-
Émile Bécat soon after
McAlmon had arrived in Paris
in 1921
(Princeton University Library)

9 (b) Robert McAlmon (left) and
Ernest Hemingway in the bull ring at
Pamplona, May 1923
(Princeton University Library)

10 (a) The terrace of the Dôme, heart of the Quarter
(BBC Hulton Picture Library)

10 (b) The Rotonde, in August 1922
(BBC Hulton Picture Library)

11 (a)   (*above*) Kiki, drawn by Hilaire Hiler (from *This Must Be The Place* by Jimmie Charters)

11 (b)   Jimmie Charters, 'Jimmie the Barman', drawn by Ivan Opffer (from *This Must Be The Place*)

12 (a) (*above*) Geniuses together: a group taken at the reopening of the Jockey Club under the management of Hilaire Hiler, 1923. Bill Bird stands at the back left-hand corner; Hiler is in the middle of the back row, in bowler hat; Ezra Pound is on the far right, in Whistler-type beret. The woman in the Russian fur hat in the middle row is Jane Heap, probably Margaret Anderson is standing between her and Pound. Kneeling in the front row (left to right) are Man Ray, Mina Loy, Tristan Tzara and Jean Cocteau
(Mary de Rachewiltz)

12 (b) Malcolm Cowley
(Princeton University Library)

13 (a)   (*above*) Summit conference for the *transatlantic review*: (left to right) Ford Madox Ford, James Joyce, Ezra Pound, and John Quinn, outside Pound's studio in rue Notre Dame des Champs
(Humanities Research Center, University of Texas at Austin)

13 (b)   F. Scott Fitzgerald and Adrienne Monnier on the doorstep of Shakespeare and Company
(University of Princeton)

14 (a) Kay Boyle, photographed by
Man Ray
(Princeton University Library; copyright
Juliet Man Ray)

14 (b) Ernest Walsh
(Princeton University Library)

15 (a)   Harold Loeb
(*Dictionary of Literary Biography*)

15 (b)   (*below*) The woman seated at
the left is Duff Twysden; the small man
standing third from left is Jimmie
Charters
(from *Being Geniuses Together* by Robert
McAlmon and Kay Boyle)

16 (a)   Harold Loeb rides aloft on the horns of the bull
(from *The Way It Was* by Harold Loeb)

16 (b)   Hemingway, head bandaged after a domestic accident, makes his departure from
Shakespeare and Company in March 1928, while Sylvia Beach looks on admiringly
(Princeton University Library)

best American book to come out of the war, it has almost nothing to do with the 'real' war of the trenches and the battlefields. Even those Americans who actually fought, says Cowley, 'retained their curious attitude of non-participation, of being friendly visitors who, though they might be killed at any moment, still had no share in what was taking place'.

So, for the young American would-be writer who had been through these experiences, by the early 1920s 'the country of his boyhood', says Cowley, 'was gone and he was attached to no other'.

★

One day Gertrude Stein went to a garage to collect her car, Gody, which had been taken in for repairs. It was not ready, and the proprietor lost his temper with the young mechanic who was supposed to have done the job. 'You are all,' he told the lad, 'a *génération perdue!*' Gertrude Stein was struck by the phrase, and when Hemingway next called at 27 rue de Fleurus she repeated it to him. 'That's what you are,' she said. 'All of you young people who served in the war. You are a lost generation.'

Hemingway expressed polite doubt, but she would not budge: 'You are. You have no respect for anything. You drink yourselves to death.' He thought this was nonsense, and said so. 'Was the young mechanic drunk?' he asked. 'No,' she admitted. 'Have you ever seen me drunk?' 'No,' she said, 'but your friends are drunk.' 'I've been drunk,' Hemingway revealed, 'but I don't come here drunk. The boy's *patron* [who had made the remark about the lost generation] was probably drunk. That's why he makes such lovely phrases.' Gertrude answered: 'Don't argue with me, Hemingway.'

He gave up, but he was irritated. 'That night walking home,' he continues, 'I thought of Miss Stein ... and egotism and mental laziness ... and thought who is calling who a lost generation?' Yet the phrase had an undeniable ring, and a little later, when he had finished his first novel, he quoted her words as an epigraph at the front of the book: '"You are all a lost generation." – Gertrude Stein in conversation.'

Harold Loeb (original of one of the principal characters in the novel) agrees that 'some of us were "lost" for a time, separated from our traditional moorings and attached to nothing whatsoever ... But at least ours was a generation that had set out to discover, a generation that had chosen to dare.' Malcolm Cowley allows that Stein's remark was pretentious, but says his generation was lost in another sense: 'School and college had uprooted us in spirit; now we were physically uprooted [by the war] ... dumped, scattered among strange people. All our roots were dead now.' And, as suddenly as it had begun for them, the war ended.

★

The Armistice at first induced a sense of relief. 'We were still alive,' writes Cowley, 'and nobody at all would be killed tomorrow.' It soon appeared, however, that the ideals for which the war had supposedly been fought were 'dissolving into quarrelling statesmen and oil and steel magnates'. Young Americans returned from Europe where they had celebrated peace by reeling through the streets with champagne, only to find that the Prohibition amendment had been passed, as if, says Cowley, 'to publish a bill of separation between itself and ourselves', as if to say that 'it wasn't our country any longer'.

The young men who had served in the war had to go back to the USA because at first there was nowhere else to go. Most of them congregated in New York, which Cowley calls 'the homeland of the uprooted, where everyone you met came from another town and tried to forget it; where nobody seemed to have . . . a past more distant than last night's swell party'. They hung about Greenwich Village, homeland of 'the proletariat of the arts', where everyone was poor. They mostly had friends living there already who had written them letters enchantedly describing the bohemian life. Also, New York seemed to be the only city where a young writer could get published, since the 'little magazines' had mostly shifted there from Chicago during the war.

Some people had reached the Village before war service. Cummings had got there after leaving Harvard in 1916, financed by his wealthy classmate Scofield Thayer. He shared a Village studio that had a high ceiling and a peephole in the door, and told his friends that it was a former gambling den. Here he painted and made experiments in unpunctuated and uncapitalised poetry – cautious efforts at modernism. Snatched away again from the Village by the army draft a few months before the end of the war (for his ambulance service and imprisonment had not made him exempt from military call-up), he wrote nostalgically from camp in New England a poem about New York life, first published by Harold Loeb in *Broom*:

> by god i want above fourteenth
>
> fifth's deep purring biceps, the mystic screech
> of Broadway, the trivial stink of rich
>
> frail firm asinine life . . .
>
> the little barbarous Greenwich perfumed fake
> And most, the futile fooling labyrinth
> where noisy colours stroll . . .

When Cummings left the army in January 1919 he went straight back to the Village, this time moving into a garret up seventy-four stairs with no running water or heating.

Cowley and his friends intended to 'continue the work begun in high school, of training ourselves as writers' in the Village. Despite the need to get jobs and earn money, the dislocation of war had left them with 'a vast unconcern for the future and an enormous appetite for pleasure', and for a time sheer hedonism prevailed. 'We danced to squeaky victrola records . . . we had our first love affairs . . . we were continually drunk with high spirits, transported by the miracle of no longer wearing a uniform'. Cowley recalls how the Villager would

wake at ten o'clock between soiled sheets in a borrowed apartment . . . On the dresser was a half-dollar borrowed the night before from the last guest to go downstairs singing . . . enough to buy breakfast for two . . . When the second pot of coffee was emptied a visitor would come, then another; you would borrow fifty-five cents for the cheapest bottle of [bootlegged] sherry. Some-body would suggest a ride across the bay to Staten Island. Dinner provided itself, and there was always a program for the evening. On Fridays there were dances in Webster Hall attended by terrible uptown people who came to watch the Villagers at their revels . . . On Saturdays everybody gathered at Luke O'Connor's saloon . . . On Sunday nights there were poker games . . . There were always parties, and if they lasted into the morning they might end in a 'community sleep': the mattresses were pulled off the beds and laid side by side on the floor . . . so that a dozen people could sleep there in discomfort . . . Always, before going to bed, you borrowed fifty cents for breakfast.

But this Village version of the *vie bohème* could not go on for ever. Allowances from families soon ran out, and there was a limit to how long one could subsist 'on borrowed money, on borrowed time, and in a borrowed apartment'. After that, it was time to support oneself as a writer – or try to. One might perhaps get hold of a friend who worked for the *Dial*, the only literary journal that was both mildly sympathetic to the Village ethos and could afford to pay its contributors. But even the *Dial* funds were strictly limited; all one was likely to get from it was, says Cowley, 'half a dozen bad novels to review in fifty or a hundred words apiece', for which one would be paid a dollar per novel when the review finally appeared – and this might not be for three or four months. Meanwhile, the thing to do was sell the review copies for 35 cents each, which often seemed more than they were worth.

Soon it was time to get a real job. In any case, the attractions of the Village would begin to pall, for the 'Greenwich Village Idea', as Cowley calls it, the twentieth-century version of Mürger's garret life, was fast becoming – in a diluted version – the lifestyle of the middle classes all over the American continent.

By 1920 'bohemian' had become a fashionable word. Wives of businessmen in Milwaukee and Pittsburgh patronised 'bohemian' antique shops, browsed in little 'bohemian' bookstores, and gave 'bohemian' parties. 'In Philadelphia,' writes Cowley, 'young married couples...would encourage their guests: "Don't stand on ceremony; you know we are thorough bohemians." All over the Western world, bohemia...was making more converts.' The Village was beginning to seem like an imitation of itself, an *ersatz* way of dropping out.

Consequently, says Cowley, soon after the war people in the Village were talking about 'the good old days of 1916' and assuming that they would never return. There had also been a collapse of political idealism. Before the USA entered the war, Greenwich Village had plenty of political life: socialism and even anarchism had rubbed shoulders with 'free love' and 'free verse'; meetings had been held in support of the IWW (Industrial Workers of the World, popularly known as 'Wobblies'); and the IWW leader Bill Haywood often held forth to an audience of avant-garde poets and Cubist painters. But in 1917 the Draft Law suddenly forced people to decide how radical they really were. Political revolution had no place in the lives of those – the majority – who accepted Woodrow Wilson's call-up and joined the fight for 'democracy'. Some Villagers evaded the draft and fled to Mexico, and others allowed themselves to be imprisoned as conscientious objectors, but the IWW was virtually destroyed when it set itself in determined opposition to the USA's participation in the war – many of its leaders were sent to prison under new legislation against 'sabotage', while other prominent IWW figures hastily left the country. To many American radicals it seemed that Wilson had drawn the USA into the international conflict largely because it provided him with an excuse to crush the labour movement. A character in Dos Passos's *The 42nd Parallel* observes: 'It's a plot of the big interests, Morgan an' them, to defeat the workers by sendin' them off to the war. Once they get you in the army you can't howl about civic liberty or the Bill of Rights. They can shoot you without trial, see?'

After the war socialism was still a live issue. The Village was deeply concerned about the case of Eugene Debs, a socialist leader imprisoned in 1918 for attacking the Wilson Administration's prosecution of persons charged with sedition under the wartime Espionage Act; and active fury was aroused when Sacco and Vanzetti, two labour leaders who had been convicted on dubious evidence of murder during a payroll robbery, were finally executed in 1927. But by the 1920s the political atmosphere was repressive; much could be contemplated but nothing could be done.

The Village sensed these things acutely, but they were felt elsewhere in America too. Sherwood Anderson wrote in his notebook: 'In Chicago...faces seen on the street...are tired faces. America wants something it cannot find. The old belief in material progress is lost and nothing new has yet been found.' And McAlmon bluntly sums up the American atmosphere in 1921 as 'postwar despairing'.

*

The unrest among young American intellectuals was expressed with considerable force in the symposium that included Lewis Mumford's and Clarence Britten's essays on modern American life. Entitled *Civilization in the United States*, it was assembled during 1921 by a group of New Yorkers under the editorship of Harold Stearns, and appeared in print the next year. Despite its grandiose title it was concerned with one simple question: why was there no satisfying career open in America to talented young men?

Stearns, born in 1891, was a Harvard-educated literary journalist and critic who had visited Europe just before the outbreak of war, had worked on the *Dial*, and in 1919 had published a study of liberalism in America. For the symposium he assembled thirty contributors, and allocated to them such topics as the law, science, economics, sex and advertising, as well as intellectual life and the various arts.

He gave the task of writing on 'The Intellectual Life' to the critic and literary historian Van Wyck Brooks, who took a thoroughly pessimistic line, summing up American writers' experience as 'sterile bitterness, a bright futility, a beginning without a future'. According to Brooks there had always been abundant literary talent in the USA, but very little of it had come to maturity. He asked of how many contemporary American authors it could be said that their work showed 'a continuous growth, or indeed any growth', and judged that the typical American writer never fulfilled his youthful promise. Brooks went on:

Shall I mention the writers – but they are countless! – who have lapsed into silence, or have involved themselves in barren eccentricities, or have been turned into machines? The poets who, at the very outset of their careers, find themselves extinguished like so many candles? The novelists who have been unable to grow up, and remain withered boys of seventeen? The critics who find themselves overtaken in mid-career by a hardening of the spiritual arteries? Our writers all but universally lack the power of growth, the endurance that enables one to continue to produce personal work after the freshness of youth has gone. Weeds and wild flowers! Weeds without beauty or fragrance, and wild flowers that cannot survive the heat of day.

Brooks ascribed this failure to 'something wanting in the soil'. American writers, he argued, had been insufficiently nourished by the arid society in which their roots had tried to grow. More specifically, he blamed it on the wrong sort of education and expectations, the fact that the USA had chosen to stimulate the competitive rather than the creative spirit, so that it was almost impossible to find a scientist or scholar who, for the sake of his subject, 'will refuse an opportunity to become the money-gathering president of some insignificant university'. Brooks thought that Walt Whitman was the sole instance of the 'force and vivacity' that American literature ought to have produced; Henry James, for all his qualities, was both an exile and 'a man of singularly low vitality'. Even Whitman 'folded his hands in mid-career'.

Brooks was following the party line of Stearns and the other contributors, who had met fortnightly for discussions while writing the book. It is possible to read the history of American literature up to 1920 in a different light, to see the achievement of the best nineteenth-century writers – such as Melville in *Moby Dick* and Twain in *Huckleberry Finn* – as reflecting with chilling accuracy the struggles of individuals against the repressions of American society, and the self-destructive compromises they have to make in order to survive within it. Whitman, for all his noisy complaints, was perhaps in the end an irrelevance. Maybe American writers had not really failed but had been too honest, had discovered the barrenness of the society they inhabited – a discovery that was likely to make them fall silent or lapse into trivia. Brooks assumed that it was the 'sustained career' that made a nation's literature, but such a career was just as likely to be evidence of a self-sufficient literary profession in which authors and critics live in each other's pockets and promote each other's work. Such a body of professional writers and critics had been found in London since the eighteenth century, but had played almost no part in the birth of literary modernism just before and during the First World War. The principal figures in the modernist movement were two Americans, T. S. Eliot and Ezra Pound, and an Irishman, James Joyce; while these three were at work, the English literary establishment had chiefly concentrated its attention on the Georgian poets. The USA lacked a close-knit 'literary world' like that of London, but arguably this was to its advantage.

Another doubt about the self-flagellation of the contributors to *Civilization in the United States* is expressed by Harold Loeb, who, after reading the symposium, wrote to a friend: 'These writers all gnash their teeth because America is not France or Germany or England; it seems to me it is rather a cause for rejoicing. What is sadder is that Europe is being Americanized which I am sufficiently romantic to regret.'

Eight years after the symposium was published, Gertrude Stein touched on the issue of the USA's headlong plunge into industrialisation and the problems it had created for writers and artists. She came up with an idiosyncratic observation that was just as pertinent as the long-winded self-reproaches of Stearns's team. Answering a questionnaire in the magazine *transition* about why so many American writers had come to Europe, she wrote: 'The United States is just now the oldest country in the world... the mother of the twentieth century civilisation... Your parents' home is never a place to work.' It was nonsense to suggest, as Stearns and his contributors did, that the USA was a young nation with growing pains. It had become an urban society long before anyone else, and had now reached the geriatric stage. Europe was only just beginning.

*

From the general discontent among young American intellectuals, one idea began to surface: 'They do things better in Europe; let's go there.' This is how Malcolm Cowley puts it; similarly the hero of McAlmon's *Post-Adolescence* longs to be 'in a place where there was color and music that caught him up'. *Civilization in the United States* proposed no single practical remedy for the malaise it believed it had diagnosed, but Harold Stearns knew what he should do. In the summer of 1921 he delivered the completed book to the publisher and then sailed for Europe. He chose his date of embarkation deliberately: the Fourth of July.

'Reporters,' writes Malcolm Cowley, 'came to the gangplank to jot down his last words. Everywhere young men were preparing to follow his example... "I'm going to Paris," they said... "I'll meet you on the Left Bank. I'll drink your health in good red Burgundy, I'll kiss all the girls for you. I'm sick of this country. I'm going abroad to write one good novel."'

A few who set off had plenty of cash at their disposal. McAlmon had Bryher's allowance; E. E. Cummings, who had left for Europe four months before Stearns sailed, was being supported by his father. Most were not so fortunate, but even if an intending writer's family could not pay for him there were ways of acquiring money: it could be borrowed from friends, raised from hopeful publishers as an advance on an unwritten book, cadged from newspapers that were interested in reports from Europe, or begged from official institutions. Cowley himself came over during 1921 on an American Field Service Fellowship for study at a French university:

It was only twelve thousand francs, or about a thousand dollars at that year's rate of exchange, but it also entitled my wife and me to a reduction of fifty per cent in our cabin-class steamship fares. We planned to live as economically as a French couple, and we did. With the help of a few small checks from American magazines, the fellowship kept us in modest comfort, even permitting us to travel, and it was renewed the following year.

In Paris, apartments and studios were not hard to find on the grapevine. John Glassco and a friend, arriving from Canada on a cattle boat, were lent one by two girls who were going into the country for the summer. It was typical of what the expatriates could afford: there was no electricity, only a cold-water tap, and the roof leaked. Everything in it belonged to different people – most of the furniture to Janet Flanner, Paris correspondent of the *New Yorker*; the curtains to an abortionist, Dr Maloney; and the beds to a mysterious man named Boomhower. 'We never knew who owned the lease, and merely paid the rent to the concierge, an old woman called Madame Hernie who lived across the street and spent all her time illuminating the entries in a folio-sized album devoted to the records of her family funerals.'

Though rudimentary, the apartment had great attractions – again typical. There was a big skylight and a tall window filling one wall, while outside, the moonlight would shine on a group of unfinished abandoned statues left by some former sculptor-tenant. 'The smell of some flowering shrub is coming in through the long window,' wrote Glassco in his journal, 'and there's a bird singing somewhere in the walled garden of the Ursuline Convent...' Afterwards, Glassco recalled the apartment with great nostalgia:

It was here that I tried seriously to write for the first time, here I brought my two or three girls, and here I met the woman with whom I at last fell in love and whom, however miserable the outcome of that love, I shall always remember in this setting as she undressed one night in a luminous haze of gaslight and moonbeams before we threw ourselves in ecstasy on one of Mr Boomhower's straw-stuffed beds. It was the theatre of my youth.

For those who could not afford apartments or be bothered to look after themselves, hotel rooms were available at the very cheapest prices, while the quality of Parisian bread and *vin ordinaire* made it possible to live delectably on virtually nothing. For the reasonably affluent, bistros and workmen's restaurants offered more than adequate meals for a few centimes, while each *charcuterie* and *fromagerie* displayed modestly priced wares that would have shamed the produce of a New York delicatessen. A few expatriates set up home in some style – the Hemingways, though they were far from rich, could afford a maid who came in twice a day and cooked their evening meal – but most, like McAlmon, perched in hotel rooms and ate in cafés. Transport was an easy matter: taxis were plentiful and cheap and drove at breakneck speed, while the Métro, with its stations at almost every major road intersection, made it possible to flit about the city for a small coin or two. Not only did Paris offer these delights: it offered them at all hours, never shutting down, and reaching a peak of gaiety around midnight. For those in flight from the Prohibition-ridden USA, it was scarcely believable.

*

Paris was not the only European city with these advantages: they could be found in some measure in Vienna, Venice, Rome, or Berlin, and some American expatriate would-be writers roosted there; but most came to Paris because Americans had always come to Paris, because James Joyce and Gertrude Stein were holding court there, and because Paris could offer a particular blend of metropolitan excitement and almost rural idyll that no other European city could quite achieve.

Sherwood Anderson, arriving there in the summer of 1921 wrote in his notebook of the 'special kind of pearly clearness' of the sky, the 'soft floating clouds and the fresh flowers for sale at marvellously low prices on every street corner', and observed of life on the Seine *quais* that there was 'something quiet, pastoral' about it: 'What a contrast to the dark black shores of the rivers that flow thro our American cities'. John Glassco, who had been brought up in Montreal, responded with even more excitement: 'For the first time I can feel the movement of my thoughts, the pulse of my youth – as you're supposed to at eighteen. I'm lucky to be here, in this city that I love more and more every day.'

Anderson was constantly struck by the nearness of Parisian life to the country: 'Wagon loads of hay go thro the streets, peasants from the country are driving in in carts, the vegetables and fruits are peculiarly fresh and delicious. The morning dew is still on these berries now for sale from a little wheeled cart under my window.' In the rue de la Glacière, near his apartment, Glassco 'met a man with a flock of goats, playing a little pipe to announce he was selling milk from the udder'. Hemingway saw the same thing outside his door in the rue du Cardinal Lemoine: a goatherd leading his flock down from Place de la Contrescarpe and householders coming out with pots into which the animals were milked.

Even the taxis were fun.

Merely to ride downtown in an open taxi [writes Glassco], over the smooth streets paved with tarred wooden blocks was a great pleasure. Almost every morning we would take a dash through the Place de la Concorde, thrilling to the absence of traffic regulations and the wild blowing of horns, and then find our way back on foot to Montparnasse for breakfast at the Dôme or the Sélect.

Most members of the expatriate community carefully avoided the tourist sights, and would only explore the back streets. Glassco and his friend spent sunny days wandering about the odd and obscure parts of Paris – the rue Mouffetard, the Place de la Contrescarpe, the little network of streets around the Place St Michel, the churches of Saint-Séverin and Saint-Julien-le-Pauvre. They became fascinated by the weird occupations and trades pursued by keepers of small shops in these back streets: producers of catskin waistcoats, fake antiques, glass eyes, curious musical instruments, woodworking machinery, martinets for punishing children. They 'agreed to regard as out of bounds' the Grand Boulevards, Passy, the Champs-Élysées, and Montmartre, 'and we absolutely refused to enter the Louvre'.* Once, having made a mistake in the mazes of the Métro, 'we surfaced at the Invalides and were so appalled by the sight of Napoleon's tomb that we fled back down the steps'.

In *Civilization in the United States*, Lewis Mumford had argued

---

* Even Man Ray said he had been in Paris for ten years before he could bring himself to look round the Louvre; eventually he spent about an hour there.

that the modern city encourages perpetual mobility and restlessness. Sherwood Anderson noted in contrast how very stable Paris life seemed: 'Everyone is settled down here. Men stay in the place to which fate has assigned them. A certain freedom of action and living is achieved ... One never sees the tired discouraged faces so characteristic of the American city.'

It was perhaps not 'democratic', not a society in which self-improvement and the attainment of riches were within the grasp of every citizen as they were supposed to be in the USA. But in some scarcely definable way the riches of Paris seemed every man's property: 'Even though a man is a waiter in a café under the shadow of the cathedral of Notre Dame,' wrote Anderson, 'he feels himself in some obscure way a part of the cathedral. Frenchmen built it. He is himself a Frenchman. He is a stockholder in the great company that is France.'

Anderson reflected that the USA, made up of every race in the world, had become a home of racial intolerance. Paris, however, was truly cosmopolitan: 'One often sees negroes dining in restaurants and walking about in the streets with their white sweethearts. The sight attracts no attention. In an American city it would cause a riot.'

On a bridge over the Seine, Anderson watched a young working man with his girl: 'They kissed oblivious to the thousands of people passing ... One sees lovers everywhere going straight on being lovers without selfconsciousness.' There was also a cheerful lack of conformity: 'The American is afraid he will, in clothes, in manner of walking, in facial adornment, in the style of his hat, not quite conform to the accepted standards. He trembles lest someone stare at him in the street. With the Frenchman it is not so. It is his passion to be an individual sharply defined, to stand forth among men.' When the American takes in this fact, continues Anderson, 'a delightful sense of freedom is at once achieved. Deeply buried within yourself is some passion for display. You have in secret hungered to wear a green feather in your cap, to adorn yourself with a red sash, to wear long fierce looking mustachios.' But the American sadly realises that there is no point in trying: 'I am Anglo Saxon. The most humble Paris cab driver can outdo me without an effort.'

Henry Miller reacted in the same way in 1930, noting with pleasure the gendarmes smoking on duty, the general nonconformity: 'Here is the greatest congregation of bizarre types. People do dress as they please, wear beards if they like, and shave if they choose. You don't feel that lifeless pressure of dull regimentation as in N.Y. and London.'

Clarence Britten, writing on 'School and College Life' in *Civilization in the United States*, remarked on this American desire to be inconspicuous, the 'universal desire to be alike ... to put on straw hats the same day, to change your clothes in Texas in accordance with the seasons in New York, to read the books everybody else is reading, to adopt the opinions a weekly digests for you from the almost uniform opinions of the daily press, in war and peace to be incontestably and entirely American'. In *This Side of Paradise* Fitzgerald reflected on the same characteristic among Princeton undergraduates: 'Anything which brought an under classman into too glaring a light was labelled with the damning brand of "running it out"... Standing for anything very strongly... was running it out; in short, being personally conspicuous was not tolerated, and the influential man was the non-committal man.' Clarence Britten puzzled over the causes of the determination to conform; perhaps it was a substitute for 'some natural background we lack but should like to have'. Whatever the root, it was a dangerous and alarming tendency, 'for it masks our ignorance of what we are and what we may reasonably become'.

Yet Sherwood Anderson was not altogether blind to the virtues of his fellow countrymen. He admitted that Americans were capable of 'real humbleness and a strange kind of rather fine sensitiveness', and a friend who was with him in Paris suggested that 'Americans are like fine children, badly brought up'; by contrast, the French seemed 'too alert, too sure of themselves. What have they found to make them so self satisfied? If Paris is beautiful, present day Frenchmen did not make it so.'

Some Americans quickly realised that the European Dream was as false as the American. Malcolm Cowley wrote to a New York friend from France during 1923: 'America is just as god-damned good as Europe – worse in some ways, better in others... New York is refinement itself besides Berlin. French taste in most details is unbearable. London is a huge Gopher Prairie. I'm not ashamed to take my coat off anywhere and tell these degenerate Europeans that I'm an American citizen.' Cowley also says that many Americans, coming in search of a France where 'poets had labored for days over a single stanza', found instead among many French writers a greed for all things American, a hunger to be told about skyscrapers.

*

Though the rate of exchange was favourable in Paris, elsewhere in Europe it was often spectacular. Europe seemed to have lost all its old certainties; instead, it had prices that changed from country to country virtually from hour to hour. On Tuesday in Hamburg, says Cowley, you could order 'a banquet for eight cents (or was it five?)'. On Thursday in Paris 'you might buy twenty cigarettes for the price of a week's lodging in Vienna'. Hemingway calculated that two people could live well and travel comfortably on $5 a day; in Germany he and Hadley had four days' room and full board for 80 cents each. In Paris a hotel room for two people cost on average a dollar a night, and a good dinner 50 cents.

Consequently there sprang into being a new race of tourists, 'parasites of the exchange' who wandered through Europe in quest of the lowest prices. 'Especially,' says Cowley, 'you saw them in the railway station at Innsbruck: Danes, Hindus, Yankees, South Americans, wine-cheeked Englishmen, more Yankees, waiting by the hundreds for the international express that would bear them toward the falling paper-mark or the unstabilized lira.' Cowley and his wife were among them; after an initial month in Paris and half a year in Montpellier where Cowley took a diploma in French literature at the university, they travelled to Brussels, Munich, Vienna, the Tyrol, and back to Germany, where inflation was rampant. The game of getting the best value for dollars, as much as restlessness or the search for literary 'copy', explains the constant journeyings about Europe of such people as Hemingway and McAlmon. 'Following the dollar,' says Cowley, 'we saw machine guns in the streets of Berlin, Black Shirts in Italy . . . and drifted down to Pamplona for the bullfights.'

For a salary of $100 a month from the USA, Matthew Josephson, an expatriate poet, lived in Berlin in a lavish apartment with two maids. He could afford riding lessons for his wife, meals in the most expensive restaurants, picture collecting, and charitable gifts to struggling German writers. Cowley, who visited him, thought it all insane, and hurried back to France on an international express full of amateur smugglers, among them an English army officer with seven suitcases full of German butter which he proposed to sell in Belgium at an enormous profit.

Thereafter, Cowley and his wife spent some months in Giverny, the village on the edge of Normandy where Claude Monet was still painting at the age of eighty; Monet's daughter had married an American artist, and a small American colony had gathered around them. From Giverny, Cowley would go up to Paris every week or so, just for the day:

You rose before dawn, breakfasted on a quart of milk-and-coffee, just caught a branch-line train full of peasants dressed for market day, then changed at the junction for the Paris express – all this hurry and loss of sleep was a stimulant like cocaine. You could not sit still in your compartment, but picked your way up and down the crowded corridor, watching the Seine unwind as the train creaked faster... Paris! You leaped into the first empty taxicab outside the station... raced from one appointment to another, from an art gallery to a bookshop... Paintings and music, street noises, shops, flower markets, modes, fabrics, poems, ideas... You drank black coffee by choice, believing that Paris itself was sufficient alcohol. Late at night, you took the last train for Normandy, happy to be returning to your country routine.

On one of these day trips Cowley was introduced to the Dada group. 'They are the most amusing people in Paris,' he wrote to a friend a few days later. He had accompanied André Breton to a play of which they approved. The 'approval' consisted of taking thirty seats in the balcony night after night, booing the curtain raiser, and applauding the main play (a banal melodrama) with such wild cheers that the police were forced to intervene. Breton would then orate for half an hour to the stalls, and the audience would break up into arguing factions. 'Really,' reported Cowley, 'it is huge fun.'

He was particularly delighted to discover Dada because he and most of his contemporaries were failing to find the guidance they had hoped for from the established masters of the older generation, resident in Europe. Up to now, T. S. Eliot had been the poet who seemed to suggest the direction they should take. He also appealed, says Cowley, as a Mid-Western local-boy-makes-good. But in the autumn of 1922 *The Waste Land* made its first appearance in the *Dial*, and simultaneously in Eliot's new *Criterion*, and while they admired it greatly Cowley and his friends were distressed by its implication that the present was inferior to the past, and that the modern age could only express itself by borrowing and patching together lines from dead poets. Hemingway felt strongly that Eliot had been overrated and was really dry as dust. During 1924, writing on the death of Joseph Conrad, he said that if he could bring Conrad to life again 'by grinding Mr Eliot into a fine dry powder and sprinkling that powder over Conrad's grave', then he would 'leave for London early tomorrow morning with a sausage-grinder'.

Joyce was widely held to be the epitome of the isolated, exiled artist, producing a work of genius without regard to physical comforts or other distractions. But when – as Cowley did, on one of his weekly visits to Paris – one actually met the man, one realised that he was not by any means averse to comfort; furthermore, said Cowley, on anything other than literature his opinions were 'those of a fourth or fifth-rate mind'. It was as if he had 'starved everything else in his life to feed his ambition'. Despite this discovery, Cowley remained deeply admiring of *Ulysses*, though certain of his friends wondered if there had been an overvaluing of the book – John Dos Passos read it 'at one gulp' while laid up with 'flu: 'Parts I found boring and parts I found magnificent.' Fitzgerald had read *A Portrait of the Artist as a Young Man* at Princeton and was 'puzzled and disappointed'. Hemingway judged Joyce to be more a conjuror than a great artist: 'It was easy to write if you used the tricks. Everybody used them. Joyce had invented hundreds of new ones. Just because they were new didn't make them any better. They would all turn them into clichés.'

Proust, who died in November 1922, seemed another symbol of fulfilled literary ambition. But he was not a model Cowley and his friends wanted to copy: 'We had neither the wish nor the financial nor yet the intellectual resources to shut ourselves in cork-lined chambers and examine our memories.'

By comparison with these men, Dada seemed wonderfully refreshing. Up to now, writers of Cowley's age had wondered if anything remained to be said in literature. Now they could take heart again, for Dada announced 'new subjects waiting to be described, machinery, massacre, sky-scrapers, urinals, sexual orgies, revolution'. Yet Dada was not really so original: F. T. Marinetti and his Futurists had done much the same thing in Italy before the First World War, and even in 'waterlogged' London the Wyndham Lewis group, with its iconoclastic magazine *BLAST*, had trodden a similar path. It was less an artistic revolution than a game of shocking the bourgeoisie in a superficial manner. By the time Cowley arrived in Paris, Dada had in any case split into its two mutually hostile factions (the Breton–Aragon group against Tristan Tzara and his adherents), and was shading off into the more restrained excesses of Surrealism. Some of Cowley's associates thought it all plain silly; a contributor to *Broom* described the Dadaists as 'merely a group of young Parisians many of whose innovations of literary capering are possibly less signs of new life than the death spasms of a movement in which the last word was practically said by Mallarmé – right at the start'. Hemingway dismissed Tzara and Dadaism as 'shit'.

Nevertheless Cowley had a lot of fun with the Dadaists, both in Paris and Giverny, where Aragon came to stay to work on a book and Tzara paid a visit. One evening after a jubilant dinner at a restaurant, at which E. E. Cummings was also present, they all went back to Cowley's studio over a blacksmith's shop, and Cowley began to make a Dadaist speech against 'book fetishism' – the fact that people collect books. He pulled some of his own collection off the shelves, or at least a few unwanted review copies and French texts, tore them in two and set the pile alight: 'It was a gesture in the Dada manner, but not a successful one, for the books merely smouldered... Cummings proved that he was a better Dadaist... by walking over and urinating on the fire.'*

Equally Dadaist and more successful in causing a stir was the punch that Cowley landed on the jaw of the Rotonde *patron* that 1923 Bastille night while McAlmon was making the rounds of the bars. Cowley,

---

* This episode is also recalled in his memoirs by John Dos Passos, a kind of *alter ego* to Cummings, who was there too. Born in 1896, Dos Passos was the illegitimate son of a prominent Mid-Western attorney of Portuguese descent. He had been educated at Choate and Harvard, where he became great friends with Cummings, and he served in an ambulance corps during the war. Like Cummings, he got into trouble through writing anti-war letters. He took himself to study at the Sorbonne in 1919, and published two novels based on his war experiences. He was a left-wing sympathiser who regarded the war as a deceit by Woodrow Wilson. Contemporaries found him rather a comic figure, peering through thick glasses. He was an incorrigible traveller and only made sporadic appearances in Paris, though he had numerous friends among the expatriates there, including Hemingway, who had first met 'Dos' during war service. His novel trilogy *U.S.A.*, published volume by volume during the 1930s, is an extended exercise in social realism.

who was due to return to America in three weeks' time, was not exercising any personal grudge against the café proprietor; he explains that he merely felt the man 'deserved to be punched' because he was thought to be a paid police informer who had reported some years earlier on the conversations of Lenin and other revolutionaries at his café table. He was also inclined to insult American girls, treating them as if they were *poules*. He was, in other words, a symbol of a certain bourgeois mentality.

The idea of hitting the man was proposed by the ever-belligerent Laurence Vail. They had all been sitting on the terrace of the Dôme when suddenly Vail said: 'Let's go over and assault the proprietor of the Rotonde.' Cowley agreed, and he, Vail, Aragon, and other members of the party crossed the road. Aragon led the first assault, which as befitted a true Dadaist was entirely verbal; in beautifully shaped sentences he expressed his opinion of all *mouchards* (stool-pigeons) and asked 'why such a wholly contemptible character as the proprietor of the Rotonde presumed to solicit the patronage of respectable people'. The waiters, sensing that a fight was coming, formed 'a wall of shirt fronts' round their employer; Laurence Vail pushed through it and, being a native French speaker, made an angry oration at such speed that Cowley could only catch a few phrases, all of them abusive. The *patron* backed away: 'His eyes shifted uneasily, his face was a dirty white behind his black mustache.' Harold Loeb looked on anxiously with an embarrassed smile.

Cowley began to be angry at these useless gestures, and was 'seized with a physical revulsion for the proprietor, with his look of a dog caught stealing chickens and trying to sneak off'. Elbowing the waiters aside he struck him a glancing blow on the jaw. Then, before he could strike again, 'I was caught up in an excited crowd and forced to the door'. He had almost forgotten about the incident when later in the evening he met Tristan Tzara at the Dôme and they went for a stroll together, arguing as to whether the Dada movement could be reunited. They passed the terrace of the Rotonde: 'The proprietor was standing there with his arms folded. At the sight of him a fresh rage surged over me. "*Quel salaud!*" I roared for the benefit of six hundred customers. "*Ah, quel petit mouchard!*"' A few moments later, recrossing the street towards the Dôme, Cowley 'felt each of my arms seized by a little blue policeman'.

One of the gendarmes was determined to amuse himself.

'You're lucky,' he said, 'to be arrested in Paris. If you were arrested by those brutal policemen of New York, they would cuff you on the ear – like this,' he snarled, cuffing me on the ear...'Ah, the police of Paris are incomparably gentle. If you were arrested in New York, they would crack you in the jaw – like this,' he said, cracking me in the jaw, 'but here we do nothing, we take you with us calmly.' He rubbed his hands, then thrust his face toward mine. His breath stank of brandy. 'You like the police of Paris, *hein?*' 'Assuredly,' I answered. The proprietor of the Rotonde walked on beside us, letting his red tongue play over the ends of his mustache.

Cowley found himself charged with assault and resisting arrest – the policeman showed a scratch he claimed had been inflicted on him – but a bribe dispensed with the second charge. He spent a night and a day in jail, was let out after a preliminary hearing, and collected 'nine young ladies in evening gowns' as witnesses for his defence. 'None of them had been present at the scene in the Rotonde the night before, but that didn't matter: all of them testified in halting French that I hadn't been present either; the whole affair was an imposition on a writer known for his serious character.' The examining magistrate was impressed; moreover Cowley got the poet and novelist André Salmon, who was also a crime reporter for *Le Matin*, to work behind the scenes. 'He managed to have my trial postponed from day to day and finally abandoned.'

The most striking feature of the affair was the effect it had on Cowley's Dadaist friends: 'They looked at me with an admiration I could not understand.' He became, instantly, a Dadaist figure, and was pressed to contribute to Dadaist reviews all over Europe. The irony of this was that his poems were not Dadaist at all, nor even faintly revolutionary in tone: 'They were poems about America, poems that spoke of movies and skyscrapers and machines, dwelling upon them with all the nostalgia derived from two long years of exile.' A typical poem describes the decaying scenery of his childhood summers in Pennsylvania:

> I watched the agony of a mountain farm,
> a gangrenous decay;
> the farm died with the pines that sheltered it;
> the farm died when the woodshed rotted away.
> It died to the beat of a loose board on the barn
> that flapped in the wind all night;
> nobody thought to drive a nail in it.
> The farm died in a broken window light . . .

The same issue of *Broom* in which this was published contained E. E. Cummings's 'Three United States Sonnets', unambiguously expressing a longing for Greenwich Village and New York. Harold Loeb writes that in the exiles' minds the USA had become 'a land transformed by distance into a place of shining towers and green hills'. Cowley, Cummings, and the rest of them had found, in Cowley's words, 'a crazy Europe in which the intellectuals of their own middle class were more defeated and demoralized than those at home'. Consequently they began to reconsider their own country: 'We had come three thousand miles in search of Europe and had found America.'

PART THREE

Fiesta

1
Iceberg principle

The Hemingways decided that their baby should be born in Toronto. Hadley thought the medical care would be better there,* and Hemingway could earn a steady wage from the *Toronto Star*, which had been printing his reports from Europe.

But arriving in the *Star* offices in September 1923 he was not exactly treated as a returning hero. The editor made it clear that he would have to work like any young reporter, refused him a by-line and sent him long distances to cover routine stories. 'The free time that I imagined in front of a typewriter in a newspaper office has not been,' he wrote to Gertrude Stein and Alice Toklas after a month of this. 'The whole thing is a sort of nightmare.' In October the baby was born – a boy, who, says Harold Loeb, was soon trained to put up his fists and assume a fierce expression – and Hemingway decided that they must return to Europe as soon as possible. 'We have both been very homesick for Paris,' he told Gertrude and Alice. And to Sylvia Beach: 'Thank Gawd we will get back to Paris.'

They sailed back in mid-January 1924. 'Have you seen Hueffer's new magazine?' Hemingway had asked Gertrude and Alice in a letter not long before leaving Toronto. 'I have been invited today in a letter by Pound to come home and direct its policy etc. I feel the invitation has been exaggerated.' But when he got back to Paris – where this time he and Hadley took a second-floor apartment at 113 rue Notre Dame des Champs, just round the corner from the Dôme and up the street from Ezra Pound's studio – he discovered that there was little exaggeration.

In a tiny balcony perched precariously over Bill Bird's antediluvian printing machine on a *quai* of the Île St Louis, the fifty-year-old English novelist Ford Madox Ford, *né* Ford Madox Hueffer, was attempting to launch a new literary journal. Thanks to Bird's whim, its title was being printed as *transatlantic review*. The use of lower case might be avant-garde but the editor emphatically was not.

Hemingway already knew Ford a little, and could not stand him.

* Although there was an excellent American Hospital in Paris (at Neuilly), founded in 1910.

Ford shared his predilection for tall stories, but unlike Hemingway, Ford expected no one to believe them. He told Gertrude Stein that people kept following him around Paris because he looked exactly like the Bourbon claimant to the throne; if so, a very moth-eaten Bourbon. Harold Loeb describes his appearance: 'Ford moved ponderously, with his feet at right angles to each other. His head resembled Humpty Dumpty's except for the walrus mustache and the rosy complexion of a retired officer of the Indian Army.' Wyndham Lewis once compared him to a seedy character out of Conrad, with whom Ford had collaborated in their early days – Ford told Lincoln Steffens he was 'the man who taught Conrad to write'.

Hemingway's mistake was to take Ford seriously and brand him a liar. Most people were amused rather than annoyed by the fact that, as Harold Loeb puts it, Ford was 'blessed with total unrecall; he remembered nothing as it actually happened'. John Glassco encountered him at a Paris party:

Ford inclined graciously towards us from what seemed to be a height of about seven feet. His reputation, his high wheezing voice, and his walrus moustache were frightening until one saw his small twinkling eyes, which were full of kindness and curiosity. 'You write poetry, my young friend,' he said. 'I wonder if you would mind my asking whether your poems are sad or joyous?' 'Mostly joyous, I'm afraid.' 'Admirable. I was talking to Willie Yeats the other day, about the communication of joy in poetry . . . Willie and I were asking ourselves what was the most joyous *modern* poem in English . . .'

Which must have been an invention, since – as Pound always pointed out – Ford and Yeats could not tolerate one another's company.

But then, Ford claimed friendship, even kinship, with anyone who was influential. Before 1914 he had been heard describing his intimacy with the Kaiser; when war broke out he abandoned his Germanic surname and volunteered for the British Army, though he was over age. After the war it got about that his mouth hung open because he had been gassed, but really it had always hung open. He made a great deal of his war experiences, and Hemingway began to learn a lesson from this: 'I'm going to start denying I was in the war,' he wrote to Pound, 'for fear I will get like Ford to myself about it.' Actually, he had already far exceeded Ford's modest degree of exaggeration about his military exploits.

The Hemingway's new apartment was near the Closerie de Lilas in the Boulevard du Montparnasse. A generation earlier this had been the café where all the French poets met, and Hemingway took to working there because it was a little distance up the road from the Dôme and the Rotonde crowds. But Ford soon discovered it too, and in *A Moveable Feast* Hemingway gives a wickedly funny caricature of one of their encounters:

I was sitting at a table outside of the Lilas watching the light change on the trees and the buildings and the passage of the great slow horses of the outer boulevards. The door of the café opened behind me and to my right, and a man came out and walked to my table.

'Oh here you are,' he said.

It was Ford Madox Ford, as he called himself then, and he was breathing heavily through a heavy, stained moustache and holding himself as upright as an ambulatory, well-clothed, up-ended hogshead.

Ford allows Hemingway to order a drink for him, changes his mind after the order has been given, and then complains that he has been brought the wrong cocktail. Hemingway – who mentions that Ford suffered from halitosis – describes Ford then inviting him to 'the little evenings we're giving in that amusing Bal Musette near the Place Contrescarpe on the rue Cardinal Lemoine'. Hemingway says he knows the place well, having lived above it for two years, but Ford pays no attention and says he will 'draw a map so you can find it'. Then he spots a passer-by, 'a rather gaunt man wearing a cape', and claims he has 'cut him' by refusing to greet him. Hemingway asks who it was, and is told: 'Belloc...*Did* I cut him!' (Later, says Hemingway, it turned out not to have been Belloc at all, but Aleister Crowley.)

I was trying to remember what Ezra Pound had told me about Ford [Hemingway continues], that I must never be rude to him, that I must remember that he only lied when he was very tired, that he was really a good writer and that he had been through very bad domestic troubles. I tried hard to think of these things but the heavy, wheezing, ignoble presence of Ford himself, only touching-distance away, made it difficult.

Ford was scarcely more charitable about Hemingway. Writing in 1927, he complained that

in Paris I have lived for years buried under mountains of Middle-Westerners who there find it necessary to assume the aspects, voices, accents and behaviours of cow-boys crossed with liberal strains of prize-fighters and old-time Bowery toughs. They may have been born in Oak Park, that suburb of Chicago that is the mildest suburb in the world; but they are determined to make you and Paris think them devils of fellows who have only left Oklahoma of the movies ten minutes before.'

In his autobiography, Ford also implies that Hemingway's stories were distinctly tall: 'Mr Hemingway shadow-boxed at Mr Bird's press...shot tree-leopards that twined through the rails of the editorial gallery and told magnificent tales of the boundless prairies of his birth.'

Pound had reason to be charitable to Ford. In his own early days in London, Ford had been the first editor to print his work, and had given him some invaluable advice about the need to modernise his poetry. As for the 'bad domestic troubles' to which Pound had alluded, fifteen years earlier Ford had abandoned his wife and daughter for the leading *femme fatale* of the Edwardian literary world, Violet Hunt – the 'Sylvia' of his *Parade's End* novels, of which the first was about to appear when Hemingway met him. That affair lasted till the First World War, when Ford took up with an Australian art student whom Ezra had introduced into London society, Stella Bowen. In 1924 he and Stella had just arrived in Paris after a period of trying to live off the land in Sussex. Ford was a prolific writer, but until *Parade's End* only his short novel *The Good Soldier* (1915) had achieved much success. He had scarcely any literary income, and he and Stella were surviving on her Australian capital. They had a baby daughter.

Hemingway found Stella almost as trying as Ford. He wrote to Pound:

Every few days Madame F comes over in her best Australian manner and while complaining in a high voice of her troubles, all her troubles, sneezes and coughs on our baby . . . On the slightest encouragement . . . she will start on the tale of her 50 hour confinement that produced Julie. I am going to interrupt some time with the story of the time I plugged the can in Kansas City . . . so that the plumbers had to be sent for . . . with a turd produced after 5 hours of effort.

Stella made no claim to be in control of Ford. She told Hadley twice in the same evening: 'You know I caught Ford too late to train him.' Hemingway wondered if she meant house-trained.

Stella is 'rather vague' in her memoirs as to how Ford's *transatlantic review* started, and how Hemingway became involved in it. She explains its birth as almost inevitable: 'Ford's name as an editor was one to conjure with, since he had been the founder and editor of the *English Review* and had there published the early work of a whole galaxy of writers who afterwards became famous. He could judge the quality of a manuscript by the smell, I believe! "I don't read manuscripts," he said, "I know what's in 'em."'

In fact Ford's editorship of the *English Review* had been years earlier (1908–9), and had only lasted a few months before he was sacked by the proprietor. Certainly during that brief period he had discovered and printed the work of Pound, Wyndham Lewis, and D. H. Lawrence, but the magazine's celebrity at the time was chiefly due to its regular contributors including such big names as Thomas Hardy and H. G. Wells. Stella is, however, quite correct in saying that Ford often did not bother to read manuscripts before sending them to the printer.

His own excuse for starting a new magazine in Paris was that 'a dozen times I was stopped on the Boulevards and told that what was needed was another *English Review*.' No doubt somebody, maybe Pound, made such a remark to him. But Ford was neither in touch nor in

sympathy with the young American exiles in Montparnasse. The only
new writer he particularly wanted to publish at that moment was an
Englishman, A. E. Coppard, whom he had just discovered living in
obscurity in Oxford; he wrote to Coppard: 'I've started this review
with you in mind as I started the *English Review* to publish stuff of
Hardy's.' Indeed he even tried to get Hardy himself to contribute once
again – and received the wise reply from Dorset: 'Don't you think you
should invite young men more particularly, and keep out old men like
me?'

Stella says that Pound had 'a whole line-up of young writers waiting
for Ford, with Hemingway at the top'. But really the list began and
ended with Hemingway. Pound did persuade John Quinn, a New York
lawyer who had been supporting various of his protégés, to put up
money for the magazine, but as far as literary contributions were
concerned Pound's only ideas were to push Hemingway in Ford's
direction and himself write articles publicising George Antheil's music,
his latest Paris discovery. After delivering his articles on Antheil and
telling Ford to get Hemingway to run the *transatlantic review* for him,
Pound left permanently for Rapallo, as he now found Paris too full of
Americans for his taste. From this safe distance he sent Ford a good deal
of abuse about the way the magazine was going.

A specimen issue of the *transatlantic review*, distributed free to
booksellers and potential subscribers, included contributions by Mina
Loy, McAlmon, and Cummings, but thereafter Ford made almost no
effort to extract manuscripts from the crowd at the Dôme. The first
number came out in January 1924, just as Hemingway was sailing back
from Toronto. 'The whole thing,' says Stella, 'was run in conditions of
the utmost confusion. Everything that could possibly go wrong with
regard to the printing, paper, forwarding and distribution, did go
wrong.' An elegant White Russian colonel appointed himself to manage
the magazine's affairs but soon departed, leaving them in confusion, and
Joyce described the first issue as 'very shabby' in appearance, while
Quinn sent angry telegrams of complaint.

As to the content, there were poems by Cummings, but by now his
work could be found in virtually all the little magazines, not to mention
the *Dial*. The issue was largely taken up with a reprint of *The Nature of
a Crime*, an ancient Ford–Conrad collaboration that had first been
published in the *English Review* in 1909; there was also an article by
Ford making much of his own part in the writing of it. The issue also
contained a memoir of Whistler by an eighty-seven-year-old friend of
Pound's mother-in-law, and many columns of ponderous editorialis-
ing by Ford, both in his own identity and as Daniel Chaucer, under
which pseudonym he began a series of articles entitled 'Towards a Re-
Valuation of English Literature'. The tone of it all was absurdly
nostalgic; Ford seemed to be trying to conjure up the pre-*Waste Land*

world. T. S. Eliot wrote ambiguously to Ford that he welcomed the appearance of the magazine 'with extreme curiosity'.

The White Russian was briefly replaced by Basil Bunting, a fierce young poet whom Pound had rescued from the Santé prison where he had been thrown after some drunken antics, but Bunting found that his duties included babysitting for Ford and Stella, so he soon made way for Hemingway. In his memoirs Ford suggests that besides Hemingway there was 'a bewildering succession of sub-editors' who 'had all been cow-boys', but this was just another attempt to belittle Hemingway.

One of Hemingway's first actions as sub-editor was to write to Gertrude Stein saying that Ford would like to print *The Making of Americans* in what he (Hemingway) referred to as the *Transportation Review*. Ford 'wondered if you would accept 30 francs a page . . . I said I thought I could get you to . . . He is under the impression that you get big prices when you consent to publish.' Hemingway did not trouble to correct him: 'After all it is Quinn's money.'

Gertrude was 'quite overcome' with excitement at getting the great work into print at last, and since she had only the one manuscript she immediately set Alice and Hemingway to work to copy it out for the printer. Hemingway must quickly have resented his joke against Ford as he laboured to transcribe the endless and frequently incomprehensible epic. Meanwhile, Gertrude contemplating the *gloire* that would result from the publication of the book she claimed was 'the beginning, really the beginning of modern writing'.

Ford soon discovered what was going on. He said that Hemingway had told him that *The Making of Americans* was just a short story, whereas 'it was not a short story but a novel, in fact several novels' – and several unreadable novels at that. Hemingway admitted to Gertrude that he was having 'a constant fight' to make Ford keep printing it, but it filled the space, and Gertrude's name was much admired in the circles where Ford wanted the *transatlantic review* to be read. Reluctantly he let it ramble on month after month.

Joyce had promised to contribute, and had allowed himself to be photographed with Ford, Pound, and Quinn to help launch the magazine. Now he gave Ford some pages from the new book he had begun in March 1923, a year after the publication of *Ulysses*. Ford did not like the future *Finnegans Wake* any more than he admired *The Making of Americans*, and he deplored the Joyce cult, but Joyce's name was of course an excellent selling-point, and Ford put the new piece of prose in a section in the April 1924 issue entitled 'Work in Progress'. Joyce liked this title and decided to use it for the book itself until it was complete. Hemingway reported to Pound that as usual Joyce was making free with his proofs; 'His manuscript started at 7 pages (printed) but by additions to the proof in microscopic handwriting eventually reached about 9 pages.'

The *transatlantic review* conducted much of its editorial business on Thursday afternoons. In fact it seemed to be chiefly an excuse for Ford to hold an 'At Home' in Bill Bird's print shop that day, with Stella making tea for everyone. 'Ford,' she writes, 'would first be observed aloft at his desk... talking to a new contributor. Presently he would descend and spread geniality among the faithful.' Ford himself writes of these Thursdays: 'You never saw such teas as mine. They would begin at nine in the morning and last for twelve hours. They began again on Friday and lasted until Saturday. On Sunday disappointed tea drinkers hammered all day on the locked doors.'

McAlmon gives a less enthusiastic account: 'Ford's teas were not highly interesting, but as Bird and I were often in the shop we dropped in.' McAlmon's view of Ford was as critical as Hemingway's: 'It was quite impossible to talk of a place or a person without Ford topping your story.' He says Ford liked telling the world that he was 'the master of prose style'. Conrad died soon after the magazine was launched, and Ford organised a memorial issue designed, says McAlmon with little exaggeration, so that 'the glory which was Conrad's appeared but a reflection of Ford's glory'.

Now and then, Ford would expand the Thursday teas into evening gatherings when literary discussion was supposed to take place. McAlmon describes one of these occasions in a Montparnasse bistro on a Saturday night. Joyce was supposed to be guest of honour and the usual crowd of Quarterites turned up, but the evening was not a success. 'Miss Hamnett arrived, primed for gaiety,' writes McAlmon, 'and then Miss Florence Martin... But, miracle of miracles, Miss Martin was cold sober.' Joyce forgot to come, so someone had to go to fetch him, and when he arrived neither he nor anyone else had much to say. Nora Joyce was heard by McAlmon to mutter: 'Jim, what is it all ye find to jabber about the nights you're brought home drunk for me to look after? You're dumb as an oyster now, so God help me.'

Slightly more successful but potentially just as embarrassing were Ford's gatherings at the grubby *bal musette* underneath Hemingway's old flat in the rue du Cardinal Lemoine. These evenings could reveal unexpected talents. 'Ezra Pound was a supreme dancer,' writes Sisley Huddleston, an expatriate who sometimes attended them. 'Whoever has not seen Ezra ignoring all the rules of tango and of fox-trot, kicking up fantastic heels, in a highly personal Charleston, closing his eyes as his toes nimbly scattered right and left, has missed one of the spectacles which reconcile us to life.'

*

Hemingway said that McAlmon had presumably written '8 or ten novels etc' since they last met. He had published Hemingway's *Three Stories and Ten Poems* during the autumn of 1923 while Hemingway and Hadley were in Toronto. The slim booklet caused no public stir, but it was at least in print, which was more than could be said for the Bill Bird pamphlet of Hemingway pieces. Bird had announced the booklet, which was to be called *in our time* (lower case was becoming fashionable), for December 1923, but the following March it was still at the binder's. 'After awaiting various dates,' Hemingway wrote to Pound, 'I have lost the fine thrill enjoyed by Benj. Franklin when entering Philadelphia with a roll under each arm. Fuck literature.'

Hemingway had hoped the *transatlantic review* would print some of the 'damn good stories' he said he was now writing, but Ford was turning out to be a very cautious editor. He had been anxious about possible suppression on account of the 'Work in Progress' stuff from Joyce – presumably just because it was by Joyce, for nobody could detect anything obscene about it, or indeed make much of it at all. Hemingway reported to Pound that, apart from Joyce and Gertrude Stein, Ford was accepting only the sort of things *Century* or *Harper's* would have printed, which seemed crazy considering the secure financial backing from Quinn. 'The only stories I've got that I know the St. Nicholas Mag.* wont publish I know damn well Ford wont too.' And such pieces of his as Ford had accepted, he 'changes ... revises ... cuts ... makes it not have sense etc.'

It is quite true that when Hemingway's story 'Indian Camp' appeared in the April 1924 *transatlantic review* it had been lopped of the first eight pages of the manuscript, but whoever performed this surgery – and it may have been Ford – knew very well what he was doing. As published in Ford's magazine, 'Indian Camp' has a wonderfully abrupt start:

At the lake shore there was another rowboat drawn up. The two Indians stood waiting.
   Nick and his father got into the stern of the boat and the Indians shoved it off and one of them got in to row. Uncle George sat in the stern of the camp rowboat. The young Indian shoved the camp boat off and got in to row Uncle George.
   The two boats started off in the dark. Nick heard the oar-locks of the other boat quite a way ahead of them in the mist. Nick lay back with his father's arm around him. It was cold on the water.

In the manuscript the story starts with the boy Nick Adams afraid of the dark and firing off a rifle to fetch his father and uncle back from fishing in the lake. Shorn of this rather pedestrian setting-up, the story becomes laden with dark significance.

It describes Nick's doctor-father going with the boy and his uncle to assist an Indian woman in labour. For Nick, the experience is implicitly

---

* Celebrated American magazine for children.

an initiation into (in T. S. Eliot's phrase) 'Birth, and copulation, and death', the three elements of life. Nick is rowed across to the other shore of the lake with his father's arm around his shoulder – a symbol of his own infancy – and is led through a wood to the place where the birth is to take place; Hemingway informs us that it 'smelled very bad' there. Nick's father, who all along behaves maternally to the boy, tries to explain about reproduction, but Uncle George can only play the brutal father-male ('Damn squaw bitch!' he snarls at the woman in labour), and the birth, a Caesarean without anaesthetic, is so disgusting as to appal the child:

Later when he started to operate Uncle George and three Indian men held the woman still...
'There. That gets it,' said his father and put something into the basin.
Nick didn't look at it.

The boy's horror is reinforced by the discovery that the baby's father, lying in the upper bunk, has cut his own throat. Uncle George, unable to come to terms with this, vanishes into the night – male authority has proved unreliable – and Nick and his father are left discussing death. Having covered the whole of life in four pages, the story finally allows Nick to revert to the false security of childhood: 'In the early morning on the lake sitting in the stern of the boat with his father rowing, he felt quite sure that he would never die.'

In this small masterpiece, as in all Hemingway's writing from now on, a sense of drama is created through the omission of all specific expression of emotion, giving the impression that comment is superfluous, that the events in the story – themselves often implied rather than clearly described – are too traumatic to require it. Hemingway said of this: 'I always try to write on the principle of the iceberg. There is seven eighths of it under water for every part that shows. Anything you know you can you eliminate and it only strengthens the iceberg.'

This 'iceberg' principle produces writing that is superficially close to the school of literature – generally thrillers or detective fiction – known as 'hard-boiled', in which the hero or narrator is a 'tough guy' who represses his feelings and does not allow himself to give way to horror or pity. Hemingway's prose in his early books is not like this: 'Indian Camp', not a 'tough' story at all, is remarkably squeamish. Nick's view of the world is fearful and cautious, and whenever possible he averts his eyes and shelters under his father's protection. '"I'm terribly sorry I brought you along, Nickie," said his father... "It was an awful mess to put you through."' Life itself is 'an awful mess', and the story, far from being 'hard-boiled', is about the trauma of discovering this.

*

Ford afterwards claimed that he had discovered Hemingway – 'I did not read more than six words of his before I decided to publish everything that he sent me' – but at the time he showed no enthusiasm, handing the task of reviewing Hemingway's *Three Stories and Ten Poems* to his secretary on the *transatlantic review*, an American girl named Marjorie Reid whom Pound had recruited from the Dôme terrace. She wrote a perceptive piece, observing that Hemingway had taught himself to seize upon 'moments when life is condensed and clean-cut and significant', and had learnt to eliminate 'every useless word'.

in our time finally emerged from the binder during the spring of 1924. Its thirty-two pages consisted of sixteen short untitled 'chapters' – prose fragments of a paragraph's length – six of which had already appeared in the *Little Review*. The book's title was an ironic reference to words from the *Book of Common Prayer*: 'Give us peace in our time, O Lord.'

The sixteen 'chapters' are presented as fragments from narratives that have otherwise evaporated, leaving these short episodes stranded, There is no obvious connecting thread betweeen them, other than that several describe incidents in the First World War, some refer to bullfights, and all are concerned with the theme of brutality – there are descriptions of executions and of refugees struggling through the mud. But though it amounts, as one reviewer said, to 'a harrowing record of barbarities', the events are described, like the birth and death in 'Indian Camp', in a manner that is the opposite of 'tough'. Here an English officer recalls the killing of Germans at an improvised barricade:

It was a frightfully hot day. We'd jammed an absolutely perfect barricade across the bridge. It was simply priceless. A big old wrought-iron grating from the front of a house. Too heavy to lift and you could shoot through it and they would have to climb over it. It was absolutely topping. They tried to get over it, and we potted them from forty yards. They rushed it, and officers came out alone and worked on it. It was an absolutely perfect obstacle. Their officers were very fine. We were frightfully put out when we heard the flank had gone, and we had to fall back.

Hemingway is trying to mimic the verbal style of an English acquaintance who had fought in the war, but it sounds more like a girl describing her pony's performance in a gymkhana. The viewpoint, like Nick Adams's in 'Indian Camp', is childlike; the speaker experiences such a revulsion from what really happened – the killing of soldiers helplessly caught in a trap – that he can only allude to it by talking about 'potting' them, an expression perhaps suggesting a children's game with toy pistols. Again, life is such 'an awful mess' that the narrator is having to retreat from it, to regress into childhood, using language itself as a defence against the world.

Some of the other 'chapters' of *in our time* seem to be concerned to explore the territory that divides journalism from literature:

They hanged Sam Cardinella at six o'clock in the morning in the corridor of the county jail. The corridor was high and narrow with tiers of cells on either side. All the cells were occupied. The prisoners had been brought in for the hanging. Five men sentenced to be hanged were in the five top cells. Three of the men to be hanged were negroes. They were very frightened...

When they came towards him with the cap to go over his head Sam Cardinella lost control of his sphincter muscle. The guards who had been holding him up dropped him. They were both disgusted...

Here the narrator seems to be a journalist covering the story for his paper, but the difference between *in our time* and real journalism is shown by the actual newspaper account in the *New York Times* from which Hemingway took the material for another 'chapter', about the execution of Greek cabinet ministers. The newspaper version opens as follows:

To begin the horrors of the morning it was discovered by the guards that one of the five had died in the van on the way out from heart failure.

On the arrival of the van, Gounaris was lifted out on a stretcher to stand up and face a firing party. It was then found that this wretched man, who, after all, had been a figure in the recent history of Europe, was unable to stand at all...

This is Hemingway's version in *in our time*, in its entirety:

They shot the six cabinet ministers at half past six in the morning against the wall of the hospital. There were pools of water in the courtyard. There were wet dead leaves on the paving of the courtyard. It rained hard. All the shutters of the hospital were nailed shut. One of the ministers was sick with typhoid. Two soldiers carried him downstairs and out into the rain. They tried to hold him up against the wall but he sat down in a puddle of water. The other five stood quietly against the wall. Finally the officer told the soldiers it was no good trying to make him stand up. When they fired the first volley he was sitting down in the water with his head on his knees.

A superficial reading of these two accounts might suggest that Hemingway was the eyewitness; the *New York Times* reporter indulges in expressions of emotion which seem contrived and histrionic. However, the newspaper report gives the plain facts, while in contrast Hemingway – as in 'Indian Camp' and the account of the shooting at the barricade – is averting his eyes from what is really happening. The rainwater, the puddles, and the 'wet dead leaves' are substitutes for the blood that is about to be shed, the hospital with its shutters nailed shut anticipates the lifeless corpses or perhaps the coffins that are to receive them, and the account stops abruptly just as the first real death is about to happen – Hemingway has cut out the detail of the man who was already dead, as this would have spoilt the effect of these substitutions for death and bloodshed. Similarly in the account of the hanging, the height and narrowness of the prison corridor suggests the gallows and the drop, which are themselves scarcely mentioned, while the climax is not the execution but the prisoner defecating in his trousers – reverting to childhood, even babyhood, for he 'lost control of his sphincter muscle' like a child not yet properly toilet-trained. The *in our time* 'chapters' are, then, exercises in the 'iceberg' principle, experiments in describing horror and brutality by keeping the real subject matter submerged.

*

Hemingway told a friend that Ezra Pound has said *in our time* was the best piece of prose he had read in forty years. The book's technique was a prose version of Imagism – described by William Carlos Williams as 'no ideas but in things'. The Imagists, too, had omitted anything that could be judged superfluous. Yet Harold Loeb wondered if Hemingway's preference for this style of writing was due less to literary fashion than to his own character. Loeb doubted if he was really able to immerse himself fully in any experience, whether he was not pathologically suited to being the uninvolved observer of other people's troubles.

Edmund Wilson, reviewing *Three Stories and Ten Poems* and *in our time* in the *Dial* in October 1924, judged the poems unimportant but called the prose 'of the first distinction'. He said Hemingway was the only American writer apart from Sherwood Anderson who had 'felt the genius of Gertrude Stein's *Three Lives*'. The characteristic of this Stein–Anderson–Hemingway school, said Wilson, was 'a naïveté of language often passing into the colloquialism of the character dealt with', but despite its flatness of time it could convey 'profound emotion and complex states of mind'. Wilson also observed that it was not just that these three writers were successful in the traditional style of English prose: 'It is a distinctively American development.'

*

By midsummer 1924 the *transatlantic review* had, as Stella Bowen puts it, 'absorbed' all Quinn's backing and her and Ford's own cash. Ford went off to New York in the faint hope of extracting some more dollars from Quinn, and left Hemingway in charge of the magazine while he was away, blandly informing his readers in a pre-departure editorial that his deputy's tastes 'march more with our own than those of most other men'.

This seemed almost an invitation to misbehaviour, and as soon as

Ford had gone, Hemingway assembled an issue (dated August 1924) calculated to annoy him. He threw out the serialisation of Ford's own *Some Do Not* (the first part of *Parade's End*), and dropped Ford's Daniel Chaucer critical *dicta*, in order to make way for contributions by Bryher, Dorothy Richardson, Nathan Asch, John Dos Passos, and William Carlos Williams. Ford got back to Paris just before the issue went to press, and squeezed in a sarcastic editorial observing that 'Mr Ernest Hemingway, the admirable Young American prose writer', had saddled the magazine with 'an unusually large sample of the work of that Young America whose claims we have so insistently – but not with such efficiency – forced upon our readers'. He reassured them that 'with its next number the Review will re-assume its international aspect'.

Hemingway had been paid nothing for the editorial work, and Hadley's income had dropped drastically, thanks to unwise investments. He badly wanted to spend some time in Spain – he and Hadley managed it in July 1924 with Bill Bird and McAlmon – but they were running out of cash, and the *transatlantic review* left Hemingway with little time for his own work. He told Pound that acting as editor in Ford's stead had 'killed my chances of having a book published this fall and by next spring some son of a bitch will have copied everything I've written and they will simply call me another of his imitators. Now we haven't got any money anymore I am going to have to quit writing and I never will have a book published. I feel cheerful as hell.'

The *transatlantic review* struggled on for a few months more, but Quinn died of cancer soon after Ford got back from New York (he had been too ill to talk business while Ford was there), and Ford wasted a good deal of effort and money trying to raise backing elsewhere; Hemingway describes him spending '100s of francs on taxis trying to get 500 francs out of Natalie Barney'. It was Hemingway himself who lifted the magazine temporarily out of its difficulties by persuading a Chicago acquaintance who had married an heiress to put up a substantial sum. (Hemingway was obliged meanwhile to borrow 100 francs each from Pound and McAlmon to survive.) By the end of the year the magazine's new cash had all been spent, and the issue dated January 1925 was the last. Ford had been persuaded to include another batch of work by young expatriates, so he sneeringly entitled it a 'children's number'.

Hemingway was at least managing to write much faster now; in August he told Gertrude Stein and Alice Toklas – who had agreed to be godparents to the Hemingway baby, christened John but nicknamed Bumby – that he had finished two long short stories. One of them, 'Big Two-Hearted River', covered 100 pages of manuscript, 'and nothing happens and the country is swell, I made it all up, so I see it all and part of it comes out the way it ought to ... but isn't writing a hard job though. It used to be easy before I met you. Certainly was bad, Gosh, I'm awfully bad now, but it's a different kind of bad.'

In October, writing to thank Edmund Wilson for his piece in the *Dial*, he said he had 'worked like hell' and had produced 'a book of 14 stories with a chapter of In Our Time between each story – that is the way they were meant to go – to give the picture of the whole before examining it in detail'. The book had been sent to a friend in the USA who hoped to find a publisher.

Whatever he might say in justification of the scheme, the 'chapters' of *in our time* fitted rather awkwardly between the short stories he had written for the new book. They seemed to have been reduced to the status of a decorative border, and have little or nothing to do with the short stories, several of which were about the boyhood and adolescence of Nick Adams. *In Our Time*, as the new collection was to be called, was therefore a less tightly constructed book than *in our time*. Nor were all the new stories entirely successful. 'The End of Something' and 'Three Day Blow' skilfully described Nick Adams's skill at fishing or his drunken evening with his friend Bill, but became mawkish when they tried to deal with the break-up of a love affair:

All he knew was that he had once had Marjorie and that he had lost her. She was gone and he had sent her away. That was all that mattered. He might never see her again. Probably he never would. It was all gone, finished.

Another piece, 'A Very Short Story', was an idealised account of Hemingway's wartime affair with the nurse Agnes in the Milan hospital: 'She was cool and fresh from the night...There were only a few patients, and they all knew about it...As he walked back along the halls he thought of [her] in his bed.'

But these defects were hugely outweighed by the good things in the book. Hemingway could now sustain the tight, narrative style of the *in our time* 'chapters' through full-length short stories – though they were often not 'stories' in the conventional sense. For example, 'The Doctor and the Doctor's Wife' simply portrays its author's irascible father as Dr Adams, having a pointless quarrel with Indians who have come to cut up logs for him, and 'Cross-Country Snow' presents a few moments from a skiing holiday with a male friend. Both are studies in atmosphere and nuance rather than constructed narratives. Best of all is 'Big Two-Hearted River', the story whose completion Hemingway had announced to Gertrude and Alice. This is an account of an entirely eventless fishing and camping holiday; the adult Nick Adams is alone in the Michigan landscape with his own reflections for company:

Nick was hungry. He did not believe he had ever been hungrier. He opened and emptied a can of pork and beans and a can of spaghetti into the frying-pan.

'I've got a right to eat this kind of stuff, if I'm willing to carry it,' Nick said. His voice sounded strange in the darkening woods. He did not speak again.

He started a fire with some chunks of pine he got with the axe from a stump. Over the fire he stuck a wire grill, pushing the four legs down into the ground with his boot. Nick put the frying-pan on the grill over flames. He was hungrier. The beans and spaghetti warmed. Nick stirred them and mixed them together. They began to bubble, making little bubbles that rose with difficulty to the surface. There was a good smell. Nick got out a bottle of tomato ketchup and cut four slices of bread. The little bubbles were coming faster now. Nick sat down beside the fire and lifted the frying-pan off. He poured about half the contents out into the tin plate. It spread slowly on the plate. Nick knew it was too hot. He poured on some tomato ketchup. He knew the beans and spaghetti were still too hot. He looked at the fire, then at the tent, he was not going to spoil it all by burning his tongue. For years he had never enjoyed fried bananas because he had never been able to wait for them to cool. His tongue was very sensitive. He was very hungry. Across the river in the swamp, in the almost dark, he saw a mist rising. He looked at the tent once more. All right. He took a full spoonful from the plate.

'Chrise,' Nick said. 'Geezus Chrise,' he said happily.

'Big Two-Hearted River' is a recapitulation of 'Indian Camp', except that this time Nick turns his back entirely on the 'awful mess' of adult life and retreats into the country of childhood. Deposited by a train in the middle of nowhere, he discovers that the town he had expected to find has been burnt to the ground; the adult world has been wiped out at a stroke. He then sets off on foot to explore a landscape that seems to be his own body: crossing a gentle ridge of hills he looks down on a country that is dotted with 'islands of dark pine trees', and in one of these he lies down to rest, looking up contentedly at the erect tree trunks, 'straight and brown without branches'. He falls asleep, and when he wakes it is almost as if he had been reborn female. Certainly he is now a homemaker:

His hands smelled good from the sweet fern. He smoothed the blankets. He did not want anything making lumps under the blankets . . . Already there was something mysterious and homelike . . . He was in his home where he had made it. Now he was hungry.

The meal he cooks for himself is the kind of food that children eat, and he suffers from a childlike impatience to begin it before it has properly cooled.

Having rediscovered the female and childlike sides of his own nature, in the second part of the story he specifically investigates his own sexuality. He goes fishing – presumably in the 'Big Two-Hearted River' itself, though the story's title is never explained; very likely it is the Indian name for Nick's trout stream, and it seems, with its hint of breasts, to emphasise the female nature of the river. Nick's actions appear superficially male – impaling grasshoppers on his hook as bait and standing with an erect fishing rod – but again he seems also to take on a female role. Plunging himself into the river, he feels 'all the old feeling' as he watches the slippery trout sliding beneath the surface of the water and catches two of them. 'They were both males,' he discovers as he slits them open with his knife, 'long grey-white strips of milt, smooth and clean.' He reacts to each catch as if it were orgasm: 'Nick's hand was shaky ... The thrill had been too much. He felt, vaguely, a little sick, as though it would be better to sit down.' He seems to be in a pre-adult state in which he can come to terms with female as well as male characteristics in himself. At the end, he chooses to remain in this state for the present, rather than to return again to adult male sexuality: 'He did not feel like going on into the swamp ... He did not want to go down the stream any further today.'

The other outstanding story *In Our Time*, 'The Battler', begins in a manner closely resembling the opening of 'Big Two-Hearted River'. Again, Nick finds himself by the railroad track in open country, this time having been thrown off a freight train on which he has been riding illicitly. 'Riding the rods' like this is a classic action of a 'tough guy', but he is not really tough and so has come to grief. Walking along the track, once again a refugee from adult life, he sees a fire with a solitary man beside it. The man comments on Nick's black eye and dishevelled appearance, and sizes him up in terms of maleness: '"You're a tough one, aren't you?" "No," Nick answered.'

The man himself is a genuine 'tough one', an ex-boxer: 'His face was misshapen ... queerly formed and mutilated ... Dead looking in the firelight.' He is the epitome of maleness: 'Call me Ad,' he tells Nick – Adam, the archetypal man; hence also Nick's surname, Adams. He exults in having been tough: '"I could take it ... Don't you think I could take it, kid?"' But he is by his own admission 'crazy' – his brains have almost been knocked out in the ring – and consequently he is as childlike as Nick; he has to depend for food and protection on a Negro who acts as his minder. While Nick is eating with him he suffers a sudden fit of meaningless rage and attacks Nick; the Negro carefully knocks him out with a blackjack and thereafter behaves with maternal tenderness: 'The Negro picked him up, his head hanging, and carried him to the fire ... laid him down gently ... splashed water with his hand on the man's face.' Apologising for his action, the Negro explains to Nick: 'I didn't know how well you could take care of yourself...' Nick, too, has been given maternal protection. At the end of the story he returns to the adult world, walking along the track towards a town, having discovered – as if he did not know it already – that 'toughness' is a mirage.

*

After such magnificent writing it is disappointing to find Hemingway descending, elsewhere in *In Our Time*, into mediocre social satire. One of the stories, 'Mr and Mrs Elliott', describes the ineptitudes of a naïve newly married American couple who have gone abroad:

Paris was quite disappointing and very rainy. It became increasingly important to them that they should have a baby, and even though someone had pointed out Ezra Pound to them in a café and they had watched James Joyce eating in the Trianon and almost been introduced to a man named Leo Stein, it was to be explained to them who he was later, they decided to go to Dijon...

Mr Elliott (the name is a silly gibe) becomes a bad poet and Mrs Elliott consoles herself sexually with a girlfriend. Hemingway is crudely mocking the sexual confusions that 'Indian Camp' and 'Big Two-Hearted River' had explored with such sensitivity.

'Mr and Mrs Elliott' does show, however, that he was beginning to regard his fellow expatriates in Paris as potential 'copy'. Up to now he had chiefly affected to despise them as a collection of wastrels. Writing in the *Toronto Star* in March 1922 he alleged that

the scum of Greenwich Village, New York, has been skimmed off and deposited in large ladles full on that section of Paris adjacent to the Café Rotonde. It is a strange-acting and strange-looking breed... You can find anything you are looking for... except serious artists... They are nearly all loafers expending the energy that an artist puts into his creative work in talking about what they are going to do.

Two years later he began to see their value as raw material for fiction.

Fairly typical of the Quarter, though with more to recommend him than some, was Harold Loeb. Hemingway first met Loeb at one of Ford's Thursday teas. He was having an affair with Kitty Cannell, and the two of them took Hemingway and Hadley out to dinner. Loeb felt well disposed towards Hemingway, and said he would try to help him find a publisher for *In Our Time*, but Kitty was wary. Perhaps she noticed how Hemingway watched intently when she scolded Loeb, as she often did. She warned Loeb that he might prove a disloyal friend.

There was already plenty of evidence that Hemingway had a disloyal streak. He was currently contributing satirical verses about the Paris crowd to a German avant-garde periodical, *Der Querschnitt*. They included a dig at Pound and a parody of Gertrude Stein: 'Short knives are thick short knives are quick short knives make a needed nick.'

He was also finding some questionable amusement in the eccentricities of an ailing American poet, Ralph Cheever Dunning, who lived like a hermit in a studio next door to Pound and wrote bad neo-Victorian verse. Dunning had been in Paris since 1905, but had only published one slim volume of poems, and that unwillingly. He occupied a bare room, smoked opium, and took his only other sustenance during occasional visits to a café, where he would sit in silence grasping a glass of hot milk. Suddenly Pound 'discovered' him and went around saying he was 'one of the four of five poets of our time', an assertion received with hilarious disbelief by Hemingway and his friends.

Pound was only trying to be kind to a sick man, and he attempted to persuade Hemingway to do the same. One day he summoned him because he was convinced that Dunning was dying. Hemingway went round to Dunning's room and found him indeed looking like a skeleton. On the other hand, said Hemingway, he appeared to be speaking in *terza rima*, and 'few people ever died while speaking in well-rounded phrases'. Ezra said it was not *terza rima*; it only sounded like *terza rima* because Hemingway had been asleep when he had sent for him.

Dunning was taken to a clinic and detoxified, all at Ezra's – or at least his wife Dorothy's – expense. Not long afterwards, when Ezra finally left Paris for Rapallo, he made Hemingway promise to keep an eye on Dunning, and gave him a jar of opium which he said he had bought from an Indian chief in the Avenue de l'Opéra. It was to be given to Dunning 'only when he needs it'. It was a large and heavy jar that had once contained cold cream. Possibly it still did, and there was really no opium in it at all, which would certainly explain what happened next.

One Sunday morning, Ezra's concierge hurried down the street and shouted up at Hemingway's window: 'Monsieur Dunning est monté sur le toit et refuse catégoriquement de descendre.' Hemingway decided that this called for the opium jar, so he went with the concierge. By the time they got there, Dunning had come down from the roof and shut his door. Hemingway knocked, and Dunning opened it:

He was gaunt and seemed unusually tall.
'Ezra asked me to bring you this,' I said and handed him the jar. 'He said you would know what it was.'
He took the jar and looked at it. Then he threw it at me. It struck me on the chest or the shoulder and rolled down the stairs.
'You son of a bitch,' he said. 'You bastard.'
'Ezra said you might need it,' I said. He countered that by throwing a milk bottle.
'You are sure you don't need it?' I asked.
He threw another milk bottle. I retreated and he hit me with yet another milk bottle in the back. Then he shut the door.
I picked up the jar, which was only slightly cracked, and put it in my pocket.
'He did not seem to want the gift of Monsieur Pound,' I said to the concierge.
'Perhaps he will be tranquil now,' she said.
'Perhaps he has some of his own,' I said.

'For a poet,' adds Hemingway, 'he threw a very accurate milk bottle'.

Hemingway got a similar degree of amusement from Ernest Walsh, an Irish-American whom he met one day in Pound's studio:

He was with two girls in long mink coats and there was a long, shiny, hired car from Claridge's outside in the street with a uniformed chauffeur... Ernest Walsh was dark, intense, faultlessly Irish, poetic and clearly marked for death as a character is marked for death in a motion picture. He was talking to Ezra and I talked with the girls, who asked me if I had read Mr Walsh's poems. I had not and one of them brought out a green-covered copy of Harriet Monroe's *Poetry, A Magazine of Verse* and showed me poems by Walsh in it. 'He gets twelve hundred dollars apiece,' she said... My recollection was that I received twelve dollars a page, if that, from the same magazine... 'It's more than anybody gets ever,' the first girl said.

Walsh, born in Detroit and brought up in Cuba, was a sick man. He had caught tuberculosis in his teens and had further weakened his lungs in a plane crash while training as an air cadet during the war. Harriet Monroe had published four of his poems, for the usual very modest fees, in *Poetry* during 1922, and Walsh had set off for Europe, intending to live on his services pension. He landed up at Claridge's in Paris, where the girls in mink coats soon abandoned him and he became virtually a prisoner because he could not pay his bill. He was discovered in this predicament by a lady who, as Hemingway puts it, specialised in 'young poets who were marked for death': Ethel Moorhead, a well-off middle-aged Scotswoman who had studied painting with Whistler and had been a suffragette. She was no fool, but could switch from violent praise to violent abuse of the same person on the slenderest of grounds. Much more attracted than Hemingway by Walsh's Byronic appearance, she paid his Claridge's bill and became his protector.

Moorhead and Walsh decided to start a Montparnasse literary magazine, *This Quarter*, and Hemingway says that a 'very substantial sum' was promised as a prize for the best work to be printed in the first four issues. Hemingway was taken for lunch by Walsh to an expensive restaurant in the Boulevard Saint Michel, fed best quality oysters and Pouilly Fuissé, and told confidently by Walsh – who on this occasion 'did not bother to look marked for death' – that he would get the award. Some time later, Hemingway was talking to Joyce at the Deux Magots, and Joyce asked if he had been promised the award. 'Yes,' said Hemingway. Joyce said he had been promised it too: 'Do you think he promised it to Pound?'

This, at least, is the story Hemingway tells in *A Moveable Feast*, but at the time he was obsequious to the editors of *This Quarter*, for motives which were obvious. 'Dear Ernest and Dear Miss Moorhead,' he wrote to them both from a skiing holiday in the Alps in January 1925. 'Hurray for the new Review... If there is anything I can do from here about helping you, let me know... I see from your prospectus that you are paying for MS on acceptance and think that is the absolute secret of getting the first rate stuff.' *This Quarter* not only paid promptly; it paid very well. Hemingway received the splendid sum of

1,000 francs for 'Big Two-Hearted River', which appeared in its first
number in May 1925. On receiving the cheque he wrote to Walsh and
Moorhead that they were 'a couple of white men'. He needed the
money very badly, for he and Hadley were trying to get by on $100
(1,200 francs) a month, so he was very willing to help see this first
number through the press, in order to help Walsh and Moorhead who
had gone down to the South of France for Walsh's health. When the
Dial turned down a new story, 'The Undefeated', Hemingway sent it to
Walsh, and another big cheque duly turned up.

However, Hemingway soon had enough of sub-editing *This
Quarter*, and asked to be relieved of his duties, suggesting a friend as
successor. Walsh wrote back angrily saying that they had paid him
lavishly because they had assumed he was going to do editorial work
too, and he had been taking money on false pretences. Hemingway did
not break off relations with them – he could not afford to – but
thereafter things were strained.

At around the same time he heard that Boni & Liveright in New
York, publishers of *The Waste Land*, were going to take *In Our Time*
for an advance of $200; and things seemed to be looking up even more
when, in April 1925, he had a letter from Maxwell Perkins, an editor at
Scribner's. Perkins had been told by one of his most successful young
authors, F. Scott Fitzgerald, that he must take notice of Hemingway.

'This is to tell you,' Fitzgerald had written to Perkins in October
1924, from the South of France,

about a young man named Ernest Hemmingway who lives in Paris (an
American) writes for the transatlantic Review & has a brilliant future. Ezra
Pount published a collection of his short pieces in Paris, at some place like the
Egotist Press. I havn't it hear now but its remarkable & I'd look him up right
away. He's the real thing.

Hemingway remarked on the 'feeling of reading an illiterate' that
Fitzgerald's letters gave him. 'I knew him for two years before he could
spell my name.'

Maxwell Perkins got hold of *in our time*, and wrote to Hemingway
asking whether he had anything he could send Scribner's. Hemingway
answered that he would love to submit a book to them one day, but at
present Boni & Liveright had the option on his next three manuscripts.
He was thinking about writing 'a very big book' on bullfighting, and
this might be his next project, but so far he had not felt like attempting a
novel: 'The novel seems to me to be an awfully artificial and worked out
form but as some of the short stories now are stretching out to 8,000 to
12,000 words maybe I'll get there yet.'

He laboured on at the stories, getting by on such cheques as he could
pick up from Walsh and Moorhead, and from the satirical pieces he was

sending to the German magazine. He describes Sylvia Beach's concern for him when he wandered into Shakespeare and Company:

'You're too thin, Hemingway,' Sylvia would say. 'Are you eating enough?'
'Sure.'
'What did you eat for lunch?'
My stomach would turn over and I would say, 'I'm going home for lunch now.'
'At three o'clock?'
'I didn't know it was that late ... Did I have any mail?'
'I don't think so. But let me look.'
She looked and found a note and looked up happily and then opened and closed a door in her desk.
'This came while I was out,' she said. It was a letter that felt as though it had money in it ...
'It must be from *Der Querschnitt* ... It's six hundred francs. He says there will be more ... It's damned funny that Germany is the only place I can sell anything ...'
'You can sell stories to Ford,' she teased me ... 'Get home now and have lunch.'

With the money in his pocket, he hurried round the corner to Lipp's, the brasserie opposite the Deux Magots. 'The beer was very cold and wonderful to drink. The *pommes à l'huile* were firm and marinated and the olive oil delicious ...'

*

One day Hemingway was sitting in the Dingo, talking to a couple of Harold Loeb's friends, when he was greeted by a stranger who identified himself as Scott Fitzgerald. Hemingway was pleased to be able to thank Fitzgerald for the introduction to Max Perkins at Scribner's, but privately he was 'on the fence' about Fitzgerald's runaway success with *This Side of Paradise*. Writing to a friend, he said that Fitzgerald's prose 'wasn't exciting'.

Fitzgerald had come into the bar with a celebrated baseball player, Dunc Chaplin, who had played for Princeton.* Hemingway immediately took to Chaplin, who was an amiable, relaxed character, but Fitzgerald aroused more complex feelings. In *A Moveable Feast* he gives a disturbing description of how Fitzgerald struck him:

Scott was a man then who looked like a boy with a face between handsome and pretty. He had very fair wavy hair, a high forehead, excited and friendly eyes and a delicate long-lipped Irish mouth that, on a girl, would have been the mouth of a beauty. His chin was well built and he had good ears and a

---

* Or so Hemingway says in *A Moveable Feast*, though it appears that Chaplin was not in Europe at the time.

handsome, almost beautiful, unmarked nose. This should not have added up to
a pretty face, but that came from the colouring, the very fair hair and the
mouth. The mouth worried you until you knew him and then it worried you
more.

He was twenty-nine, three years older than Hemingway, and had made
his name with *This Side of Paradise* at the age of twenty-four.

Besides being disturbed by Fitzgerald's girlish looks, Hemingway
quickly became embarrassed by what he was saying: 'It was all about
my writing and how great it was.' The enthusiasm was quite unfeigned;
Fitzgerald had never regarded himself as a stylist – he had modelled
This Side of Paradise, stylistically as well as thematically, on Compton
Mackenzie's *Sinister Street* (1913–14) – and he was very impressed by
Hemingway's experiments in prose. What he said when they met in the
Dingo may be guessed at from a review he wrote of *In Our Time*,
printed in the *Bookman* a few months later:

When I try to think of any contemporary American short stories as good...
only Gertrude Stein's 'Melanctha', Anderson's 'The Egg', and Lardner's
'Golden Honeymoon' come to mind...I read [*In Our Time*] with the most
breathless unwilling interest since Conrad first bent my reluctant eyes upon the
sea...You are immediately aware of something temperamentally new...the
awakening of that vast unrest that descends upon the emotional type at about
eighteen...And many of us, who have grown wary of admonitions to 'watch
this man or that' have felt a sort of renewal of excitement at these stories
wherein Ernest Hemingway turns a corner into the street.

Hemingway had picked up the ethic of the Quarter that 'praise to the
face was open disgrace', and was embarrassed by Fitzgerald's effusive
congratulations. Also, he was disturbed that Fitzgerald 'did not look in
awfully good shape, his face being faintly puffy', and was wearing a
Guards tie. 'I thought I ought to tell him about the tie, maybe, because
they did have British in Paris.' Fitzgerald said he had bought it in Rome.

Fitzgerald ordered champagne, first one bottle, then another. When
his speech about Hemingway's writing ran out, the questions started.
Fitzgerald believed a novelist could find out what he needed to know
by asking questions, and according to Hemingway the interrogation
began like this:

'Tell me, did you and your wife sleep together before you were married?'
    'I don't know.'
    'What do you mean, you don't know?'
    'I don't remember.'
    'But how can you not remember something of such importance?'
    'I don't know,' I said. 'It is odd, isn't it?'
    'It's worse than odd,' Scott said. 'You must be able to remember.'
    'I'm sorry. It's a pity, isn't it?'

'Don't talk like some limey,' he said. 'Try to be serious and remember.'
'Nope,' I said. 'It's hopeless.'

It sounds like one of Hemingway's taller stories, except that John Dos
Passos had a similar experience with Fitzgerald and his wife: 'Scott and
Zelda both started plying me with questions. Their gambit was to put
you in the wrong. You were backward in your ideas. You were
inhibited about sex. These things might perfectly well have been true
but my attitude was that they were nobody's goddamn business.'

Hemingway noticed that Fitzgerald was sweating in a peculiar way:
drops were coming out on 'his long, perfect Irish upper lip'. An
alarming change suddenly came over him: 'The skin seemed to tighten
over his face . . . The eyes sank and began to look dead and the lips were
drawn tight and the colour left the face.' Hemingway asked if he was all
right, and received no reply. He suggested that maybe Fitzgerald
should go to a first-aid station, but Chaplin – or whoever the companion was – said 'That's the way it takes him' and put Fitzgerald into a
taxi, adding that he would be all right by the time he reached home.

Hemingway ran into Fitzgerald again a few days later at the Closerie
de Lilas, and said he hoped he was all right, and that maybe they had
drunk too much while they were talking. Fitzgerald said there had
been nothing whatever wrong with him: 'I simply got tired of those
absolutely bloody British you were with and went home.' Hemingway
got nowhere when he tried to pursue the matter, so they talked about
writers instead, and Fitzgerald was 'cynical and funny and very jolly
and charming and endearing'. He was lightly dismissive of his own
work, though he said he wanted Hemingway to read his new book, *The
Great Gatsby*: 'He had the shyness about it that all non-conceited
writers have when they have done something very fine.'

Like Hemingway, Fitzgerald came from the Mid-West. He was the
son of a failed Procter & Gamble salesman from St Paul, Minnesota, but
some family money on his mother's side – from an Irish immigrant
great-grandfather who had made a fortune in wholesale groceries – had
sent him to private school, and to Princeton, where he was a considerable social success. He entered the army too late to see the First World
War, then after demobilisation drifted to New York, where he frequented the smarter circles in the Village and wrote *This Side of
Paradise*. Shortly afterwards he married Zelda Sayre, daughter of an
Alabama judge. He and Zelda delighted to behave like characters from
his own novel, seeking publicity by doing handstands in the Biltmore
lobby because Fitzgerald had not been in the news for a week, and
riding to parties on the roof of a taxi. Zelda's behaviour as a latter-day
Scarlett O'Hara charmed some people but alarmed many. A Princeton
friend of Fitzgerald's wrote in 1920 that she was just a 'temperamental
small town Southern Belle' who 'chews gum – shows knees'. He did not

think the marriage would succeed, for both were drinking heavily, and he guessed that Fitzgerald would write 'something big', then 'die in a garret at 32'.

The 'something big' emerged faster than might have been expected, considering that Zelda prevented her husband from working most of the time. His second book, *The Beautiful and the Damned* (1922), took its story too closely from their own marriage to be a success – it describes a young artist and his wife wrecking themselves in dissipation – but *The Great Gatsby*, published in April 1925 just before Fitzgerald met Hemingway, brought off the trick.

Fitzgerald explained to Hemingway that he always wrote his first drafts to the best standard he could achieve, but before submitting stories to magazines would often deliberately make them more commercial. Hemingway was shocked; he did not believe it was necessary to go in for prostitution of this sort. He was sure that, as Sherwood Anderson had told him four years earlier, he could write really well and still make his name and fortune. He realised that he could not prove this to Fitzgerald simply by producing more short stories; he now felt he needed 'a novel to back up my faith and to show him and convince him, and I had not yet written any such novel'.

*

Fitzgerald proposed a trip on the train to Lyon to pick up a car that he and Zelda had abandoned there because of bad weather. Hemingway agreed, and they decided to go the next morning. Hemingway was enthusiastic about the trip: 'I would have the company of an older and successful writer, and in the time we would have to talk in the car I would certainly learn much that it would be useful to know.'

When Hemingway got to the Gare de Lyon, Fitzgerald was not there. The trip was supposed to be at Fitzgerald's expense; however, Hemingway decided to set off, paying for his own ticket, in case Fitzgerald had caught an earlier train. He arrived in Lyon and managed to discover that Fitzgerald had left Paris, but could not find where he was staying. The next morning Fitzgerald turned up at Hemingway's hotel, full of apologies and looking rather the worse for drink. They collected the car, which proved to be entirely roofless; Fitzgerald explained that Zelda liked fresh air at all times and had insisted on abandoning the hood. Hemingway, who had not been warned about this, had not brought an overcoat. They set out for Paris, and it soon began to drizzle. To keep themselves warm, they bought and drank a great deal of white Mâcon, swigging from the bottle while Fitzgerald drove. As the wine took effect, Fitzgerald decided that he was suffering from 'congestion of the lungs'. Hemingway, speaking as a doctor's son, said there was no such thing unless he meant pneumonia. Fitzgerald disagreed, and they quarrelled. Hemingway eventually won the argument, with the consequence that Fitzgerald said he must be dangerously ill and would probably collapse before they reached the next town. When he was not announcing his own imminent death, he spent the journey describing his recent anguish over an affair Zelda had had at St Raphael with a French aviator. Hemingway was still a novice in such matters, and wondered how, if it was true, 'could Scott have slept each night in the same bed with Zelda?'

It was now raining heavily, and they took refuge in a hotel, Fitzgerald feeling certain he was dying. Hemingway took his pulse, listened to his chest, felt his temperature, and said there was nothing whatever wrong with him. They had another quarrel about this. Hemingway comments: 'I was getting tired of the literary life, if this was the literary life.'

Fitzgerald cheered up enough to go down to dinner, but kept on drinking, and at the table passed out completely. Hemingway got him to bed. The next day they completed the journey back to Paris without event, Fitzgerald entertaining Hemingway by telling him the plots of Michael Arlen's novels. A few days later he lent him a copy of *The Great Gatsby*; Hemingway read it and decided that he had to put up with the man on account of the writing, 'whether I could be of any use to him or not'.

Fitzgerald had abandoned the rather effete manner of *This Side of Paradise* for a much terser narrative style in the new novel; but *The Great Gatsby* interested Hemingway less for the way it was written than for its subject matter. It showed that a narrator like Nick Adams – to whom Fitzgerald's Nick Carraway bore no small resemblance – could be used in a story with a sophisticated social setting. Also, the other characters in the book – the oddly assorted Buchanans, the cool golfing girl Jordan Baker, and the questionable, mysterious playboy Jay Gatsby – were just the sort of people among whom Hemingway was moving in the Quarter. Clearly, a lot of good copy lay to hand.

Soon after the Lyon trip the Hemingways were invited to lunch at the Fitzgeralds' Paris apartment not far from the Champs-Élysées. Hemingway took a dislike to Zelda, who seemed to be jealous of him, perhaps for being invited on the journey to Lyon which she evidently assumed had been a great success. To Fitzgerald, it had. He wrote to Max Perkins: 'Hemminway is a fine, charming fellow'; and to Gertrude Stein he described it as 'a slick drive'. Fitzgerald had been introduced to Gertrude Stein by Hemingway. Rather surprisingly, she admired *This Side of Paradise*, or at least she described it as the book that 'really created for the public the new generation', which was a sound commercial judgement if not a literary one. She and Fitzgerald struck a rapport, largely because, like Hemingway, he refused to take her very seriously.

Meanwhile, as soon as he had finished reading *The Great Gatsby*,

Hemingway started writing a novel of his own – the first he had attempted since the loss of his manuscripts two and a half years earlier. It was to be called *Along With Youth* – a phrase from one of his poems that Harriet Monroe had printed – and it began with Nick Adams on an American troop ship in 1919. Presumably it was going to deal with war experiences. But he abandoned it after two dozen pages, for *The Great Gatsby* suggested to him that he could write a novel about the life he and his friends were leading at that moment.

2

La vie est belle

In June 1923, Kay Boyle, a twenty-year-old American girl married to a young French engineer who had been an exchange student in the USA, set off for France with her husband. She was going to write a novel in the quiet and peace of Brittany, where his family lived, while he worked out his future. She hoped ultimately to get to Paris, meet Sylvia Beach and James Joyce, and make her name in the Quarter.

During two years in New York, Kay Boyle had done a little reviewing for the *Dial* – unsigned and almost unpaid, just as Malcolm Cowley describes it – and had had a poem published in McAlmon's and William Carlos Williams's *Contact*. She had worked in the New York office of Harold Loeb's *Broom*, meeting some of those who had gone to Paris, hearing about others. She had developed a particular obsession for Robert McAlmon, though they had never met. She read his work in the little magazines and heard that he was 'wild and daring and hard as nails'. She saluted him as 'a man of rebellion', a symbol of what she and her husband Richard hoped to find on their French trip.

Their Atlantic crossing was paid for by Harold Loeb's estranged wife Marjorie, though they expected to be able to repay the loan very soon. 'Richard would look for a temporary job,' writes Kay, 'I would begin my novel, and after the first few chapters were done a New York publisher would pay me an advance.'

They arrived at Le Havre, and immediately, thanks to their lack of money, Kay found herself in the grip of Richard's *hautbourgeois* family – who were distressed at her Greenwich Village costume of startling lipstick and gigantic white hoops of earrings, and hinted that she should buy a sober grey suit and hat. 'The next morning, as tough and determined as McAlmon, I put my lipstick and earrings away, and I did not put them on again for a long time.'

Immured for the summer in her father-in-law's mansion in Brittany, learning the proper *haut-bourgeois* lifestyle, Kay would keep asking Richard what the time was in New York, and would take refuge in her memories of the Village. She began to write her novel – about the USA, 'about all that had happened to me as I grew up in Philadelphia, in Atlantic City, in the Pocono Mountains, and in Cincinnati, as if a recounting of these experiences must finally reveal to me who I was'.

In September she and Richard set off for Paris so that he could find a job. They travelled overnight, third class, Kay refusing to eat on the journey, telling Richard she was train-sick. 'I had taken a vow in silence to eat only one meal a day until we had money of our own to live on'. Richard went for job interviews and Kay resumed her white hoops and lipstick. On the third or fourth day she went up the rue de l'Odéon towards no. 12, thinking that 'I might catch a sight of James Joyce', but 'once I actually saw the sign, *Shakespeare and Company*, I did not have the courage to approach the door'. She went back to her cheap hotel behind the Opéra and scrubbed off the lipstick and brushed her hair into a tight knot: 'This was the guise in which I would present myself to Sylvia Beach.' As soon as Richard had found his job in Paris, 'I would ask Miss Beach to let me sell books for her'.

Next morning she rang Harold Loeb's doorbell. He had been asleep (with Kitty Cannell) 'and he stood there in the partly opened door in a silk dressing gown, a bit put out, but suggested that we meet on the terrace of the Café de la Paix that afternoon at four'. Nervously, Kay turned up early for this appointment and walked round the block until she saw Loeb arrive and make his way across to one of the tables, joining a young man in a grey suit who was drinking an apéritif. Numb with shyness and feeling that she looked like a whore – she had put the lipstick back on again – she had to go once more round the block before she could summon the nerve to approach them. Still nervous as she sat down, she failed to catch the name of the young man in the grey suit, who was American and in his late twenties, with steel-blue eyes. She thought his profile not unlike John Barrymore: 'His lips were thin, and there was a half-humorous, half-mordacious twist to them as he talked.' The effect was to make Harold Loeb seem to have 'no more personality than a clean, expensive blanket lying folded across the café chair'.

The young man was talking about Gurdjieff's 'school' at Fontaine-bleau, saying that the cult had been spreading among people he had thought too sensible to dabble in it: 'Jane Heap got involved out there, and Margaret Anderson. It's mass hypnotism of some kind. The pupils, sitting in a circle, repeat "twilight", or "dawn", or "tragedy", or "labour", or "love", over and over, in their different languages. In the middle of the circle are placed bottles of armagnac, and the Master is disturbed if these bottles are not emptied, and this adds to the hypnotism. It sounds pretty much like what we do every night in Montparnasse.' Kay, sipping Pernod, felt that the young man was really talking about something else: 'His eyes had scarcely left my face, and their icy blueness had not altered.'

Loeb shifted in his seat, and turned to the young man: 'McAlmon, I'm going to have another drink. What about you?' McAlmon said yes, but Kay, overtaken with panic at realising that this was the man who symbolised so much to her, got up quickly and said that Richard was waiting and she had to go. Loeb muttered something about telephoning her at the hotel to arrange dinner, but Kay knew he did not mean to. 'I could not bring myself to look at McAlmon when I said goodbye.'

She fled to the hotel, and when Richard came back from job-hunting she told him: 'We must find our people and commit ourselves to them! We must *know!*' To which Richard replied: 'Know what?' In reply, Kay ran out into the street and spent the night on a bench in the Bois de Boulogne.

With the dawn, she decided to go back to rue de l'Odéon and ask Sylvia Beach for Robert McAlmon's address. 'And once I had found him, I would ask him to give me a job. I could type, I could take dictation, I could read proof. I would tell him that I wanted to give a shape to life.' She reached the shop, but realised that it was only 7.15 a.m. – and that Miss Beach would not be opening for two or three hours. So she wandered away again, bought a novel at a bookstall, and, losing her nerve for action, read it all day in the Tuileries garden. At last she went back to the hotel. Richard, distraught as to what had become of her, told her that he had found a job, but it was not in Paris.

*

They set up home in Le Havre on the pittance Richard was being paid for his work there with an electric company. Their apartment was cold and primitive; all the water had to be carried from a pump half a mile up the hill, they shared a stinking outside lavatory, and it took Kay most of the morning to get the coal stove alight so that she could begin to cook.

One day, Richard's wealthy brother-in-law sent his chauffeur with a limousine full of fruit and vegetables from the family château. Kay had just finished the week's wash in the stone sink, and had hung Richard's shirts and underwear and their sheets and pillowcases on an improvised line in the kitchen. Pools of water had collected on the linoleum, and the chauffeur, too polite to comment, ducked under the hanging sheets. Suddenly the clothes-line slipped from its mooring and down came the washing in a sodden mess. The chauffeur fought his way free of it and left, and Kay began picking the sheets out of the pools of filthy water and coal dust. 'And now I began crying for everything in the world, for the great hopes we had had for our life in France that had come to nothing . . .'

Gradually, she learnt how to survive, lying to the landlady when the rent was overdue. She stole a cat which had befriended her in the street, taking it home for company: 'It was an exceptionally beautiful cat, with eyes of a transparent jade, a grey and ebony striped coat, and the mindless face of a chorus girl.' Sometimes the live crabs she had brought home from the market would escape from their basket, scuttling under the bed, and the cat would help her to round up and subdue them.

One day – it was in January 1924 – William Carlos Williams and his wife landed in Le Havre on their way to Paris. Kay, who knew Williams from the Village, met them at the quay and implored them to stay for lunch; but Williams said McAlmon was waiting for them in Paris, that he was expecting them on the boat train, and they must not disappoint him. 'Kay Boyle had come down to the train at Le Havre,' Williams writes in his autobiography, 'where she was so lonely, knowing only her grocer, as she said. But we couldn't do it. We had to get to Paris where she, poor girl, would gladly have followed us.'

Later, she and Richard moved to Harfleur. 'There we lived for two years, and so totally French did I become that I scarcely recognized the look of my own features when I happened to catch sight of them in the glass.' She developed what seemed to be tuberculosis, and 'almost lost my mind in anguish' when one of her neighbours, a railway guard, annoyed by the mewing of her cat, drowned it in the communal cesspool. The cat's death became 'symbol and sign for me of all we had forgotten to defend, of all we had allowed to perish, to vanish, from our lives'.

She began to correspond with Ernest Walsh and Ethel Moorhead, who had read her poems and wanted to print her work in *This Quarter*. When Walsh learned about her tuberculosis he sent a telegram from the South of France: 'INSIST YOU SEE MY LUNG SPECIALIST. I WILL TAKE CARE OF EVERYTHING. LA VIE EST BELLE. WE WANT YOU TO JOIN US HERE. COME QUICKLY.' She went, so blinded by tears that she could scarcely see Richard standing on the station platform.

3
Some fiesta

Hemingway set off south with Hadley, heading towards Spain. All through the winter of 1924 to 1925 he had been looking forward to his third visit in as many summers to the *fiesta* of San Fermín in Pamplona. 'Why don't you come over,' he had written to a friend from Oak Park days, Bill Smith, 'and we'll go down to Spain in June...fish the Irati...and then go to Pamplona for the big bull fight week. It would be a swell trip.'

Bill Smith, who had been Hemingway's best man, featured in several stories in *In Our Time*. He said he would come, and two other Americans were co-opted into the party: Don (Donald Ogden) Stewart, a professional writer of humour, and Harold Loeb. Bumby, now aged nearly two, was dispatched to Brittany with friends, and the party left Paris towards the end of June 1925. Loeb sent word that he would join them in Pamplona, as he had already gone south to stay at a small resort near Biarritz. He did not tell them why he had made this trip.

Kay Boyle's 'clean, expensive blanket' was an all too apt description of Loeb. The son of a Wall Street broker – one of his cousins was the sponsor of the Loeb Classical Library and his mother was a Guggenheim – he had been brought up in great affluence. His father encouraged him to do something worthwhile with his life, but Harold found it hard to make a mark on the world. At Princeton he took up boxing – Hemingway alleged that this was to 'counter the feeling of inferiority and shyness he had felt on being treated as a Jew' – but he made no impression on his contemporaries, and Hemingway adds: 'I never met anyone of his class who remembered him.'

On his twenty-first birthday he inherited $50,000, swiftly married the daughter of another Wall Street broker, and began to try his hand at various forms of business, including the Guggenheim-owned lead and smelting industry, without much success. In 1919, having used up most of his capital, he and his wife Marjorie took over a little New York bookshop, the Sunwise Turn, and this prospered reasonably – Peggy Guggenheim, Harold's cousin, was among those who worked for it. But Harold was no more comfortable in literary and bohemian circles than he had been at Princeton or in the smelting business, and he describes the Villagers he met at bookshop parties as 'flaunting their new liberties . . . with all the dogmatic piety of Tennessee mountaineers'.

After a while his marriage broke up, and he decided to sell the bookshop and start a little magazine with a poet named Alfred Kreymborg as joint editor. It was to be called *Broom*, though Loeb scarcely seems to have known why. 'Clean sweep – elemental rhythm?' he suggests uncertainly in his autobiography. He decided to go off to Europe to edit it, believing he could 'recognize America's significant aspects more easily by . . . observing them from a distance'. He sailed in June 1921, and he and Kreymborg first went to Paris. There, they met the Dadaists; talked to Ezra Pound, who, says Loeb, 'was dressed like one of Trilby's companions'; saw McAlmon, 'a handsome young Westerner with clear blue eyes and the straightest of noses'; visited Joyce, who 'did not seem to be interested in anything until the subject of cooking came up'; and called upon Gertrude Stein – 'no suggestion of her writing style appeared in her conversation'. She wrote a word-portrait of Loeb, which seems to say that he made absolutely no impression on her, or that she could not distinguish him from his companions, Kreymborg and his wife:

Harold Loeb

In front of me and can you see readily. There were three. Three of them were there. I found that he was there and the two others . . . I said that there were three of them and what interested me was that they were seated next to each other . . .

Since Loeb had found Greenwich Village too bohemian for his taste, he was not likely to be comfortable in the Quarter, so he decided to do his share of the running of *Broom* from Rome. The first issue, which came out in November 1921, was nearly a hundred pages long with nine plates on art paper. But Loeb soon realised that very little distinguished it from the other experimental magazines apart from elegance and its large size. The writers came from all schools, Malcolm Cowley and E. E. Cummings jostling with Amy Lowell and even Walter de la Mare. The magazine sold quite well but lost money, and Kreymborg soon resigned. Loeb appealed for funds to his uncle Simon, who some years later was to establish the Guggenheim Foundation, but the request was turned down. Other rescue attempts included an offer by Kay Boyle, then still in the New York office, to work without pay – this was a year before she sailed for France – and Malcolm Cowley in Paris setting up an editorial board to help run the magazine; but *Broom* eventually petered out during 1924 and Loeb began to write novels instead. He moved to Paris, but took an apartment well away from the Quarter, near Les Invalides. His first book, *Doodab*, a *Babbitt*-like story based on his experiences in the smelting industry, was accepted by Boni & Liveright, and Loeb was just putting the finishing touches to it when he met Hemingway.

They were introduced at one of Ford's *transatlantic review* teas in Bird's print shop. Loeb liked Hemingway's 'shy, disarming smile', and thought he had never before encountered an American so unaffected by living in Paris. Kitty Cannell, Loeb's mistress, warned him that Hemingway was putting on an act, but Loeb answered: 'Who isn't?' He and Hemingway began to play tennis together and went on a walking tour. Loeb easily succumbed to the stories Hemingway was now writing; when he read 'Big Two-Hearted River' he was moved to take up fishing. They also boxed together; Loeb was nervous – 'Hem was some forty pounds heavier' – but he could usually tell from a shift in Hemingway's eyes when a big punch was coming.

Marvellous as Loeb thought them, Hemingway's stories were still bringing in rejection slips from the magazines, and Loeb gave him some advice: 'What you've got to do is bring in women. People love to read about women and violence. You've got plenty of violence in your stories. Now all you need is women.'

*

One day at a cocktail party in the Quarter, Loeb was introduced to Lady Duff Twysden and her companion, a Scotsman named Pat Guthrie – the 'two bloody British' who had been in the Dingo the day that Scott Fitzgerald first met Hemingway. 'I had first noticed Duff some months earlier,' writes Loeb, 'at the Sélect Café, where I had often gone to work on a chapter of *Doodab*. One afternoon I heard a laugh so gay and musical that it seemed to brighten the dingy room. I looked up.'

McAlmon was in the Sélect that day, so Loeb went over and asked him who she was. 'Bob, who knew everybody, said that her name was Duff Twysden* and that she had picked up a title by marriage. She was British, and went around with Pat Guthrie.' McAlmon did not like her. 'Of all the various "ladies" who were on the loose in Paris,' he writes, 'she was the most imitated, the least witty or amusing, and she could switch to acting "Her Ladyship" at the most dangerous moment.' He calls her 'entirely a product of London and England and she had nothing to do with the spirit of Montparnasse'. On the other hand Don Stewart thought her 'enormously attractive', and says 'she had a kind of style sense that allowed her to wear with dignity and chic almost anything – I mean a man's felt hat, or a matador's hat, maybe even a lamp shade'.

Duff Twysden had been born Mary Smurthwaite, the daughter of a Yorkshire wine merchant, and in 1925, when the Hemingway set began to take notice of her, was in her early thirties. She was sometimes heard to claim that her surname at birth had been Stirling and that she had

---

*In his autobiography Loeb changes a lot of names; for example Duff Twysden is called 'Duff Twitchell'. I have restored the real names.

been a débutante, also a musical prodigy who had given a piano recital in London at the age of twelve. Her first husband was a man named Byrom, and she later married a baronet, Sir Roger Twysden, a year younger than her, by whom she had a son. She left the child and his father and eventually turned up in Paris.

Harold Loeb says that the heroine of Michael Arlen's *The Green Hat* (1924) was 'partly based on her', and Don Stewart writes that she was 'right out of the gay brave hell of Michael Arlen'. Stewart describes her companion Pat Guthrie as 'another *Green Hat* character from the overdrafts of Mayfair . . . whose charming worthlessness immediately won my heart'. In fact, Nancy Cunard was Arlen's model for Iris March in *The Green Hat*. Scott Fitzgerald guessed, however, that Duff had read the book and and was deliberately playing the part.

Loeb was bowled over by her, and so was Hemingway. 'She was not supposed to be beautiful,' Hemingway writes, 'but in a room with women who were supposed to be beautiful she killed their looks entirely.' Jimmie Charters was greatly puzzled by Hemingway's evident infatuation: 'She was one of those horsey English girls with her hair cut short . . . rather masculine physically . . . I never could see what he saw in her.' The few photographs and drawings of her which survive emphasise her boyishness, even mannishness. She usually wore a man's slouch hat and a sailor's jersey. Pat Guthrie was rumoured to be homosexual.

Loeb, who often fell in love and admired from a distance, would 'find myself looking to see if Duff was there when I entered a café, and then watching her when I should have been working . . . Her features had a special appeal for me.' According to Loeb, she talked like a member of the Drones Club in the stories of P. G. Wodehouse: 'Would one of you gents give a chap a spot of gin?' Pat Guthrie, invariably by her side, was tall and narrow-shouldered and, adds Loeb, 'usually tight'. Loeb thought him a detestable parasite, one of the nastiest specimens of the British upper class, but Don Stewart calls him 'a nice enough fellow for a drunk'.

Having worshipped Duff for weeks at a distance, Loeb was so disconcerted at finally being introduced to her at the cocktail party that he came over faint and had to leave. It distressed him to realise how obsessed he was with 'a woman whose life exemplified what I most disliked about the Quarter'. He saw her again at one of Ford's *bal musette* evenings, but she and Pat soon left for another party. A couple of evenings later, Loeb was playing bridge in the Sélect when she turned up at the bar, with friends, but for once without Pat. Loeb abandoned the game and went to sit near her. After a while her friends left, and Loeb prepared to get up and join her, 'but before I could move she turned to me and said, "It is the only miracle."'

From the start, Loeb's account of his involvement with Duff – unlike the one Hemingway was to write – is in the manner of a romantic novelette: 'Her deep gray eyes . . . seemed to be holding and to be held by mine . . . I moved three stools down to sit beside her . . . "How long have you known?" She smiled. I said, "Will you see me tomorrow . . . ?"'

They arranged to meet at the Falstaff. The only person there when Loeb arrived was the barman – Jimmie Charters, who had just moved from the Dingo. When Duff came in she introduced Jimmie to Loeb. 'I can count on Jimmie,' she said. 'A good chap.' Loeb gathered that when she was in a spot, Jimmie lent her money. Jimmie says this is true, though 'it was a strain on me'. She also borrowed money from Hemingway; on one occasion she wrote to him: 'Ernest my dear . . . I am in a stinking fix but for once only temporarily and can pay you back for *sure* . . . Am living in the country on nothing – but owe the pub a packet and dare not return without it . . . As ever, Duff Twysden.'

She insisted on telling Loeb all about her past life, or at least her preferred version of it: 'She came from a small village in Scotland. She told me all about her disastrous first marriage to an older man; she should have known better, but she wanted to get away. On a second wedding day she had eloped with the best man, a naval officer . . . She had had a child by him, but they couldn't live together. He would get blind when on leave and stay that way until it was time to return to his post. Her mother had the child now.'

Loeb saw her three times in three days, and finally said: 'We can't go on this way . . .' He suggested that as Kitty Cannell was about to visit friends in England, and Pat Guthrie was in Scotland trying to squeeze money out of his family, they could both go away together – there was just time before Loeb was supposed to join Hemingway and his friends in Pamplona for the bullfighting. They agreed on St-Jean-de-Luz, on the coast near Biarritz, and Loeb bought the tickets.

They were able to go to bed together before leaving Paris, for Flossie Martin went away for a weekend and lent them her room. 'It was a small room and messy,' says Loeb, 'not at all the kind of place I would have chosen.' Also, Loeb was feeling guilty about Kitty, which made him temporarily impotent. However, in the *wagon-lit* on the way to St-Jean-de-Luz, 'enchantment enveloped us'. At St-Jean, 'after unpacking our bags and making love again on the bed beneath the window, Duff and I strolled over to the beach. The sea sparkled under a blue sky . . .' The next morning, says Loeb, Duff told him that her feelings for him were more serious than she had thought: 'It is like that first time we dream of, that first time which never is.' And so, in Loeb's account, the idyll continued: 'The moon rose like morning from the sea. Her hands were soft and tender . . .'*

* After reading this, one might almost feel that Hemingway's version of the Loeb–Duff romance in *The Sun Also Rises* is a justifiable revenge on appalling writing, were it not that Loeb's book about the affair, *The Way It Was* (1959), was written more than thirty years after Hemingway's novel.

After a couple of weeks Duff left Loeb at St-Jean and went back to join Pat in Paris. She wrote to Loeb, who was still at St-Jean, that she had some 'doubtful glad tidings': she and Pat were 'coming on the Pamplona trip with Hem and your lot. Can you bear it?'

Hemingway, ignorant of Loeb's affair with Duff, wrote to him from Paris on 21 June 1925 with the same news:

Pat and Duff are coming too. Pat has sent off to Scotland for rods and Duff to England for funds. As far as I know Duff is not bringing any fairies with her. You might arrange to have a band of local fairies meet her at the train carrying a daisy chain so that the transition from the Quarter will not be too sudden.

This was an innuendo about Duff preferring the company of homosexuals. Hemingway added: 'Pamplona's going to be damned good.'

Loeb thought the letter 'altogether Hemingway', but for some reason 'the exuberance seemed a little forced'. He was suspicious of Hemingway's motives in inviting Duff and Pat to join the party; Duff had told him that she sensed that he was interested in her, but she was careful to have little to do with him 'because of Hadley'. In fact Hemingway was beginning to fret at monogamy; he wrote to Scott Fitzgerald that his idea of heaven would be a bullring with a trout stream outside, his wife and child in one house, and 'nine beautiful mistresses on 9 different floors' in another; and to Ernest Walsh he remarked that he wished he could go to Venice for some 'romantic fucking'.

Meanwhile McAlmon, sensing what Hemingway was up to, suddenly announced that he was coming too – and would be bringing Kitty Cannell. Hemingway 'turned a terrifying purple', and McAlmon had to explain that it was a joke.

*

Loeb was supposed to join Hemingway, Hadley, Don Stewart and Bill Smith for a few days' fishing at Burguete up in the Pyrenees before they all went on to Pamplona, but he decided to skip this and stay at St-Jean-de-Luz. He arranged with Duff that she should bring Pat down there from Paris, and they could all drive on to Pamplona together. But when Duff and Pat arrived, Pat said icily to Loeb: 'Oh, *you're* here, are you?' Duff herself seemed to have lost interest in Loeb. 'Pat broke the spell,' she told him. 'He worked hard at it.'

From St-Jean they set off across the Spanish border in a hired car. 'It was a long drive and no fun at all,' writes Loeb. 'Most of the country was not much to look at, nor was Pat.' They talked of people in the Quarter: 'Of Flossie . . . of Cheever Dunning who had been sent to a hospital . . . of Ezra Pound who had actually composed an opera, of Peggy Vail who had thrown a wild party'.

Arriving at Pamplona a day before Hemingway and the others, they checked in at the Quintana Hotel, where Hemingway always stayed because the proprietor Juanito Quintana treated him flatteringly as an *aficionado* of the bullfight. Loeb was given what he calls 'a small cubicle' on the second floor; Pat and Duff had a double room on the fourth.

Hemingway and his group arrived next morning. 'Been trout fishing,' he wrote to Fitzgerald. 'God it has been wonderful country.' The trip had really been a complete failure; Hemingway admitted to Loeb that construction work on a reservoir had 'played hell' with the trout, and the party had not caught a single fish. But after reporting this, he 'turned cheerful', ordered a good lunch, and made Loeb drink his first real absinthe. Then they all hurried out to the railroad yards to see the bulls unloaded.

They all admired the bulls. 'Hem pointed out their good points,' says Loeb, and indicated the small spot on the shoulder through which a sword could reach the heart. The party 'stayed and watched long after I had lost interest'. He began to be thoroughly depressed; Bill Smith was friendly enough to him, but never said much, and Pat was perpetually irritating; on the walk back into town he bought a goatskin full of wine and managed to drench his shirt while drinking it. 'Everyone roared as if it were funny. Duff called out: "Give a chap a swig, won't you?"'

The next morning, they watched the bulls being driven through the streets to the stadium; one spectator among the Spaniards was gored and taken to hospital. 'Then,' says Loeb, 'the ring opened for the amateur frolic' – an hour or so during which the local menfolk were allowed in the ring to try being matadors. Don Stewart had broken a rib in this event when he came to Pamplona the previous year, and had no intention of doing it again. Pat would not consider going in, but Loeb 'went up to the fence with Hem and Bill, determined to go over. It took a bit of a will, but when Hem climbed in, Bill Smith and I climbed in too.'

The Pamplona men pranced about the ring, waving their jackets as if they were capes and making a pretence of challenging the bulls, but always running away when the animals started to charge. One bull made for Bill Smith, who tried to stand up to him, but then changed his mind and was butted in the rear as he ran off. 'Then,' writes Loeb, 'the bull turned to me.' Not having a jacket, Loeb had taken off his Fair Isle sweater for a cape, and as the bull charged him he swung it around like a matador: 'He pierced the sweater with one of his horns and carried it off.' More concerned about his sweater than his safety, Loeb chased the animal around the arena. 'When he finally shook it off, it had a large hole through the middle.' After this excitement, the first formal bullfight turned out to be a shoddy business. 'The comic-opera costumes looked worn,' writes Loeb, 'and the horses would have shamed a Philadelphia cab driver.' The star matador was a nineteen-year-old named Cayetano Ordóñez, who was making his Pamplona début under the professional name of Niño de la Palma. Hadley was greatly taken with the lad, and so was Hemingway.

At apéritifs that evening, Loeb remarked *sotto voce* to Bill Smith that Hemingway had not exactly plunged into the affray in the ring. He had simply stood watching. 'Why do you think Hem kept so far from *les animaux?*' asked Loeb. Smith answered: 'He's not milked many cows.'

Loeb sensed that Hemingway was resentful towards him, and wondered why. 'It's that *wagon-lit!*' said Bill. 'You should have seen his face when Jo Bennett told him you and Duff had gone off in a *wagon-lit.*' Bill thought it was because Hemingway had a mean streak, and regarded a sleeping-car as an extravagance, but Loeb began to wonder if he really fancied Duff himself. Smith admitted that he could sense a *frisson* between them.

The next morning there was another 'amateurs' at the bull ring. Hemingway, Smith, and Loeb went along, but the rest of the party stayed at the hotel. Again, there were photographers present. To spare his sweater, Loeb had brought a hotel towel. 'The towel didn't work so well either. The bull started coming. It wasn't a big bull, but it was black and coming fast. I held the towel up in front of me, waving it slightly, and looked over it at the charging animal. Suddenly I realized that the bull's mean little eyes were not looking at the towel; they were looking at me. I had no time to think. When the bull lowered his head I dropped the towel, twisted around so that my back was facing him, and sat down hard on his head, grasping the horns for support. The bull lifted me up, carried me across the arena in three long, rolling lopes, and then tossed his head. I went up into the air and landed on my feet, upright.'

The photograph of this in Loeb's memoirs shows him in his Fair Isle sweater, white trousers, sneakers, and horn-rimmed glasses, riding aloft on the bull's horns. He looks like his namesake Harold Lloyd in some ridiculous film predicament. The picture, says Loeb, was printed in the *New York Times*, 'much to the excitement of my family'.

Hemingway decided he himself was not to be outdone: no sooner had Loeb's bull tossed him than Hemingway 'caught one of the animals from the rear, seized his horns, twisted his neck, and threw him to the ground'. But it was too late; Loeb was the hero of the day. When he went into town to smarten himself up after his adventure, neither the barber nor the shoeblack boys would take money for their services. 'They recognized me, and apparently no one had ever ridden a bull's head before.' One of the local *aficionados* said to Hemingway: 'You would have thought he had done it on purpose.'

Despite this sudden celebrity, Loeb felt half inclined to go back to Paris. He did not much like the bullfights, and clearly his presence was an irritation to Pat, perhaps also to Hemingway since his success in the ring. He asked Bill Smith what he ought to do. 'Why don't you do what you want to do?' suggested Bill. 'That's obscure,' Loeb answered. That evening, he managed to lure Duff away for a drink, and they were both seized on by convivial Spaniards and kept up very late. Next morning

Loeb woke with a hangover, and at lunch 'Duff appeared with a bruised forehead and black eye. When I asked her about it, Hem interrupted, saying that she had fallen against the railing...Pat was sour, ugly. Hadley had lost her smile...Bill looked grim.' At the bullfight that afternoon, Loeb deliberately sat in a different row from Duff, Pat and Hemingway. The tension and silence persisted into the evening.

After dinner they all took a table on the square and began drinking brandy. Hemingway described the fine bulls that were to arrive the next day, but then turned to Loeb: 'Harold, I suppose you'd like it better if they shipped in goats.'

Loeb said he didn't mind the bullfighting, but 'I just find it hard not to sympathize with the victims'.

Pat said it was nice of him to be considerate of the bull's feelings, 'but how about ours?' And now Hemingway joined in:

'Harold is very considerate. You should see him with Kitty. I've listened to him taking it by the hour.'

Loeb had not particularly minded Pat disliking him, but it hurt to have Hemingway taking Pat's side. He began to fight back verbally at Pat, but Hemingway joined in again. 'You lay off Pat,' he told Loeb. 'You've done enough to spoil this party.' Loeb gripped the table hard.

'Why don't you get out?' Pat asked Loeb. 'I don't want you here. Hem doesn't want you here. Nobody wants you here, though some may be too decent to say so.'

'I will,' answered Loeb, 'the instant Duff wants it.'

'You lousy bastard,' said Hemingway. 'Running to a woman.'

Loeb got up unsteadily. Struggling to keep his voice calm, he said to Hemingway: 'Do you mind stepping out for a moment?'

'Oh, willingly, willingly,' Hemingway said.

Hemingway got up and followed him. 'The square was full of light,' writes Loeb, 'though most of the celebrants were now seated at tables. There was an unlit corner diagonally across from us. The streets beyond the plaza would be dark and empty.'

They crossed the open space towards the darkness. Loeb was 'scared – not shaken or panicky, but just plain scared. I had boxed enough with Hem to know that he could lick me easily; his forty-pound advantage was just too much...I would just have to stand up and take it.'

They went down some steps into a side-street lit only by widely spaced lamps. 'I took my glasses off and, considering the safest place, put them in the side pocket of my jacket. Then I stopped, faced Hem, and took my jacket off...I looked around for someplace to put my jacket.

'"Shall I hold it for you?" he asked.'

Loeb smiled, and there was just enough light for him to see that Hemingway was smiling too, 'the boyish, contagious smile that made it so hard not to like him'.

'"If I may hold yours," I said. We stood hesitantly looking at each other. "I don't want to hit you," I said.

'"Me neither," said Hem. We put on our jackets and started back.'

Hemingway once told Ernest Walsh he would never hit anybody. 'Have never hit but 2 gents outside of boxing in my life. Then only because they wanted to hit me. I don't brawl.' Besides, Loeb had been middleweight boxing champion of Princeton.

Leob says that 'everyone pretended not to notice our return. The drinking continued. I avoided Pat, Pat avoided me. Duff no longer seemed to matter.' The next day Hemingway put a letter in Loeb's pigeon-hole at the hotel:

Dear Harold:

I was terribly tight and nasty to you last night and I dont want you to go away with that nasty insulting lousiness as the last thing of the fiestas. I wish I could wipe out all the mean-ness and I suppose I cant but this is to let you know that I'm thoroly ashamed of the way I acted and the stinking, unjust uncalled for things I said.

So long and good luck to you and I hope we'll see you soon and well.

Yours
Ernest

Loeb thought the apology almost excessive: 'I wondered if he had said anything that I had missed. When we were alone for a moment after luncheon I told him that I was glad he felt as he did.'

The *fiesta* ended. 'Some fiesta,' observes Loeb. Hemingway and Hadley were going on to Madrid; Hemingway 'seemed to be in high spirits, and overdid the heartiness'. Pat and Duff did not have enough money to pay their hotel bill, so Don Stewart paid it for them. Stewart went to Antibes; he says that on the way it occurred to him 'that the events of the past week might perhaps make interesting material for a novel'.

4

Just a damn journalist

Hemingway's high spirits as they were leaving Pamplona suggest that the idea of writing something about the week had occurred to him too. A few days later he started work on a narrative set in Pamplona. He was probably still angry about what had happened during the *fiesta*; someone once said: 'His temper has to go bad before he can write.'

At first he did not write about his friends. He began a piece of prose about the young matador:

Cayetano Ordonez
'Nino de la Palma'

I saw him for the first time in the Hotel Quintana in Pamplona. We met Quintana on the stairs as Bill and I were coming up to the room to get the wine bag to take to the bull fight. 'Come on,' said Quintana. 'Would you like to meet Nino de la Palma?' He was in room number eight, I knew what it was like inside, a gloomy room with the two beds separated by monastic partitions. Bill had lived in there and gotten out to take a single room when the fiesta started. Quintana knocked and opened the door. The boy stood very straight and unsmiling in his white shirt ...

The other members of the party soon appeared in the story, and their reactions to the *fiesta* and Pat's resentment of Loeb's presence were described, but they were all given their real names – Hem, Pat, Duff, Don, Harold, Bill, Hadley – and the young bullfighter remained the centre of attention. After a description of Pat and Duff, Hemingway wrote: 'I do not know why I have put all this down. It may mix up the story but I wanted to show you what a fine crowd we were; what a good crowd for a nineteen year old kid [the matador] to get in with.'

However, two things soon happened. First, he realised that the narrative was going to be long, stopped using loose sheets of paper, and began the first of a series of notebooks. Also he developed a different personality for the narrator. Not very far into the first notebook, the storyteller stops being 'Hem' and becomes Jake Barnes. It appears that Jake is in love with Duff, but that he has a mysterious war wound, apparently some sort of sexual injury, which inhibits him from having an affair with her. Meanwhile, other characters have their names changed. Loeb becomes Gerald Cohn, later Robert Cohn. Pat is renamed Mike Campbell, and Bill Smith and Don Stewart are fused into one person – Bill Gorton, a cheerful boozy man-of-the-world. Duff retains her own name for a while, then becomes Brett Ashley. Hadley disappears altogether.

Hemingway also realised that, if he was to explain everything that had happened in Pamplona, he must say a good deal about his characters' life in Paris. After all, the events during the *fiesta* in Spain had simply been a dramatic climax to the continual *fiesta* of life in the Quarter. He began to see that the novel – if it was to be a novel – would show the expatriates' fundamental inability, despite their superficial *joie de vivre*, to cope with the *fiesta* spirit. In this first draft he wrote: 'I do not think English and Americans have ever had any seven day fiestas. A prolonged fiesta does strange things to them.' He started to realise 'how much of what happened can be laid ... to the natural progress of events starting in Paris', to feel that 'if it had not been the Fiesta' that had prompted the crisis, 'it would have been something else'.

*

He now tried to explain to himself that he intended to write a novel that was not a novel, just as he had been writing short stories that were not short stories – at least not in the conventional sense. A little way into the first notebook, in the middle of the narrative, he observes:

In life people are not conscious of these special moments that novelists build their whole structures on. That is most people are not. That surely has nothing to do with the story but you cannot tell until you finish it because none of the significant things are going to have any literary signs marking them out. You have to figure them out by yourself.

He had already practised this in some of his short stories, and in the 'chapters' of *in our time*, anti-narratives deliberately deprived of 'signs' to the reader of an event's dramatic importance or its significance. But though he had perfected this technique for the small-scale narrative, at first it proved hard to eliminate 'literary signs' from a full-length novel. The early drafts include a number of passages where the narrator analyses and considers his characters in a literary manner. For example, lying awake in the Pamplona hotel, Jake contemplates Brett and the consequences of her trip to San Sebastian (St-Jean-de-Luz) with Cohn, and decides that since the trip

she seemed to have lost that quality in her that had never been touched before. All this talking now about former lovers to make this seem quite ordinary. She was ashamed. Really ashamed. She had never been ashamed before. It made her vulgar where before she had been simply going by her own rules.

Jake also reflects on his own feelings for her:

There had been a time when I had loved her so much that it seemed there was nothing else in the world. That there could never be anything else. The world was all one dimensional and flat and there was nothing but Brett and wanting Brett. I killed that with my head.

There was also some difficulty in getting away from the novelist's convention of having a hero. Even the Nick Adams stories had had a hero of sorts, but this did not seem appropriate to the events that had occurred in Pamplona, nor to Hemingway's intention of eliminating 'literary signs'. In the persona of Jake, he now wrote:

I looked as though I were trying to get to be the hero of this story. But that was all wrong. Gerald Cohn is the hero. When I bring myself in it is only to clear up something. Or maybe Duff [*sic*] is the hero. Or Nino de la Palma. He never really had a chance to be the hero. Or maybe there is not any hero at all. Maybe a story is better without any hero.

One option was to cut himself out altogether. 'I did not want to tell this story in this first person,' says Jake. 'I wanted to stay well outside... and handle all the people in it with that irony and pity that are so essential to good writing.' But 'I made the unfortunate mistake, for a writer, of first having been Mr Jake Barnes' – that is, Hemingway had been a protagonist in the events he described, and could not cut himself out. At one stage he tried third-person narration, but the result was lifeless. *The Great Gatsby* had demonstrated that authorial detachment was possible even with an involved first-person narrator; Fitzgerald had shown Hemingway a review of his book by Gilbert Seldes in the *Dial*, which described the novel as 'regarding a tiny section of life and reporting it with irony and pity', and Bill Gorton echoes these words in the Pamplona novel:

'Work for the good of all.' Bill stepped into his underclothes. 'Show irony and pity... Aren't you going to show a little irony and pity?'... As I went downstairs I heard Bill singing, 'Irony and Pity. When you're feeling —, Oh, Give them Irony and Give them Pity. When they're feeling —, Just a little Irony. Just a little Pity . . .' He kept on singing until he was downstairs. The tune was: 'The Bells are Ringing for Me and my Gal.'

This snatch of Gorton–Jake dialogue shows that, despite the application of certain of Gertrude Stein's principles to the novel, Hemingway had decided to loosen up his narrative technique, at least to the extent of representing his friends as they really were. In the first draft, Jake addresses himself on this topic: 'Gertrude Stein once told me that remarks are not literature. All right, let it go at that. Only this time the remarks are going in and if it is not literature who claimed it was anyway.'

*

Hemingway wrote to his father from Paris on 20 August 1925, six weeks after the end of the Pamplona trip: 'Been working day and night and done about 60,000 words on a novel. About 15,000 more to do.' By mid-September he was able to tell Ernest Walsh: 'I've finished my novel – have to go over it all this winter and type it out.'

The draft he had completed was entitled *Fiesta*, and it occupied seven notebooks and some loose sheets. As soon as it was finished, he put it aside and hurriedly wrote a satirical novella, *The Torrents of Spring*. The plan was to offer this to Boni & Liveright, to whom he was under contract; he knew they would turn it down, because it was chiefly a parody of one of their most successful authors – none other than Sherwood Anderson – and when they rejected it he would be free to take *Fiesta* to Maxwell Perkins, Scott Fitzgerald's editor at Scribner's.

Sherwood Anderson himself appears in *The Torrents of Spring* in the guise of 'Scripps O'Neill, a tall, lean man with a tall, lean face . . . tall and lean and resilient with his own tenuous hardness'. Scripps walks into a small town in Michigan with a bird under his shirt (he is giving it shelter), and explains: 'My wife left me . . . I write stories. I had a story in *The Post* and two in *The Dial*. Mencken is trying to get ahold of me . . . Scofield Thayer was my best man.' Scripps gets a job in a pump factory – with the bird still under his shirt – and marries an ancient waitress. At this point Hemingway parodies Ford Madox Ford:

The story will move a little faster from now on, in case any of the readers are tiring. We will also try to work in a number of good anecdotes . . . If any of the readers would care to send me anything they ever wrote, for criticism or advice, I am always at the Café du Dôme any afternoon . . .

Another section is entitled 'The Passing of a Great Race, and the Making and Marring of Americans'.

The three of them striding along the frozen streets . . . Going somewhere now. En route. Huysmans wrote that. It would be interesting to read French. He must try it sometime. There was a street in Paris named after Huysmans. Right around the corner from where Gertrude Stein lived. Ah, there was a woman! Where were her experiments in words leaving her? What was at the bottom of it? All that in Paris. Ah, Paris. How far it was to Paris. Paris in the morning. Paris in the evening. Paris at night. Paris in the morning again. Paris at noon, perhaps.

There are passing swipes at other writers; the narrator explains that one chapter was written after an extensive and bibulous lunch with 'John Dos Passos, whom I consider a very forceful writer' – Hemingway thought very poorly of Dos Passos's books – and another was allegedly interrupted when 'Mr F. Scott Fitzgerald . . . suddenly sat down in the fireplace and would not (was it could not, reader?) get up and let the fire burn something else.' There is a passing parody of *The Great Gatsby*, and the book concludes: 'Well, reader, how did you like it? It took me ten days to write it. Has it been worth it?'

Some while later, after *The Torrents of Spring* had been published, Hemingway wrote a semi-apologetic letter to Sherwood Anderson: 'Dear Sherwood . . . It is a joke and it isn't meant to be mean . . .' The joke was not only against Anderson and the other writers parodied, for *The Torrents of Spring* was a necessary exercise by Hemingway in laughing at a whole side of his own writing personality, that which was indebted to Anderson. The exorcising of Anderson's ghost from his own writing, at least temporarily, was a necessary accompaniment to developing in the Pamplona novel a much more Fitzgerald-like, knowing, even urbane style.

Indeed it seems doubtful how much he really wanted to leave Boni & Liveright, who had done him no harm. When they published *In Our Time* in October 1925 – just after he had finished the first draft of the Pamplona novel – they gave it a decent send-off, soliciting compliments on the book, to be printed on the dust-jacket, from Sherwood Anderson, John Dos Passos, and other successful writers. It attracted plenty of critical attention; H. L. Mencken in the *American Mercury* sneeringly described it as 'written in the bold bad manner of the Café Dôme', but most reviews were laudatory. The New York *Sun* critic, Herbert J. Seligman, wrote:

Ernest Hemingway is abrupt, at times, as only an American can be. He wants his moments direct. The fewer words the better. What words there are must yield explicitness. It is like people talking. His vocabulary is close to the happening. It fits the mood of young men who had to face war, were killed and mutilated.

The review shows that the Hemingway style was already infecting his readers. D. H. Lawrence, reviewing *In Our Time* in an English journal, pretended to have caught it badly:

Mr Hemingway does it extremely well. Nothing matters. Everything happens. One wants to keep oneself loose. Avoid one thing only: getting connected up. Don't get connected up. If you get held by anything, break it. Don't be held, break it, and get away. Don't get away with the idea of getting somewhere else. Just get away, for the sake of getting away.

*

Over Christmas 1925, at a hotel in the Alps with Hadley and Bumby, Hemingway resumed work on the Pamplona novel. To Horace

Liveright he wrote of 'the long novel which, so far, I am calling THE SUN ALSO RISES and which I am now re-writing and will be working on all this winter'; and to Scott Fitzgerald on New Year's Eve: 'I am rewriting The Sun Also Rises and it is damned good. It will be ready in 2–3 months for late fall.'

The new title had been arrived at by accident. He had thought of calling the book *The Lost Generation: A Novel* – Gertrude Stein had made her celebrated remark to him only a few months earlier – but he also remembered the biblical words about 'Vanity of vanities' and decided to look them up in full in the Book of Ecclesiastes 1: 2–5.

Vanity of vanities, saith the Preacher, vanity of vanities; all is vanity...One generation passeth away, and another generation cometh; but the earth abideth forever...The sun also ariseth, and the sun goeth down, and hasteth to the place where he arose...

He told Maxwell Perkins that, in calling the book *The Sun Also Rises*, he meant to refer to the words that precede this phrase in the Ecclesiastes passage: 'The point of the book to me was that the earth abideth forever.' This seems an eccentric message to derive from the novel. The British edition was published as *Fiesta*, which in the end seems the best title.

Resuming work on the book, he decided to add a whole new series of chapters at the beginning, set in Paris. The new version had the plainest of openings:

This is a novel about a lady. Her name is Lady Ashley and when the story begins she is living in Paris and it is Spring. That should be a good setting for a romantic but highly moral story...

There follows a description of Brett Ashley's two marriages. It is implied that she would like to have married Jake Barnes; instead, she has taken up with Mike Campbell (Pat Guthrie):

Brett went off with Mike Campbell to the Continent one afternoon, she having offered to at lunchtime because Mike was lonely and sick and very companionable, and, as she said, 'obviously one of us.' ... They came to Paris on their way to the Riviera, and stayed the night in a hotel which had only one room free and that with a double bed. 'We'd no idea of anything of that sort,' Brett said...That was how they happened to be living together.

This loose, chatty narrative style is a little suggestive of Fitzgerald, also of Michael Arlen. It seems a long way from *in our time*.

The second chapter of the new version opens with Jake explaining that he is an American newspaperman living in Paris, the European director of the Continental Press Association – Bill Bird ran just such a bureau. He turns to the subject of Montparnasse:

I never hung about the Quarter much in Paris until Brett and Mike showed up. I always felt about the Quarter that I could sort of take it or leave it alone. You went into it once in a while to sort of see the animals . . . and on hot nights in the spring when the tables were spread out on the sidewalks it was rather pleasant. But for a place to hang around it always seemed awfully dull. I have to put it in, though, because Robert Cohn, who is one of the non-Nordic heroes of this book, had spent two years there.

Jake explains that during these two years Cohn had lived with a lady who thrived on gossip, Frances Clyne (Kitty Cannell). She had 'a constant fear and dread' that he was seeing other women and was about to leave her, and it is implied that she made his life hell.

After *The Sun Also Rises* was published, Kitty Cannell tried to pretend that she had had only a brief and insignificant affair with Loeb, and that they had 'occupied separate apartments in the same building near the Eiffel Tower, where we quite comfortably led double lives'. She alleged that Hemingway did not have her in mind at all for the character of Frances Clyne, who, she said, was really based on a *Broom* secretary who had travelled to Europe with Loeb and Alfred Kreymborg. However, Bertram D. Sarason, who has investigated the lives of the real people behind the novel, was shown Kitty's letters to Loeb, and says that Hemingway's account of the 'Frances Clyne' affair in the novel is closely based on the Kitty–Loeb affair, is indeed an astonishingly accurate record of it; he is mystified as to how Hemingway discovered so much, unless Loeb told him everything.

The narrative goes on by explaining that, despite Frances Clyne's constant interference in his life, Cohn has somehow managed to write a novel – Loeb's *Doodab*: 'He was the hero of it, but it was not too badly done and it was accepted by a New York publisher.' Jake says that Cohn, at that time, 'had only two friends, an English writer named Braddocks, and myself, with whom he played tennis'. Braddocks is Ford Madox Ford, and there follows an account of him promising to help Cohn improve his novel. Braddocks never actually gets round to reading it – a dig at Ford's laziness – and asks Jake to look at it for him. Now comes the account of Ford at the Closerie de Lilas, making a nuisance of himself to Hemingway and the waiter and wrongly identifying Belloc, which – considerably expanded and with Ford's real name restored – finally appeared in *A Moveable Feast*. Hemingway seems to feel a little guilty at having sidetracked himself into this story, for he makes Jake apologise for including it; Jake says of Braddocks:

I should avoid as far as possible putting him into this story except that he was a great friend of Robert Cohn and Cohn is the hero.

Robert Cohn was middleweight boxing champion of Princeton. Do not think I am very much impressed by that as a boxing title, but it meant a lot to Cohn...

Jake now gives us a picture of Cohn's aimless life in the Quarter. He struggles to get away from Frances, and pours out his troubles to Jake as he hangs around Jake's newspaper office. It is also mentioned that he used to edit 'a review of the arts' *(Broom)*. As a portrait of Loeb it is neither kind nor very unfair, just studiedly neutral, a touch sardonic, and – judging from Loeb's autobiography – all too accurate. Not that it was easy to convey the sheer indeterminacy of Loeb's character and behaviour; Jake feels that he has failed to portray Cohn clearly:

The reason is that until he fell in love with Brett, I never heard him make one remark that would, in any way, detach him from other people...He had a funny sort of undergraduate quality about him. If he were in a crowd nothing he said stood out.

As if to emphasise Cohn's naïvety, Jake's own first romantic encounter is with a *poule* whom he picks up on a café terrace out of sheer *ennui*. He takes her to dinner and runs across Braddocks, to whom he facetiously introduces her as his fiancée, 'Mademoiselle Georgette Leblanc' – the celebrated singer and Paris beauty. They all go on to Braddocks's weekly gathering at the *bal musette*, and Brett now makes her first entry, in the company of a crowd of 'fairies', dancing ostentatiously with them while Robert Cohn watches from the bar: 'Brett was damned good-looking...Her hair was brushed back like a boy's.'

Brett realises that Cohn has fallen in love with her, but it is Jake she chooses to go off with. It becomes clear that they are in love with each other, but have not had an affair because of Jake's war wound. Brett asks him:

'Don't you love me?'
'Love you? I simply turn all to jelly when you touch me...And there's not a damn thing we could do,' I said.

The novel does not make it precisely clear what is wrong with Jake, but many years later Hemingway explained that Jake had been injured in the groin during the war, rather improbably losing his penis – or at least the use of it sexually – but not his testicles, therefore being capable of sexual desire without being able to do anything about it.

Within the context of the story, Jake's physical impotence offsets the character-weakness of Cohn, who gets his woman physically but is totally unable to achieve any union of minds. The sexual wounding seems a grotesque way of achieving this contrast, but it is also in the story because Hemingway badly needed to express his own private predicament. On a simple level, it is a manifestation of his desire to have an affair with Duff but his fear of extra-marital involvement; more deeply, there is something in it of the Oak Park boy adrift among the sexually liberated; and at a fundamental level, Jake's wound is a way of portraying a confused sexual identity: Hemingway's terror of homosexuals but his attraction to boyish women – perhaps to actual boys such as the young matador – and his worship of maleness from a viewpoint that, as 'Indian Camp' and the first part of 'Big Two-Hearted River' suggest, was essentially feminine.*

Yet one should be wary of making too close a narrator–author identification. In the finished novel, Jake is not much like Hemingway. His role as the detached observer, ironic and hard-boiled (Jake's own epithet for himself – 'it is awfully easy to be hard-boiled,' he says in chapter 4) – wary of close involvements and sexually inactive, bears a striking resemblance to Robert McAlmon.

*

Wandering into the Sélect after Brett has failed to meet him for a drink at the Hôtel Crillon – traditional Right Bank haunt of American journalists – Jake runs across Harvey Stone:

He had a pile of saucers† in front of him, and he needed a shave.

'Sit down,' said Harvey, 'I've been looking for you... Do you want to know something, Jake?'

'Yes.'

'I haven't had anything to eat for five days.'

I figured rapidly back in my mind. It was three days ago that Harvey had won two hundred francs from me shaking poker dice in the New York Bar...

I felt in my pocket.

'Would a hundred help you any, Harvey?'

*The sexual act described in one of his first short stories to deal explicitly with sex may be sodomy; see *The Nick Adams Stories*, Scribner, 1972, p. 227; 'He...moved Kate over...She pressed tight in against the curve of his abdomen...Nick kissed hard against her back..."Isn't it good this way?" he said.' Hemingway's fourth wife Mary gave a heavy hint, in a mock-interview that she wrote in 1953, about his preferred form of sex: '*Reporter*: Mr Hemingway, is it true that your wife is a lesbian? *Papa [Hemingway]*: Of course not. Mrs Hemingway is a boy. *Reporter*: What are your favourite sports, sir? *Papa*: Shooting, fishing, reading and sodomy. *Reporter*: Does Mrs Hemingway participate in these sports: *Papa*: She participates in all of them.' (Quoted in Jeffery Meyers, *Hemingway: a biography*, Macmillan, 1985, pp. 436–7.) In the posthumously published Hemingway novel *The Garden of Eden*, written during his later years, a writer and his wife pretend to interchange sexual identities: '"You are changing," she said. "... You're my girl Catherine. Will you change and be my girl and let me take you?"'... He lay there and felt something and then her hand holding him and searching lower and he helped with his hands and then lay back in the dark and did not think at all and only felt the weight and the strangeness inside and she said, "Now you can't tell who is who can you?"' (*The Garden of Eden*, Scribner, 1986, p. 17.) The wife cuts her hair short and dresses like a boy.

†In Parisian cafés a waiter bringing each order of drinks places before the customer a saucer containing the bill.

This is Harold Stearns, who in 1921 had delivered his symposium *Civilization in the United States* to the publisher and then made his much-publicised departure to Europe on the Fourth of July. Despite the fanfare on that occasion, Stearns says in his memoirs that he had only intended to come to Europe for a short summer trip, and his journey was motivated as much by the recent death of his wife as by any ideological dissatisfaction with the USA. He had various literary projects in mind, and was lent some money by Sinclair Lewis, off which he lived for a while in Paris. Deciding to stay a little longer, he began to write some pieces for the newspapers, including the *Paris Herald* – the European edition of the *New York Herald*. 'The work was fun, it was easy; and at the then rate of exchange it paid well... How could one be bored or miserable?'

But he quickly became bored with the journalism, and gradually gave it up. By 1925, still in Paris, he was unemployed and almost destitute, a sponger who was avoided by most of his former friends in the Quarter. He ate almost nothing, drank continuously, touched strangers at the Dôme and the Sélect for loans, and sold racing tips to gullible American tourists. John Dos Passos observes that 'even his pursuit of drink and women seemed to lack conviction'; Harold Loeb says he had become 'a landmark' in the Quarter.

Kay Boyle, who met him in 1928, gives a vivid picture of Stearns when he had reached these depths:

The stubble-covered jowls packed hard from drink... the stains of food on his jacket lapels, and the black-rimmed fingers holding his glass... The collar of Harold's black and white striped shirt was frayed, and the side of his face was in need of a shave.

Quarterites, recalling the grand title of his symposium, would sneer: 'There goes American civilization – in the gutter.'

John Glassco describes a typical encounter with him in the Dôme. Glassco had just been reciting to a Spanish girlfriend a forty-line surrealist poem he had written:

'It's awful,' she said. 'But it's very beautiful too.'

'Excuse me,' said a grating, boozy voice at my elbow. 'It's good and it's not beautiful. Send it to the *Dial*...'

'You mustn't pay any attention to this man,' said Adolf. 'He is Harold Stearns, and he knows less about poetry than any living man.'

'I am not a living man,' said Stearns.

At the end of 1925 Stearns took over the 'Peter Pickem' racing column in the *Paris Tribune* (the European edition of the *Chicago Tribune*) and proved to be an erratic but sometimes inspired tipster, scorning the obvious favourites for outsiders that occasionally fulfilled his prophecies. Of the *Tribune* staff, he observes that half of them did not come to work because they were drunk, while the other half turned up drunk: 'It was a sheer miracle that the paper came out at all.' Stearns was now drinking so much that he sometimes saw racehorses flying over the grandstand.

'How did your plan of having Harold Stearns make good in two weeks – after all these years – turn out?' Hemingway asked Scott Fitzgerald in a letter in December 1925, while he was at work on *The Sun Also Rises*. Hemingway said he was 'sorry as hell' for Stearns, 'but there's nothing anybody can do for him except give him money and be nice to him'.

*

After the establishment of the Jake–Brett frustrated romance and the encounter with Harvey Stone, the new draft of the novel introduces Bill Gorton, a necessary comic antithesis to the hard-boiled Jake and the vapid Cohn. Jake takes Gorton to the Sélect, where Brett is sitting at the bar with Mike Campbell. Mike's attitude to Brett is coarse, asexual, non-romantic – perhaps a dig at Pat's supposed homosexuality. He treats her like a comic pet dog:

'You *are* a lovely lady, Brett. Where did you get that hat?...It's a dreadful hat...I say, Brett, you *are* a lovely piece...Don't you think so, Jake?'

Brett and Mike agree to join Jake, Bill, and Robert Cohn in Pamplona, after Jake has taken Bill and Cohn fishing in the Pyrenees. 'Won't it be splendid,' Brett says. 'Spain! We *will* have fun.' When she learns that Cohn will be on the trip, she suggests it may be 'a bit rough' on him, and lets out that she has just been staying with him in San Sebastian. Jake's reaction is terse:

'Congratulations,' I said.
　We walked along.
　'What did you say that for?'
　'I don't know. What would you like me to say?'
　We walked along and turned a corner.

Brett explains that she went away with Cohn because 'I rather thought it would be good for him'. Jake remarks: 'You might take up social service.'

Jake and Bill go down south and meet up with Cohn in Pamplona. Jake takes Bill off to Burguete for the fishing – which goes splendidly, there being no mention of spoiled trout-streams – and Jake now admits his feelings about Cohn's affair with Brett: 'I was blind, unforgivingly jealous...I certainly did hate him.' Bill, too, has little time for Cohn. 'How did you ever happen to know this fellow, anyway?' he asks Jake. 'Haven't you got some more Jewish friends you could bring along?...

The funny thing is he's nice, too. But he's just so awful.' (Don Stewart says this is a fair reflection of his feelings about Loeb: 'I liked Harold all right, but undoubtedly I had a patronizing attitude towards him.') Cohn's Jewishness is harped upon several times, and Jake no longer distances himself from his friends' behaviour, allowing himself to be drawn into the contempt for Cohn and the resentment of his presence in Pamplona. Tension begins to build up as the party, having assembled for the *fiesta*, watches the bulls being unloaded:

'I say,' Mike said, 'they *were* fine bulls... Did you see the one that hit that steer?'...
   'It's no life being a steer,' Robert Cohn said.
   'Don't you think so?' Mike said. 'I would have thought you'd loved being a steer, Robert.'
   'What do you mean, Mike?'
   'They lead such a quiet life. They never say anything and they're always hanging about... Come on, Robert. Do say something... Don't sit there like a bloody funeral. What if Brett did sleep with you? She's slept with lots of better people than you.'
   'Shut up,' Cohn said.

Mike complains to Brett, not about her affair but about her choice of Cohn: 'Brett's had affairs with men before... But they weren't ever Jews, and they didn't come and hang about afterwards.' Bill Gorton calls Cohn 'That kike!' and Mike says of Brett: 'If she would go about with Jews and bull-fighters and such people, she must expect trouble.' Jake begins to become uneasy at the baiting of Cohn; he admits that he 'liked' to see Mike hurting him, but 'I wished he would not do it... because afterwards it made me disgusted at myself. That was morality; things that made you disgusted afterwards. No, that must be immorality.'
   Cohn is repelled by the goring of the horses in the bullring. He tells the others: 'I wish they didn't have the horse part.' His own situation is much like the horses'; he is being gored by everyone as a minor diversion before the big fight. 'I'm not sorry for him,' Jake tells Brett. And she replies: 'I hate his damned suffering... that damned Jew.'
   The *fiesta* and the bullfighting now begin to dominate the narrative, and Cohn slips temporarily into the background. Despite Jake's claim to be an *aficionado*, he and his party behave like any bunch of tourists, rushing about to see the sights. Strikingly, Hemingway entirely omits the 'amateurs' episode in which Loeb had ridden on the bull's horns and become a local hero. Cohn, the despised, could here have been drawn into the *fiesta* in the way that Jake and his friends were failing to be; but evidently Hemingway was too jealous of what Loeb had done to put it in the book, even though some such compensation for the maltreatment of Cohn is badly needed.

Instead, he went back to his original scheme and made the young matador, whom he now calls Pedro Romero, the 'hero' of the remainder of the novel. Brett falls in love with the lad; she tells Jake, 'I'm a goner. I'm mad about the Romero boy,' and goes off with him for the evening. This is based on Duff disappearing with Loeb for the evening at Pamplona and in consequence being beaten up by Pat. In the novel, however, Cohn beats up the matador because he is jealous of the boy's affair with Brett. Jake finds Cohn weeping remorsefully on his hotel bed, and the next morning Cohn leaves abruptly in a hired car, back to Paris.

Don Stewart comments of all this invented part of the narrative: 'He had to make some of it up ... otherwise it wouldn't have been a novel.' Maybe Stewart is right, and Loeb's aborted fight with Hemingway would not have provided a sufficiently dramatic climax. Yet it is hard to convince oneself that Hemingway's rewriting of history in the final chapters is much of an improvement, either dramatically or in any other respect, on the real events. When Loeb's account of what actually happened is compared with the novel, the fictional version seems both melodramatic and muddled, as if Hemingway were trying to settle too many personal scores.

Hemingway told Scott Fitzgerald that the book's moral was 'how people go to hell'. But Mike and Bill leave Pamplona cheerfully enough, and Jake and Brett are allowed at least a low-key happy ending: there are some pages describing Jake meeting up with Brett in Madrid, where she has persuaded the boy matador to abandon her because she knows she will do him no good; and the novel ends with Jake and Brett enjoying lunch with several bottles of rioja and cuddling in a taxi. No one has gone to hell except Cohn, the character who least deserves it.*

★

Boni & Liveright duly rejected *The Torrents of Spring*, and Maxwell Perkins at Scribner's accepted both it and *The Sun Also Rises*. 'He wrote an awfully swell contract,' Hemingway reported, 'and never even asked to look at *The Sun*.'

Hemingway now lent Fitzgerald a carbon copy of *The Sun Also*

---

*Early in the novel Cohn seems to be an *alter ego* for Jake–Hemingway. He is described as a passive, almost female figure: 'He had been taken in hand by a lady ... She was very forceful ... Cohn never had a chance of not being taken in hand.' Jake says that Cohn 'was married by the first girl who was nice to him' – note the passive – and describes Frances as 'the lady who had him'. At this stage Jake is patient, even affectionate towards Cohn; he plays tennis with him, plans a walk with him, and says he 'rather liked him' – which for Jake is a strong statement of feeling. One might almost suspect that Jake–Hemingway has a sexual interest in Cohn–Loeb, which might add to his resentment when Cohn pairs off with Brett. Certainly the baiting of Cohn in the final chapters seems almost orgiastic and beyond reason, with anti-Semitism as a conventional excuse for it rather than the real cause.

Rises; Fitzgerald was markedly unenthusiastic about some of it. He told Hemingway, face to face in Paris, that he thought parts of it were 'careless and ineffectual', and that in particular there was a feeling of 'condescending *casualness*' about the opening chapters, a lot of 'mere horseshit', bad writing that '*honestly* reminds me of Michael Arlen'. He repeated all these criticisms in a letter the next day, warning Hemingway that 'the very fact that people have committed themselves to you will make them watch you like a cat'. It was true that 'almost everyone is a genius' in the Quarter, or at least they thought they were, but this did not mean that a really 'good man' like Hemingway should take things easy. He must realise that the people who had been telling him that he was a genius were frail and unreliable, mere 'professional enthusiasts', and he must develop 'a lust for anything honest' that he could get people to say about his work. It was an odd reaction: Fitzgerald was attacking that part of the novel – the opening section – which most resembled his own writing; quite unjustifiably, for these chapters were excellently done in themselves, though in a rather different manner from the rest of the book. Maybe Fitzgerald felt Hemingway was straying threateningly into *Gatsby* territory and becoming a potential rival.

He gave Hemingway some detailed notes on what he particularly disliked in the opening fifteen pages of the typescript. These included the anecdote about Ford and Belloc, which he said was 'flat as hell without naming Ford which would be cheap'. He continued:

Why not cut the inessentials in Cohens [*sic*] biography?... When so many people can write well & the competition is heavy I can't imagine how you could have done these first 20 pps. so casually... From p. 30 I begin to like the novel but Ernest I can't tell you the sense of disappointment that beginning with its elephantine facetiousness gave me. Please do what you can about it in proof.

Fitzgerald explained that he had 'decided not to pick at anything else' in the remainder of the novel 'because... I was much too excited'. He said the greater part of the book was 'damn good'.

Maxwell Perkins wrote to say he liked the novel. Replying to Perkins, Hemingway did not mention what Fitzgerald had said – all he told Perkins was that Fitzgerald was 'very excited' about the book – but he said he had now decided to 'start the book at what is now page 16 in the Mss.' There was nothing, he told Perkins, in those first sixteen pages that was essential to the rest of the narrative. 'Scott agrees with me.' Perkins did not agree; he wanted to retain the opening because he thought it provided necessary background to the characters. Hemingway himself did not altogether like performing such surgery. 'I believe the book loses by eliminating the first part,' he admitted to Perkins, 'but it would have been pointless to include it with the Belloc eliminated – and I think that would be altogether pointless with Belloc's name out.'

Fitzgerald had not asked him to eliminate these pages; he had merely recommended that he rewrite them. But Hemingway was evidently not prepared to take instructions, even from Fitzgerald. Probably he was furious; no letter from him to Fitzgerald survives until September 1926, several months after he had received the criticisms. Writing then, he mentions quite casually that he has 'cut' the novel to 'start with Cohn', and offers no thanks or even acknowledgement to Fitzgerald for having initiated this.

Though the cutting was probably done in a mood of pique and anger, it did the novel no harm. Hemingway decided to begin abruptly with the account of Robert Cohn boxing at Princeton, and this gives the novel an intriguingly low-key start that recalls 'Indian Camp' and 'Big Two-Hearted River'. Just as Cohn appears without preamble, so a few pages later does Brett. The reader is plunged straight into Jake Barnes's world, the Quarter in the spring of 1925, and is treated as a true Quarterite who knows everybody without needing to be introduced.

*

The book was published during October 1926, and at once began to attract a cult following. Thornton Wilder describes undergraduates at Yale mimicking Jake, while Malcolm Cowley recalls their opposite numbers at Smith College adopting Brett as a model. 'Bright young men from the Middle West,' he writes, 'were trying to be Hemingway heroes, talking in tough understatements from the sides of their mouths.' Gossip-columnists hinted at the real identities of the novel's characters. 'For those who know the stamping ground of the American expatriates in Paris,' wrote Herbert Gorman in the New York *World* a month after the book had been published, 'it will become speedily patent that practically all of these characters are directly based on actual people.' Janet Flanner wrote in her 'Letter from Paris' in the *New Yorker*: 'The titled British declassée and her Scottish friend, the American *Frances* and the unlucky *Robert Cohn* . . . are . . . to be seen just where Hemingway so often placed them at the Sélect.'

Harold Loeb was in the South of France when the novel was published. Hemingway had not given him the slightest warning about the book, and Loeb says that it 'hit like an upper-cut'. Not that he read it right through:

At first I had difficulty getting into it. I confined my reading to the passages that had to do with Cohn, seeking to discover if I talked like Cohn. Evidently I didn't act like Cohn, never having knocked anyone down or even hit anyone except with gloves on. I didn't seem to talk like Cohn either. But it is difficult to see oneself as another sees you; so I couldn't be sure. Then, having read the book, I tried to understand what had led my one-time friend to transform me into an insensitive, patronizing, uncontrolled drag.

He felt that despite all that had happened at Pamplona, 'nothing in our relationship justified the distortion of the real friend I was into the Robert Cohn of *The Sun Also Rises*'.

Rumours began to circulate the Quarter that Loeb and the others wanted revenge. Someone suggested that the novel should be called *Six Characters in Search of an Author – with a Gun Apiece*.* It was even said that Loeb really had a gun and was looking for Hemingway, and that Hemingway, hearing this, had sent him a telegram saying he would be in a certain bar for three nights running if Loeb wanted to get him. Hemingway wrote to Fitzgerald six months after the book had come out that there was a story that he had gone to Switzerland 'to avoid being shot by demented characters out of my books'. Loeb's own version is that, some months after the novel was published, he was having a drink in one of the bars in the Quarter when Hemingway walked in. Hemingway saw him, smiled uneasily, and went over to the bar and drank there by himself. Loeb was 'amazed at the colour of his neck. Red gradually suffused it – and then his ears – right to their tips.'

The other characters did not resent the book at all; they were flattered to be in it. Hemingway told Fitzgerald that Duff had said she 'wasn't sore' about the novel; she 'said the only thing was she had never slept with the bloody bull fighter'. Nor did they object when friends in the Quarter credited them with all the exploits of their fictional selves. Kitty Cannell, though she disclaimed identity with Frances, says with pride that 'everyone in Montparnasse' kept asking her if she had done everything Frances did in the novel. To Don Stewart it seemed as if they had all been 'busily playing their roles' for the book at Pamplona. Even Loeb, writing about *The Sun Also Rises* and the real events behind it in a 1967 article in the *Connecticut Review*, uses the names from the novel to describe himself and his friends, as if they had all merged into the Hemingway characters. Whatever his feelings about Hemingway's maltreatment of him, he admits in his autobiography that nothing after Pamplona seemed quite so exciting: 'All that came afterward was anti-climactic, even the high spots.'

Though there were doubters, reviewers of *The Sun Also Rises* were mostly very impressed by the book. Conrad Aiken in the *New York Herald Tribune* said that 'if there is better dialogue being written today I do not know where to find it'. No critic – not even Aiken, who was Jewish – commented on the Jew-baiting of Cohn or Jake's complicity in it, nor did they mention Jake's impotence, the one element of the novel that still worried Fitzgerald after Hemingway had cut the open-

---

* Pirandello had been a contributor to *Broom*.

ing; he told Hemingway: 'He isn't like an impotent man. He's like a man in a sort of moral chastity belt.' Robert McAlmon did not care for the novel, or what he bothered to read of it. Writing many years later, he said: 'Beginning with *The Sun Also Rises* I found his work slick, affected, distorted... himself always the hero.'

The Sun Also Rises has a strong claim to be regarded as Hemingway's best novel. When Duff Twysden's brother-in-law, Sir William Twysden, was questioned in the 1960s about Hemingway's portrayal of Duff, he snorted that Hemingway was 'just a damn journalist'. This is really a compliment, for the novel is a supreme piece of journalism. In a passage rejected from 'Big Two-Hearted River', Nick Adams asserts that 'the only writing that was any good was what you made up, what you imagined... Everything good he'd ever written he'd made up. None of it had ever happened.' *The Sun Also Rises* proves that this is nonsense. As Don Stewart remarks, the novel is 'so absolutely accurate ... What a reporter, I said to myself. That's the way it really was.'

5

These rocky days

While Hemingway was revising *The Sun Also Rises* in February 1926, Kay Boyle arrived at Grasse in the South of France to join Ernest Walsh and Ethel Moorhead, in the hope of recovering from tuberculosis. They met her on the station platform. Walsh proved to be 'tall and slender and ivory-skinned, with bold, dark, long-lashed eyes, and his black eyebrows met savagely above his nose'. Moorhead was middle-aged and severe-looking; 'the pince-nez she wore gave her an air of authority'. They were living in a hillside villa rented from a shoe manufacturer. 'If I was going to die of tuberculosis,' writes Kay, 'it would be easy to die in the white blaze of the plaster and stone of the walls... with drifting curtains of wisteria.'

Walsh did not like to be called Ernest; the name he preferred was Michael. Kay describes how 'that first night Michael read for a long time to us...' He read two of his mock early-English sonnets:

> How coulde I call thee wife no thou art notte
> For the quicke violent steps of a husbande
> In thy chamber nor the lawful claiminge
> Hands of a husbande atte thy brests nor marriage
> Speeches or the vulgar nameplate mistress
> Thou ladye thou dame thou girlbrested thou art
> Thighplumed sweeteyed thou loitering assent...

He also read aloud from his editorial for the forthcoming issue of *This Quarter*: 'Outside of *This Quarter*, the Three Mountains Press of William Bird in Paris, and the Contact Publishing Company of Robert McAlmon, there is at present no place in the English-speaking world to which an artist may bring his work...' Walsh approved of McAlmon. He read some of McAlmon's poetry aloud to Kay as well as his own, and when Pauline Pfeiffer, an old friend of Hadley Hemingway, came to stay and told Walsh that McAlmon was spreading outrageous stories about Hemingway, and that Hemingway was fed up with him, Walsh was furious: 'You're talking through your hat! Ernest is as close to me as a brother, and he's never had anything but good to say of McAlmon and his work!... Christ! McAlmon was the first to publish Hemingway.'

But Hemingway really had turned against McAlmon. He wrote to Scott Fitzgerald in December 1925:

McAlmon is a son of a bitch with a mind like an ingrowing toe nail. I'm through defending that one... He went around for two nights talking on the subject of what a swine I was, how *he* had done everything for me, started me off etc. (i.e. sold out an edition each of that lousy little book and In Our Time... the only books he ever sold of all the books he's published) and that all I did was exploit people emotionally... Am going to write a Mr and Mrs Eliot* on him. Might as well give his emotional exploitation story some foundation.

John Glassco describes an encounter between Hemingway and McAlmon at the Coupole bar. McAlmon opened the batting:

'If it isn't Ernest, the fabulous phony! How are the bulls?'

'And how is North America McAlmon, the Unfinished Poem?'† He leaned over and pummelled McAlmon in the ribs, grinning and blowing beery breath over the table. 'Room for me here, boys?'

'It's only Hemingway,' said Bob loudly to both of us. 'Pay no attention and he may go away.'

Hemingway gave a lopsided grin and moved into a seat at the next table... 'Seen anything of Sylvia these days?' he asked diffidently.

'The Beach? Rats, no! We had a row last year. I don't like old women anyway.'

'No one could accuse you of that, Bob.'

'Leave my friends out of this.'

'Me? You brought them in. Anyway, go to hell.' Hemingway got up and moved heavily to the bar.

'Watch,' said Bob. 'Pretty soon he'll be twisting wrists with some guy at the bar...'

*

Soon after Kay's arrival at Grasse, Ernest Walsh and Ethel Moorhead quarrelled, and Walsh and Kay set off together, journeying through the villages of the Alpes-Maritimes, looking for somewhere they could settle for a while. Walsh's own tuberculosis was far more advanced than Kay's illness, and 'once a hotel-keeper had heard Michael clear his throat or cough there would be no room available'. During their wandering, the two talked a great deal of McAlmon, whom Walsh had never set eyes on, and whom Kay had only seen once. 'We wanted to know what the man was like...'

---

*The satirical short story in *In Our Time* about the couple trying to have a baby.

†A sneer at McAlmon's long unfinished poem *North America, Continent of Conjecture*.

Walsh wrote to Ezra Pound that he was in love with Kay. Ezra replied from Rapallo in his usual Pound-language: 'Corresponse suspended herwith until without'er of ((pssbl.?)) yu cummup for air.' It seemed to mean he disapproved. Ethel Moorhead was in a white rage about it; she told Walsh she was removing his name from the masthead of *This Quarter*. He responded by refusing to hand over the material for the next number, and when they met again he threw a carafe of water at her.

Kay's health was improving, but under these strains Walsh's got rapidly worse. During October 1926 – the month in which *The Sun Also Rises* was published – he died, aged thirty-one. 'And what will you do now, you poor forlorn girl?' Moorhead asked Kay, with more than a touch of malice. But when Kay said she would go back to the USA, Moorhead broke down and told her: 'Stay here. I had only him, and now I have only you and the baby that's coming.' Kay was expecting his child.

She moved into Moorhead's Monte Carlo flat, and Moorhead perjured herself that Kay had been Walsh's legal wife, so that the baby, Sharon, born in March 1927, could be registered as his legitimate offspring. Moorhead's temper could be terrible. On the day of Walsh's funeral she shouted with rage because a man named Eugene Jolas had sent a telegram to Kay from Paris saying he was 'going to go on with what Ernest Walsh had not been able to finish'. He was going to start a magazine called *transition*, and would Kay send him her stories and poems 'as quickly as possible for the first number'. Moorhead cried out that the telegram should have been sent to *her*. Another time she implied to McAlmon that Sharon was really Kay's husband's baby, and not Walsh's.

McAlmon arrived more or less unannounced and stayed for three days. 'During that time,' says Kay, 'he and I exchanged not more than a dozen sentences,' even though 'there was so much to ask him... so much to enquire about Paris, and what Eugene Jolas and Elliot Paul, the editors of *transition*, were like,* but I found it impossible to ask him anything... He spoke so cynically of the great with whom he was intimate... I quailed before his icy gaze.'

While Kay listened in silence, McAlmon spoke of the Quarter that she had never seen, and the goings-on there. Dorothy Pound, after years of childless marriage, had come back to Paris to give birth to a son

---

* Jolas, born in New Jersey and brought up in Alsace-Lorraine, was a journalist on the Paris *Tribune*, as was his co-editor, the American writer Elliot Paul. They started *transition* during 1927 as a monthly. Later it became a quarterly, surviving until 1939, publishing segments of Joyce's 'Work in Progress' *(Finnegans Wake)* and writings by Gertrude Stein as well as work by younger authors and poets. Paul soon left the magazine because it became too serious. He was a portly bearded man who played the accordion – said Gertrude Stein – like a native. His book on Paris, *A Narrow Street* (1942), entirely ignores the expatriates and describes the life and character of the French.

in the American Hospital, and 'life was striking Ezra as complicated'. Everyone had been to see Cocteau's *Romeo and Juliet* at the Cigalle, but that was only because Yvonne Georges was in it and there was a bar at the back of the auditorium. Louis Aragon was going about with Nancy Cunard, the wild daughter of Lady Maud, and people were calling her *le Cunard sauvage*. Ezra's opera had been performed – it was about François Villon – and everyone had come to hear it, even Eliot, over from London, though typically he had hidden in the back row. Mina Loy wanted to meet him, but he ran away before the end. The music had been much better than most of them had anticipated. Afterwards they'd all gone on to the Boeuf-sur-le-Toit, and then up to Bricktop's. Ezra loved being a musician. He'd persuaded Natalie Barney to have one of George Antheil's works performed at her Friday salon, though it was bound to deafen the neighbours. Sylvia Beach had got it into her head that Antheil – who lived above her shop – had tuberculosis, so she had made everyone contribute to send him to a sanatorium. Then they all found out that there was nothing wrong with his lungs at all. By that time most of the money had gone. So people's enthusiasm about his music was rather fading away.

Satie the composer had died. One evening, said McAlmon, he was drinking at the Stryx with Nina Hamnett, the next day – or so it seemed – they were all marching in his funeral procession. Over the years he'd bought drinks for most of the *poules* in the Quarter, so they all turned up to see him off. It was marvellous, it could only have happened in Paris.

Hemingway's Lady Brett, as everyone now called her, had acquired an American boyfriend. He was much younger than her, and they'd moved into an empty studio on the rue Broca. They couldn't afford the key money, let alone the last occupant's few sticks of furniture, so McAlmon had helped out: 'I took it on a year's lease.' They were supposed to pay him rent, but he told Kay and Moorhead that he didn't hold out much hope.

Jimmie the barman was said to be writing his memoirs. They ought to make better reading than *The Sun Also Rises*. Nowadays Hemingway would only talk about bullfighting and 'how a man needs to test himself to prove to himself that he can take it'. McAlmon had been down to Pamplona with Hemingway the year before the trip that inspired the book, and it was crazy the way they'd all climbed into the ring for the amateurs' event. McAlmon had been persuaded to do it, but his only idea was 'to avoid getting butted'.*

Hemingway had split up with Hadley. They'd been apart since

---

* Bill Bird had been on that 1924 Pamplona trip too, and after reading *The Sun Also Rises* he suspected that Hemingway had intended McAlmon for the role Loeb eventually played in 1925, 'the goat of the trip'. However, since McAlmon was paying all the bills, this was not so easy.

August 1926, a couple of months before *The Sun Also Rises* was
published, and now the divorce had come through. He had married
Pauline Pfeiffer. She wasn't bad-looking, the new Mrs Hemingway,
'small-boned and lively as a partridge,' said McAlmon. Kitty Cannell
had introduced them to each other, though Pauline had known Hadley
for years, and she'd been machinating to win him from Hadley as soon
as she could see he'd got bored with 'Lady Brett'. Like Hadley, Pauline
would be able to support him. Her cash came from an Uncle Gus who
was very big in perfumes and liniments. 'Stiff with money,' as Dos
Passos put it. Pauline was four years older than Hemingway, but she'd
reduced her age on the marriage certificate. They'd taken a smart flat
near the Jardin du Luxembourg, with two bathrooms, so Hemingway
could say goodbye to the cold-water tap and the outside lavatory.

Pauline was a Catholic, so Hemingway had converted. Or rather
he'd somehow convinced the Catholic authorities that he'd been one all
along. He said he'd been baptised by a Catholic priest after being shot
up in Italy. It was no more improbable than his other war stories, and
no one could disprove it, so he'd managed to get off all that tedious
instruction. But he couldn't be much of a Catholic, judging by a two-
liner he'd just written for Ezra's new magazine in Rapallo:

> The Lord is my shepherd,
> I shall not want him for long.

The bar where everyone in the Quarter now went was a place near
the Hotel Foyot, the Trois et As, because Jimmie was working there.
One evening Lady Brett had been sitting at the bar with her new man
when in came the first Mrs Hemingway, and then a few minutes later
the second Mrs Hemingway. It was like a Keystone movie. But Hadley
was very dignified and quite witty about it.

Gertrude Stein said that Contact Editions ought to publish the entire
Making of Americans, and somehow McAlmon had found himself
agreeing, though she was right at the top of his list of megalomaniacs,
and it was infuriating to think that she could pay the entire printing bill
just by selling one of those over-valued pictures from her collection.
She'd been pestering Darantière with corrections ever since his men
started typesetting.

To be fair, she'd actually admitted that she wondered how anybody
could read her stuff. 'It seems to me quite meaningless at times,' she had
said, though she explained it had felt pretty fine when she'd actually
been writing it. You had to hand it to the old girl, said McAlmon to Kay
and Moorhead, she'd got 'vitality and a deep belief in the healthiness of
life, too great a belief for these rocky days'.

McAlmon said he'd had an argument on a cross-Channel ferry with
Scott Fitzgerald about Eliot's poems. 'When Scott discovered that I

didn't dote on them, he sorrowingly gave me up as a hopeless cause.' Someone called Mary Butts, who was with them, had said: 'But you don't know the depths of Europe. What will become of us all?' McAlmon said he was sure he didn't know: 'Rats! If the world's going to hell, I'm going there with it, and not in the back ranks either.'

As McAlmon talked, Ethel Moorhead decided he was falling for Kay. 'I'll never understand it,' she said to Kay afterwards. 'You're not really that beautiful, you're really not. How in the world or why in the world . . .' Moorhead told McAlmon he should go away before Kay ruined a third man's life. To which McAlmon replied: 'Hell's bells, my life was born ruined.' And went.

The next day he wrote to Kay from St Tropez:

I don't want to butt into anybody's life, and you've certainly been around long enough to know what you're doing. But you don't belong there. You haven't asked me, but I would say get out. Write me to Paris, c/o Sylvia Beach. If you need money, which I would think to be the case, Williams and I between us will get it to you, and quickly.

They were, says Kay, 'undoubtedly the words I had been waiting to hear'. She asked McAlmon for $50, and he sent it. But she did not use it to go to Paris. She went to Stoke-on-Trent, where her husband Richard was working for the Michelin tyre company.

*

In Stoke, trying to make her marriage work again, Kay read the early numbers of *transition*, to which she herself was contributing, and wrote endless letters to Jolas, its editor; and to McAlmon, who rarely answered. She lived as French a life as she could manage, in the little enclave of Michelin employees and their wives, and tried to ignore the eternal gloom of Arnold Bennett's Five Towns. On the day in August 1927 when the anarchists Sacco and Vanzetti were finally executed for alleged murder in the USA, after years of left-wing outcry in their defence, she set out to burn the American flag in front of the US Consulate in Stoke. And 'England went away, and the English people who passed us in the street were suddenly not there'.

In the spring of 1928, at last she had a direct invitation to go to Paris, not from McAlmon, but from a man called Archibald Craig, who wanted her to help him edit a yearbook of poetry, and had fixed her up with a job ghosting a princess's memoirs. 'So at the end of April, Sharon and I set off again. Richard and I told each other again that it would only be for a little while; but we must have known . . .'

She arrived in Paris, met Jolas and the *transition* crowd, and went to a party where she was introduced to James and Nora Joyce. There was a sudden hush in the conversation, and in came a formal procession:

Jolas's wife Maria leading Gertrude Stein and Alice B. Toklas. Kay noticed that Joyce seemed unaware of them, though they passed within a few feet of him. He and Gertrude had never before been seen in the same room. A little later in the evening, Sylvia Beach brought them together; she says they shook hands 'quite peacefully'.

Kay liked the Joyces, who assumed that she travelled from country to country all the time, 'like our friend McAlmon', and kept recommending cheap *pensions* in Switzerland. After a while Sylvia came over and sat on a footstool at Joyce's feet, in her grey mannish suit. But someone was missing. 'McAlmon was not anywhere around.'

*

He was not around all spring, nor in the early summer. Kay got on with writing the princess's book, and with editing the poetry anthology with Archie Craig. Kay suggested they might get it produced by Darantière, McAlmon's printer. 'But Archie always fell silent when I mentioned this man he had never clapped eyes on.'

The princess gave a tea party for Gertrude and Alice, and everyone was stricken with shyness, Gertrude worst of all – she kept nervously touching the short hair at her temples and forehead. Kay said how marvellous the weather was, and then dried up. 'I could have asked her how her Ford was running, and told her I had had one like it in Cincinnati...I could have asked her what she meant on page nine of "An Elucidation" which *transition* had published in April...But my tongue was dry in my mouth.'

The maid came in with the tea wagon, and everyone pecked silently at rum babas and chocolate éclairs. Then, miraculously, the doorbell rang, and in came Isadora Duncan's brother Raymond, in his invariable tunic and sandals, looking like a Roman emperor and speaking like a Mid-Western farmer. (John Glassco on Raymond Duncan: 'A walking absurdity who dressed in an ancient handwoven Greek costume and wore his hair in long braids reaching to his waist, adding, on ceremonial occasions, a fillet of bay-leaves.' McAlmon said he was 'trying to prove he's something else besides being Isadora's brother'.)

Raymond and Gertrude had grown up together in California, and had scarcely met since. They started talking about baseball games: 'You weren't much good at bat, Raymond!' 'You weren't too good yourself at home runs!' Gertrude reminded him how he had once drunk stronger liquor than his present diet of goat's milk. 'You have an excellent memory, Gertrude,' came the answer, 'probably due to the fact that you keep repeating things over and over.'

*

By the summer, Kay, whom a Paris specialist had diagnosed as not being tubercular after all, had been swept into a hectic social life, but there was still no sign of McAlmon. At first she gathered that he was away. Then she learnt from Archie Craig that he was back in Paris. Sylvia Beach had told McAlmon that Kay was in town, and wasn't it strange, said Archie, that such a good and devoted friend shouldn't come looking for her?

Surely she would run into him soon. But he was not at the Bal Nègre when Jolas took her there one midnight to meet two new friends of his, Harry and Caresse Crosby; nor in the shooting galleries of the fête she went to on the Champs de Mars. Then, one night, she was eating with a crowd at Lipp's when she looked up and saw him searching from face to face across the brasserie. 'And if his cold eye gave a sign of recognition when he saw me, or even if he saw me, I could not tell.' He did not turn his head again in her direction, so she got up and left the others and went over to where he stood alone at the bar, ordering a beer.

'Bob,' she said, unable for the moment to think of anything more to say.

He scarcely turned his head, but he put some francs for the un-finished beer down on the bar. 'Come on,' he said. 'Let's go up to Le Grand Écart. There may be some lively people there.'

6

Summer's almost ended

They made their exit from Lipp's and took a taxi up to Montmartre. In the cab, McAlmon began mocking what he called the pseudo-intellectuality of the *transition* crowd with whom Kay was hanging out: 'How can you sit for hours listening to the talking about the "revaluation of spirit in its intercontinental relations", and the "destruction of mechanical positivism"? Rats!'

He was still in the same mood when they reached Le Grand Écart* and he ordered gin fizzes for both of them. Kay listened as he went on lecturing her about what she was and what she wasn't and what she ought to be, and she tried to make a joke of it. 'The dimmed lights and the muted music made a dreamy shadowy place of the night club, but McAlmon didn't ask me to dance.' It was the son-in-law of the *patron*, tall and built like a prize-fighter, who came up to the bar in his dinner jacket and bowed to Kay and McAlmon. 'Go ahead,' McAlmon said to her. And she, disturbed by his disparagement of her new friends, 'danced with this man I did not know'.

The couples were packed on to the small highly polished square of dance floor. Looking beyond it, out into the darkness behind the rows of tables, Kay could see the figure of McAlmon sitting aloof at the bar. Her partner asked about him: was he an American newspaperman, or maybe a novelist? 'What's he looking for, wandering around night after night, alone?' Kay was hurt by the question: 'That night, I made the mistake of believing he had actually put the pieces of himself together and that he was seated in high and mighty and inaccessible security somewhere.'

When she got back to the bar, he had switched from gin fizz to Scotch, 'and we were sitting there silenced and saddened and embittered by the ugliness and opulence of the middle-aged people, French and American and English, who danced, and ate, and drank, and threw their money away instead of giving it to the poets and beggars of the world'. And then, suddenly, through the green silk draperies that concealed a window which had been opened to the summer night, 'a miserable hand

*Le Grand Écart ('the splits' in dance terminology) was named after Cocteau's novel of that title – a latter day *Scènes de la Bohème* – published in 1923.

reached in from the deserted street, a black-nailed, dirty, defeated hand, with a foul bit of coat sleeve showing at the wrist. Without a word McAlmon placed his fine, tall glass of whisky and soda into the fingers of the stranger's hand, and the fingers closed quickly on it and drew it back through the draperies into the lonely dark.' It was, as Kay says, 'a parable acted out for exactly what this man was'.

*

From Le Grand Écart they went on to Bricktop's, and Bricktop herself sat down and had a drink with them. 'And here was a woman to be cherished, her tinted brick-coloured hair, her cocoa flesh, her lively and almost impossibly beautiful legs, her dogwood-white teeth, her clear-eyed poise in the dancing, drinking, worldly turmoil of the place.' A decade later it was said she had entered a convent in California. Kay thought it quite plausible.

McAlmon talked of Montparnasse. 'The good days of the Quarter were finished, Bob kept telling me; I had come too late.' Nina Hamnett had gone back to London and was holding court at a pub in Fitzrovia. Flossie Martin was still around, but her beauty and exuberance were on the wane. All the same, said McAlmon, from Bricktop's they would go back to the Quarter, to the Coupole, to see who was around.

As they walked through the Coupole door, Kay immediately identified Flossie, 'her voice clamorous as an excited child's, her milk-white arms and throat, her bosomy flesh, packed with care into a baby's flawless, silken skin. A green straw hat with an enormous brim was over one eye, and there were orange tendrils of hair curling in the sea shells of her ears.' Seeing McAlmon, she seized him in her arms, and placed lipstick kisses like little footprints all over his brow.

Forty years later, says Kay, somebody picked up in a secondhand bookstore in Los Angeles a handful of postcards and letters that must once have lain about in Flossie's room, since they were all addressed to her. They were in different handwritings, written by different men in different countries, most of them sailors, and they were addressed in such fashions as

Miss Flossie Martin, Café du Dôme, Paris, France.

Mme la Marquise de Montparnasse, née Florence Martin, somewhere near the Dôme or Dingo, France.

La Belle Martin, Reine du Quartier Montparnasse, Royaume de France.

One letter was written half in French and half in English from a French sailor on leave near Toulon, who began: '*Ma petite Flos*,' and signed himself 'your very small friend JEAN, who loves you always and kisses

you very much'. Below his signature had been added those of a naval
electrician from the battleship *Edgar Quinet*, a second lieutenant from
the cruiser *Yser*, and a British sailor, all of whom (wrote Jean) were
eager to go to Paris to meet Flossie at the Dôme. There was also a typed
letter dated 5 February 1924, dictated by the American Consul General
in Paris:

> Madam:
>   I have to inform you that I am in receipt of a telegram from M. Martin,
> 362 Commonwealth Avenue, Boston, Mass. requesting me to report
> relative to your welfare.
>   Will you please call at this Consulate-General to see me at your earliest
> convenience.
>   I am,
>   Very respectfully yours . . .

Whoever 'M. Martin' may have been, says Kay, father or mother, uncle
or aunt, brother or sister, he or she 'must have been there at the bar with
her that night in 1928, unseen and perhaps unanswered, and every time
she gave a thought to M. Martin, she ordered another drink, and
whooped aloud, and talked about getting up early tomorrow or maybe
the day after that, and going on with her operatic career'.

Sitting at the bar while McAlmon ordered drinks for himself and
Kay, Flossie began to sing some absurd hit remembered from her
Ziegfeld days:

> Is there something wrong with Otto Kahn,
> Or something wrong with me?

'Wiz Otto Kahn, definitely,' said a voice from the end of the bar. It was
the first time Kay had seen and heard Kiki. That night her eyelids had
been painted in opaline. 'She was heavy-featured and voluptuous,' says
Kay, 'her voice as hoarse as that of a vegetable hawker.'

It was the first time, too, that Kay met Hilaire Hiler, who had come
round from his Jockey Club and was standing absorbed in his own
thoughts at the Coupole bar. 'But Bob said that Flossie and Kiki and
Hiler were no more than three survivors of another and far gayer
company and of a wilder, more adventurous time. The lines that people
spoke now were flat as stale beer, he said, and the props, the scenery, no
longer had any meaning.' There was nothing to do except have another
drink. If only Djuna Barnes or Mina Loy would turn up, the evening
might be saved. They had better both go across the road and see if there
was anyone worth drinking with in the Sélect. It was only later, when
Kay knew him better, 'that I learned that whomever he was with, Bob
was always seeking another name, and another face, in quite another
place . . .'

                                    *

Over at the Sélect they found Harold Stearns, drinking at the bar in his brown felt hat, 'in a shabby parody of respectability'. McAlmon ordered drinks for the three of them. Kay knew it must be nearly dawn.

Stearns began to talk of a horse that had fallen in a steeplechase and broken its leg. He had persuaded them not to destroy it but to let him take it home. He'd borrowed the money to get a horse van to haul it into Paris, and now he was looking after it in the overgrown courtyard behind his apartment. The leg had been set, and the *vétérinaire* said it was going to mend all right, but meanwhile the horse was eating him into the poorhouse. It needed oats, alfalfa, not to mention the rye straw for its bedding. (Stearns 'talked quickly, looking straight ahead,' says Kay.) And then there were the fees for the *vétérinaire*, who had to visit the horse every day.

'Stearns, I admire you!' said McAlmon, and began to laugh.

Stearns solemnly went on saying: 'So several times in the evening I have to take up a collection for him. I have no choice.' And he wandered out on to the terrace of the Sélect, in search of the truly gullible; and McAlmon went on laughing his mirthless laugh.

Soon Stearns was back, with banknotes in his pocket. 'I'd like you to come and see him sometime,' he said to McAlmon and Kay, buying drinks for the three of them out of his takings.

'Better not tempt fate too far,' said McAlmon. 'We might take you up on that.'

McAlmon had begun to sing to himself. 'Me and My Shadow', he was singing. 'Next time I'll tell you about another horse,' Harold Stearns was saying to Kay, looking straight ahead across his glass.

> Me and My Shadow,
> Strolling down the avenue . . . .

'I'll tell you,' Stearns was saying, 'about an American horse who happened to be travelling with us on a freighter as flat as an ark that was passing through the French Sudan, and when the natives laid eyes on him they dispersed like leaves before the customary storm . . .'

> Me and My Shadow,
> All alone and feeling blue . . .

'. . . The fact was, they'd never seen a horse before, never so much as seen the picture of a horse, they'd never put money on a horse, never attended a cinder classic, if you can believe it . . .'

> And when it's twelve o'clock,
> We climb the stair . . .

'. . . They'd never heard ponies thundering into the stretch . . .'

We never knock,
For nobody's there . . .

'. . . Those natives, they were untouched by civilization.'

Stearns paused, and drank, and there was a sudden silence. Kay realised that McAlmon had stopped singing. 'I looked quickly around and he was no longer there.'

EPILOGUE

Homeward Trek

It was not, of course, the end of the Quarter; not yet. There were other nights, other parties. One summer evening Hilaire Hiler held one in the open air. 'Kiki sat under a grand piano that had been placed under the green branches of the trees,' says Kay, 'and hoarsely sang or spoke her famous bawdy songs, while Hiler played... and Harold Stearns, still wearing his brown felt hat, appeared and reappeared, taking up a collection for a steeplechase racer that did not exist.'

That night Kay first met the heroine of Michael Arlen's *The Green Hat*, the real one, and she wore broad ivory bracelets from wrist to shoulder. Nancy Cunard was 'straight as any stick,' writes William Carlos Williams, 'emaciated, holding her head erect, not particularly animated, her blue eyes completely untroubled, inviolable in her virginity of pure act. I never saw her drunk; I can imagine that she was never quite sober.' Nancy was notable for having taken as lover a black jazz pianist, Henry Crowder, whom she had picked up from a band in a Venice café. (Lady Asquith, meeting Nancy's mother one day in Mayfair, growled at her: 'What is it now, Maud, whisky, opium, or niggers?') Nancy had bought Bill Bird's printing press, and she was going to publish an edition of Ezra Pound's *Cantos*. She was said to be a nymphomaniac, but she seemed unable to involve herself deeply with anyone. In one of his few passable poems, McAlmon describes her:

> ... your straw pale hair,
> your brittle voice machine-conversing,
> allotted speeches, no neglect,
> a social sense of order,
> a sharp dry voice
> speaking through smoke and wine,
> a voice of litheness;
>   a hard, a cold, a stern white body.

The poem might have been about himself.

Another evening there was a St Patrick's Day dinner at the Trianon, organised by Sylvia Beach and Adrienne Monnier. McAlmon had been invited, but he did not much fancy the prospect of dining with Joyce's 'adulators, imitators, editors, translators and explainers', so he sat aloof at the end of the table, refusing to eat anything and drinking Armagnac. Somebody persuaded him to sing his Chinese Opera. Inspired by it, Joyce gave a rendering of several ballads, and later wanted to climb a lamp-post. Nora manoeuvred him into a taxi.

New bars opened, others closed. One day an enterprising *madame* announced the commencement of business at a *de luxe* establishment not far from the Dôme. A shiny *bar américain* was proudly displayed, and the girls took prospective customers on a tour of the bedrooms, 'And we were supposed to bring our wives!' says Samuel Putnam. Downstairs, in the middle of a floor crowded with the clientele of the Dôme and the Sélect, Kiki and the painter Pascin did their own furious version of the Charleston.

For Kay, there was sometimes the excitement of new friends, like Harry and Caresse Crosby. Harry came from an upper-class Boston family and had caused a great scandal by marrying a divorcée, Polly Jacob, who now called herself Caresse. In Paris they had set up the Black Sun Press, where under the appropriate imprint of Editions Narcisse they printed their own poems – and also those of D. H. Lawrence, Hart Crane, and fragments from Joyce's 'Work in Progress'. (In 1929, in the USA, Harry Crosby shot himself in an apparent suicide pact with another woman; his death was regarded as another sign of the ending of the expatriate era.)

McAlmon took up for a while with John Glassco and his friend Graeme Taylor, whom Morley Callaghan calls 'those two willowy graceful young men'; Callaghan was rather shocked at the way they continually laughed at McAlmon behind his back. Glassco ran out of money and took a job as a gigolo for a Montmartre *madame*. He had to bed elderly women at all hours of the day and night, and it completely wore him out. He acquired a rich mistress, caught tuberculosis, and decided it was time to return to Canada. He was not yet twenty.

Before he left Paris, he sold the beginning of his memoirs to *This Quarter*, which had been restarted by Edward Titus who ran another of the private presses. Glassco gave a party on the proceeds, but it was not a great success. An organ-grinder who had been hired to provide the music consumed most of the drink before the party had properly begun, so Glassco and McAlmon and Glassco's girl slipped away, leaving the guests and the almost empty bottles. It was Bastille night once again and the whole city was seething with celebration. Everywhere people were dancing in the streets, and many of the women had taken off their clothes.

'What a good idea it was,' said Glassco's girl, 'to capture the Bastille in July.'

'They were probably thinking ahead. They're a practical people.'

*

But McAlmon did not revise his opinion. 'Paris,' he writes, 'was by now, as it probably always has been to "old-timers", completely finished . . . What Paris had once offered was no longer there so far as I was concerned.' People began to realise that *The Sun Also Rises* had been a watershed: Hemingway had embalmed the spirit of the Quarter in the novel, and now they all seemed to be playing the parts he had written for them. They began to talk about two eras of Montparnasse, B.S. (Before *Sun*) and A.S. McAlmon had heard rumours about some vital art movement in Mexico City. He had friends there, so 'why not go and see?'

One August afternoon in 1929, Kay was sitting on a high stool in the empty bar of the Coupole. Suddenly Gaston the barman remembered that McAlmon had left a note for her when he took off for Mexico a month earlier. Gaston gave it to her. It was written in pencil, on ruled paper. It did not say very much; only that her typewriter had looked in pretty bad shape to him, and so he had left her his: 'It's with the *patronne* of the Café du Metro at the corner of the Boulevard St Germain and the rue de l'Odéon. It's a fairly new Remington portable, so it ought to last through several books.'

*

Smitten with a social conscience at living off the princess and her memoirs, Kay decided to join Raymond Duncan's vegetarian colony at Neuilly, and learn how to milk goats and weave tunics and make sandals out of raw hide. She endured it for six months, long enough to discover that it was simply a commercial operation to manufacture goods for Duncan's Paris shops. No tunics were woven: Duncan sold those that his dead wife had made years earlier. The nearest thing to weaving in the colony was Kay's darning of Harold Stearns's collars and cuffs.

One day she went with Archie Craig to tea at Gertrude Stein's. It all seemed to be going well, and Kay got into earnest conversation with Alice about recipes for *gazpacho*, which Alice had been gathering all over Spain. But Archie told her afterwards that Gertrude had asked him not to bring her back again; she had found her 'as incurably middle-class as Ernest Hemingway'.

Hemingway had quarrelled with Gertrude, though no one could quite make out why. He said she had been offended when he and Hadley turned down an invitation to go on holiday with her and Alice. Then one day he had called at the rue de Fleurus and heard the two of them quarrelling: 'Don't, pussy. Don't. Don't, please don't.' (This was Gertrude.) 'I'll do anything, pussy, but please don't do it. Please don't. Please don't, pussy.' He had run away quickly; he hinted that he had heard more, and worse. (Is it possible that until now he had not come to terms with Gertrude's lesbianism?)

Hadley said it was Gertrude who had broken off the friendship. Hadley had come to rue de Fleurus one day with Bumby and had been told by Alice at the door: 'I'm very sorry. Gertrude can't see you today.' The quarrel was probably due partly to *The Torrents of Spring*. Gertrude thought it in deplorable taste, and agreed with Sherwood

Anderson that Hemingway had written it through jealousy. Eventually, in 1933, she got her own back in *The Autobiography of Alice B. Toklas*: 'Gertrude Stein and Sherwood Anderson are very funny on the subject of Hemingway ... Hemingway had been formed by the two of them and they were both a little proud and a little ashamed ... But what a book, they both agreed, would be the real story of Hemingway ...'

*

Hemingway did not quarrel with Scott Fitzgerald, even though Fitzgerald took almost as much pleasure in interrupting Hemingway's work as Zelda did with his own. By now, he was drunk in the daytime as well as at night. He blamed his failure to work on Paris. One day he came with his small daughter Scottie to Hemingway's flat; out on the stairs she announced that she needed to go to the bathroom. Fitzgerald started to undress her there and then, and the landlord appeared and said: 'Monsieur, there is a *cabinet de toilette* just ahead of you to the left of the stairs.' Fitzgerald answered: 'Yes, and I'll put your head in it too, if you're not careful.'

Another day he asked Hemingway to have lunch with him. He said he had something very important to ask, that meant more than anything in the world to him, and that Hemingway must answer absolutely truthfully. They had finished lunch before Fitzgerald worked up courage to talk about it. Over a final carafe of wine, he said: 'You know I never slept with anyone except Zelda.' 'No, I didn't.' 'Zelda said that the way I was built I could never make any woman happy and that was what upset her originally. She said it was a matter of measurements. I have never felt the same since she said that and I have to know truly.'

Hemingway took him off to the *cabinet* and examined him. 'You're perfectly fine. There's nothing wrong with you. You look at yourself from above and you look foreshortened. Look at yourself in the mirror in profile.' 'But why should she say it?' 'To put you out of business.' They went to the Louvre, and Hemingway showed Fitzgerald that none of the statues had big ones. 'It is not basically a question of the size in repose,' he told Fitzgerald. 'It is the size it becomes.'

*

Hemingway published one more book while living in Paris, *Men Without Women* (1927). It contained several short stories as good as anything he had written. Pauline became pregnant late in 1927, and, like Hadley with Bumby, decided she wanted the baby born on the other side of the Atlantic. The Hemingways left France the following March, he having posed for a farewell photo with Sylvia outside the bookshop. In the picture, Sylvia looks admiringly at a large bandage swathing Hemingway's temples; once again he has the appearance of a returned war hero. He had accidentally pulled a skylight down on his head. 'How the hellsufferin tomcats,' wrote Ezra Pound from Rapallo, 'did you git drunk enough to fall *upwards* thru the blithering skylight?'

Hemingway and Pauline decided to settle on Key West, an island just off the Florida peninsula. They were back in Paris during 1929, but Hemingway realised that the end of his marriage to Hadley had been 'the end of the first part of Paris. Paris was never to be the same again.'

★

During 1929 the *Little Review* finally folded. Apart from *transition*, most of the other little magazines had now petered out. During 1930 Kiki's memoirs were published; Hemingway contributed the introduction, and said that their appearance definitely marked 'the era of Montparnasse' as 'closed'. The very expression 'An American in Paris' had become a cliché now that George Gershwin's tone-poem of this title (1928) had been performed. Gershwin had composed most of it in New York before even setting eyes on Paris.

On his infrequent return visits, Hemingway found the Quarter becoming 'a dismal place'. Laurence Vail grumbled that the Dôme had been overrun by 'barbarians, happy German families in ulsters, hardy Scandinavian raw fish eaters, trans-Mississippi school teachers, and too many pretty little girls and boys from Yale, Oxford, Bryn Mawr'. They would sit on the *terrasse* and take hours to consume a couple of beers, 'a morose contrast to the old days,' said Vail, 'when, in less than two hours, Flossie Martin and other notables could pile towers of saucers half a metre high'.

There were still American writers in the Quarter, a whole new generation of exiles who had arrived in the late 1920s and did not want to go home yet. Many of their antics had a familiar ring to the older expatriates. Hart Crane arrived in 1929 and one evening had a savage, furniture-smashing battle with police at the Sélect, resulting in his imprisonment in the Santé. As with Malcolm Cowley six years earlier, his friends got him out again. Such goings-on were recorded, in what was virtually a private language, by Wambly Bald, a Chicago-ite who had begun a weekly gossip column in the *Paris Tribune* and would wander in and out of the Quarter like an alcoholic ghost. Bald's column of 14 October 1932 introduced a new figure to the Montparnasse stage: 'Miller is not a son of badinage. He is a legitimate child of Montparnasse, the salt of the Quarter. He represents its classic color that has not faded since Mürger and other optimists. A good word is *esprit*.'

Henry Miller had come to Paris in 1930 at the age of thirty-eight with several novels that nobody would publish and next to no money in his pocket. Later he moved from Montparnasse to Clichy, on the outskirts of the city, later still to Villa Seurat in the fourteenth *arrondissement*.

He worked for a while as a proofreader of stock-market reports on the *Paris Tribune*, and Samuel Putnam remembers him wandering into the 'vinous-streaked dawn' at the Coupole after the paper had gone to press, 'a broad ingenious grin on his face'. At the bar he would 'expound his *Weltanschauung*, principally in words of four letters'. Its gist was that prostitutes were about the only pure beings in a world of reeking garbage. 'Not a highly original conception,' says Putnam, 'but provided his listeners had had a sufficient number of Pernods, he could lend it all the force of novelty. Once in a while, someone would mutter: "For Christ's sake, Hank, why don't you write a book?"'

One day Miller wandered into Shakespeare and Company and showed Sylvia 'an interesting novel he had been working on, *Tropic of Cancer*'. As with Frank Harris, she sent him off to Jack Kahane at Obelisk Press, who brought it out in 1934. Miller soon became the centre of attraction to a group of expatriate writers in Paris – Lawrence Durrell among them – just as Joyce had been for the previous generation.

The Paris of Miller's sexual odyssey is scarcely recognisable as that of the Lost Generation, but it is identifiably the same city as was inhabited by George Orwell from the spring of 1928 until the end of 1929. Orwell ran out of money and took a job as a hotel dishwasher. He describes the penury he experienced during these weeks in *Down and Out in Paris and London* (1933), his first published book.

*

'Slowly but surely,' writes Samuel Putnam, 'the Depression was making itself felt among us. The great homeward trek had begun.' As Harold Loeb puts it, 'one by one we went on to recognized achievements or succumbed to the attrition of our dreams.' Loeb returned to the USA and became a civil servant in the National Survey of Potential Product Capacity; Bill Smith, who had been with him in Pamplona, worked on his staff there for a time, and later became a speech writer for Harry Truman. Duff Twysden and her American boyfriend also went to the USA; Loeb saw her once in the late 1930s: 'She looked terrible and died shortly afterwards.' Kay Boyle married Laurence Vail, who had divorced Peggy Guggenheim. Later she divorced him and married an Austrian baron. She became a successful novelist. Hadley Hemingway married a Chicago journalist; Hemingway continued to write to her so affectionately that her second husband had to ask him to stop.

Harold Stearns went on working the racetracks for a while, until suddenly one afternoon he went blind. He was sacked by the newspaper that was currently employing him – the London *Daily Mail* – and though his sight recovered he became completely destitute, sleeping on benches around Paris. His health broke down, and at a friend's recommendation he had all his teeth removed. 'With no teeth, few friends, no job, and no money, I naturally decided that all I could do was return to my own country.' The American Aid Society paid for his passage home, and a man he met on the boat fixed him up with a hotel room in New York. He went to *Scribner's Magazine* and offered them an article called 'A Prodigal Returns'. They bought it, and he began to get some book-reviewing work. Gradually he put his life together again.

In 1938 he edited another symposium, *America Now: an Inquiry into Civilization in the United States*. In the introduction, Stearns referred ironically to 'my thirteen years' French Sabbatical', but otherwise made no mention of his Parisian experiences, nor gave any indication of what he had learned in Europe. None of his 1921 contributors reappeared in the new symposium, which by comparison with its predecessor was blandly, shallowly optimistic.

*

Early in 1929, a year after he had left Paris, Hemingway finished his second novel, *A Farewell to Arms*, which quickly became a commercial success; the film rights were disposed of for $24,000, a Gary Cooper–Helen Hayes movie was released in 1932, and sales eventually passed the one million mark. But with his next book, *Death in the Afternoon* (1932), which is a celebration of bullfighting, his reputation began to suffer a little. One reviewer suggested that he had developed 'a literary style, you might say, of wearing false hair on the chest'. The trouble was, indeed, the assumption of false masculinity and the increasing repression of the ambiguities of his real nature. By the 1940s the name Hemingway had become, even among his admirers, something of a joke. Raymond Chandler, himself a skilled Hemingway follower, defined the word 'Hemingway', in *Farewell My Lovely* (1940), as meaning, 'A guy that keeps saying the same thing over and over till you begin to believe it must be good'.

The critic Alfred Kazin describes Hemingway's visible decline from the mid-1930s:

As the years went by, one grew accustomed to Hemingway standing like Tarzan against a backdrop labelled Nature; or, as the tedious sportsman of *Green Hills of Africa*, grinning over the innumerable beasts he had slain, while the famous style became more mechanical, the sentences more invertebrate, the philosophy more self-conscious, the headshaking over a circumscribed eternity more painful. Many of the lost generation had already departed to other spheres of interest; Hemingway seemed to have taken up a last refuge behind the clothing advertisements in *Esquire*, writing essays in which he mixed his fishing reports with querulous pronouncements on style and the good life.

But he was aware of what had happened to him. In his long short story 'The Snows of Kilimanjaro', written in the late 1930s, a dying

author contemplates his failure to live up to early promise, a failure
chiefly caused, he believes, by affluence and the companionship of the
very rich:

... You made an attitude that you cared nothing for the work you used to do,
now that you could no longer do it. But, in yourself, you said that you would
write about people; about the very rich; that you were really not of them but a
spy in their country; that you would leave it and write of it and for once it
would be written by someone who knew what he was writing of. But he would
never do it, because each day of not writing, of comfort, of being that which he
despised, dulled his ability and softened his will to work so that, finally, he did
no work at all ...

It was not quite as bad as that; Hemingway kept on writing, and two
of his 1930s books, *To Have and Have Not* (1937) and *For Whom the
Bell Tolls* (1940), deal with serious contemporary themes – the
Depression and the civil war in Spain. The first, a portrait of a Key West
tough guy struggling to survive in bad times, is too obviously the work
of a Have rather than a Have Not, a hasty response to Hemingway's
critics' demand for social commitment; but *For Whom the Bells Tolls* is
many people's opinion the best book about the Spanish Civil War –
Hemingway went to Spain as a journalist with Martha Gellhorn, who
eventually became his third wife. Yet there is something disquieting
about the novel if it is read as a serious political book; it is too lush,
too self-indulgent; its real subject is 'going native' with the band of
guerrillas in the hills, and sleeping with the girl Maria. The best thing in
the book is the portrayal of Pilar, the wife of the guerrilla leader who
herself takes over the leadership when her husband shows signs of
treachery. Hemingway describes her as 'a woman of about fifty ... almost as wide as she was tall, in black peasant skirt and waist, with heavy
wool socks on heavy legs, black rope-soled shoes and a brown face like
a model for a granite monument'. Later in the book she says: 'Life is
very curious ... I would have made a good man, but I am all woman and
all ugly.' She is, of course, a portrait of Gertrude Stein.

*

Sylvia Beach continued to minister to Joyce throughout the 1920s, but
by 1932, ten years after the publication of *Ulysses*, she and Adrienne
were worn out by his incessant requests for money, and told him so.
Joyce was wounded by this rejection, but once when someone belittled
her role in the publication of *Ulysses*, he said quietly: 'All she ever did
was to make me a present of the best years of her life.'
      Gertrude Stein and Alice Toklas lived on in the rue de Fleurus.
Gertrude became an international celebrity, giving lectures at Oxford
and Cambridge, and in America. In 1933 she spent the proceeds of

The Autobiography of Alice B. Toklas on a new eight-cylinder Ford.
Leo Stein said of the book: 'God what a liar she is!'

Henry Miller left Paris at the end of May 1939, first for Greece, then
the USA. Joyce, having completed *Finnegans Wake* and seen it published in the spring of 1939, left France for Zurich in mid-December
1940 after the German occupation had begun. He died there less than a
month later, of a perforated ulcer.

McAlmon, who had quickly tired of Mexico, spent the 1930s travelling the world as restlessly as he had roamed the bars of the Quarter –
Munich, Berlin, Majorca, Barcelona, Strasbourg, Texas, Los Angeles,
Paris again – always in search of that missing face, that riotous party
that must be going on somewhere, if only he could find it. He was in
France when war broke out, and he too stayed until the Germans
arrived. When he went back to the USA, his brothers gave him a job
with their Southwest Surgical Supply Co. He became a travelling
salesman in the Arizona desert, selling trusses.

★

Having struggled along through the Depression, Sylvia Beach was still
open for business at Shakespeare and Company when the Germans
arrived in Paris in the summer of 1940. She was interned for six months,
then lived in hiding, still in Paris, for the rest of the Second World
War.

Paris was liberated by the Allies in August 1944. Leon Edel had a
glimpse of the Quarter that day:

The snipers were still at their work when our vehicle rounded into Montparnasse in the long cavalcade that brought de Gaulle back to the French
capital. Across the gay glass fronts of another day . . . the Dôme, the Sélect, the
cavernous Coupole and the boarded-up Rotonde . . . chairs and tables were
heaped in earthquake disorder. Down the way, at the Gare Montparnasse,
Nazis in field-green – the dishevelled unhelmeted children of Hitler's 'master-
race' – were surrendering in terror or glum despair . . . I suddenly remembered
Kiki of Montparnasse; in the midst of war, in the thronged street, I could smell
chicory and Pernod.

That day, says Sylvia, 'there was still a lot of shooting going on in the
rue de l'Odéon, and we were getting tired of it, when a string of jeeps
came up the street and stopped in front of my house. I heard a deep
voice calling: "Sylvia!"

' "It's Hemingway! It's Hemingway!" cried Adrienne. I flew downstairs; we met with a crash; he picked me up and swung me around and
kissed me while people on the street and in the windows cheered.' He
had managed to get to France as a journalist, and had somehow taken
command of some soldiers. They dealt with the remaining Nazi

snipers; then Hemingway drove the jeep off to the rue de Fleurus to greet Gertrude and Alice, and to the Place Vendôme, 'to liberate,' he told Sylvia, 'the cellar at the Ritz'.

*

After the war, Sylvia lived on in the rue de l'Odéon, doing a little bookselling from her apartment, and presiding over a great exhibition of American writers in Paris held there in 1959. She died in 1962. Today another shop, on the *quai* of the Left Bank opposite Notre Dame, sells American and English books and bears the name 'Shakespeare and Company'.

In the 1950s Samuel Beckett inherited the role of Joyce to the latest generation of exiled writers in Paris, many of them Irish. Unlike Joyce he always insisted on paying for every round of drinks; like Joyce, he often needed to be helped home from the Falstaff, his favourite bar. After one such occasion he wrote to thank a friend for 'your invaluable help up that blazing boulevard'.

Gertrude Stein died in 1946; Alice survived her by twenty-one years, living on alone in Paris. Kiki ended up selling matches and safety-pins on the terrace of the Dôme; Nina Hamnett threw herself out of a window in London; Robert McAlmon died of pneumonia at Desert Hot Springs, California in 1956, at the age of sixty.

Hemingway shot himself in June 1961, just before his sixty-second birthday, leaving his fourth wife Mary to see his final book through the press. She chose its title from something he had said a few years earlier: 'If you are lucky enough to have lived in Paris as a young man, then wherever you go for the rest of your life, it stays with you, for Paris is a moveable feast.'

A Moveable Feast is better than anything else he wrote in his later years – far better than his last novel *The Old Man and the Sea* (1952), though that book helped to win him the Nobel Prize for Literature. The idea of writing his reminiscences of Paris in the 1920s came to him after he had discovered his notebooks from those days, mouldering in a trunk he had forgotten and which had lain for thirty years in the basement of the Paris Ritz. Only the description of Ford Madox Ford at the Closerie des Lilas, originally written for *The Sun Also Rises*, actually came from those notebooks; the rest was a brilliant recapturing of the flavour of his earliest work – a recovery of sensitivity, almost, one might say, a recovery of the feminine side of Hemingway:

It was a wonderful meal at Michaud's after we got in; but when we had finished and there was no question of hunger any more, the feeling that had been like hunger when we were on the bridge was still there when we caught the bus home. It was there when we came in the room and after we had gone to bed and made love in the dark, it was there. When I woke with the windows open and the moonlight on the roofs of the tall houses, it was there. I put my face away from the moonlight into the shadow but I could not sleep and lay awake thinking about it. We had both wakened twice in the night and my wife slept sweetly now with the moonlight on her face...

*

Natalie Barney had continued to hold her Friday evening salon all through the 1920s and 1930s, and she resumed after the war. The last was held when she was ninety-one. She refused to be deterred by the student riots that were disrupting Paris that day, for this was May 1968. A young writer who was present, Jean Chalon, recalls how 'the corks popped, keeping time with the explosions in the street.'

*

Malcolm Cowley made himself a reputation as a critic and man of letters in the USA. 'Ten years after the first migration to Montparnasse,' he writes:

I met a talented, rather naive young woman just returned from London, where she had published her first novel. Yes, it had been fairly successful – it was good enough for the English, she said, but she didn't want to publish it over here until she had time to rewrite it completely; it wasn't good enough for New York. I knew she did not intend to be smart; she was a simple person trying to state her impressions and those of the circle in which she moved.

In the 1930s American writing certainly began to hold its head high, but it is questionable how much this had to do with what had happened in Montparnasse. The chief authors to emerge in this decade – William Faulkner, grand master of Southern Gothic, Thomas Wolfe, creator of sprawling semi-autobiographies, and John Steinbeck, who wrote the fine Depression novel *The Grapes of Wrath* (1939) – had none of them been members of the Lost Generation, and had little in common with it. Malcolm Cowley, reviewing the 1930s, argues that the exiles had played their part in the strengthening of American literature; yet some words in his *Exile's Return* about the failure of the Dadaists could also be applied to his American friends in Montparnasse during the 1920s.:

Here was a group of young men, probably the most talented in Europe: there was not one of them who lacked the ability to become a good writer or, if he so decided, a very popular writer. They had behind them the long traditions of... literature (and knew them perfectly); they had all the examples of living masters (and had pondered them); they had a burning love of their art and a fury to excel. And what, after all, did they accomplish? They wrote a few interesting books, influenced a few others, launched and inspired half a dozen good artists, created scandal and gossip, had a good time. Nobody can help wondering why, in spite of their ability and moral fervor and battles over principle, they did nothing more.

Far more fruitful in terms of literature was another exile, which had been going on long before the Lost Generation beached itself in Paris, and which accelerated in the 1930s with the menace of Hitler: the flight of Europeans, especially Jews, to the USA. This was the 'movement' that played the vital part in rehabilitating American literature, as these exiled Europeans began to write, or gave birth to children who became outstanding authors – Saul Bellow, J. D. Salinger, Joseph Heller, Philip Roth, Kurt Vonnegut and Vladimir Nabokov.

*

The symbolic figure for the return of the Lost Generation to America is not Hemingway leaving Paris for an affluent life in Florida, but Harold Stearns, broken and destitute, staggering back steerage class. The geniuses had mostly turned out not to be geniuses after all. Yet they had been geniuses at being together, drinking together, sleeping together, and quarrelling together; and that was something worth remembering.

Most of them could not help remembering it. In 'The Snows of Kilimanjaro', the dying writer, lying on his camp bed in the African bush as his leg rots with gangrene, realises that over the years he has methodically destroyed his talent. But he can still look back with a kind of euphoria to his early days in Paris. Hemingway – for of course he is writing about himself – can still summon up an untarnished vision of it all:

'...The Place Contrescarpe...and the Bal Musette they lived above...And in that poverty, and in that quarter...he had written the start of all he was to do. There never was another part of Paris that he loved like that...There were only two rooms in the apartment where they lived and he had a room on the top floor of the hotel that cost him sixty francs a month where he did his writing, and from it he could see the roofs and chimney pots and all the hills of Paris...'

THE END

Appendices

Appendix A:
Biographies in Brief

This is merely a list of people who recur frequently in the story, and is intended simply as an aid to the reader in identifying them within this book. It makes no pretence of providing comprehensive information about them.

Anderson, Margaret (1886–1973), co-editor of the *Little Review*. Came to Paris in the mid-1920s.

Anderson, Sherwood (1876–1941), left his family and job in Ohio and went to Chicago to be a writer. Made his name with *Winesburg, Ohio* (1919) and *Poor White* (1920); spent the summer of 1921 in Paris, and recommended Hemingway to go there too. Hemingway parodied him in *The Torrents of Spring* (1926).

Barnes, Djuna (1892–1982), New York-born poet and author; came to Paris in the early 1920s and was a friend of Natalie Barney; wrote the satirical *Ladies Almanack* (1928) about Natalie. Her most celebrated book is the novel *Nightwood* (1936).

Barney, Natalie Clifford (1876–1972), heiress and lesbian; notable for her salons at 20 rue Jacob.

Beach, Sylvia (1882–1962), proprietor of Shakespeare and Company, and first publisher in 1922 of Joyce's *Ulysses* in book form.

Bird, William (1882–1963), journalist; proprietor of the Three Mountains Press in Paris, which printed one of Hemingway's first books.

Bowen, Stella (1895–1947), Australian painter; lived with Ford Madox Ford during his years in Paris, and had a daughter by him.

Boyle, Kay (1903–   ), born in Minnesota; came to France with her first husband in 1921. Author of many novels and volumes of short stories beginning with *Wedding Day* (1930). She added her own reminiscences to Robert McAlmon's *Being Geniuses Together* (1968 edition).

Bricktop (Ada Smith), black American jazz singer; proprietor of a night club in Montmartre.

Bryher (Annie Winifred Ellerman) (1894–1983), novelist and poet; married from 1921 to 1927 to Robert McAlmon.

Cannell, Kitty (Kathleen) (1891–1974), came to Paris after her marriage to Skipwith Cannell had broken up, and had an affair with Harold Loeb. Original of Frances Clyne in Hemingway's *The Sun Also Rises*.

Charters, Jimmie, came to Paris from Liverpool and worked as a barman in various Montparnasse bars. Published his memoirs in 1934.

Cowley, Malcolm (1898–   ), critic and poet, born in Pennsylvania; spent two years in Paris (1921–23), punched the proprietor of the Rotonde in the jaw, and wrote *Exile's Return* (1934) about the Lost Generation. Has published other books of essays and literary reminiscence.

Cummings, E. E. (1894–1962), poet; imprisoned in France during the First World War, and wrote *The Enormous Room* (1922) about this experience. His early books also included *Eimi* (1933) about a visit to the USSR, and he published many collections of poems.

Darantière, Maurice, proprietor of a Dijon firm that printed *Ulysses* for Sylvia Beach in 1922, and also McAlmon's Contact Editions, including Hemingway's first book, *Three Stories and Ten Poems* (1923).

Dos Passos, John (1896–1970), novelist, friend of E. E. Cummings; author of the *U.S.A.* trilogy (1930–36) and many other novels.

Dunning, Ralph Cheever (1878–1930), obscure poet discovered by Ezra Pound and mocked by Hemingway.

Fitzgerald, F. Scott (1896–1940), had published his first novel *This Side of Paradise* (1920), and also *The Great Gatsby* (1925) when he came to Paris and met Hemingway. His other major novels were *Tender is the Night* (1934) and *The Last Tycoon* (1941).

Ford, Ford Madox (1873–1939), English novelist; his original surname was Hueffer. Collaborated with Joseph Conrad in the early 1900s, and was best known for *The Good Soldier* (1915). Came to Paris in 1923 and started the *transatlantic review*, taking on Hemingway as sub-editor. Is widely admired for his *Parade's End* tetralogy (1924–1928).

Guthrie, Pat, Scotsman, companion of Duff Twysden and original of Mike Campbell in Hemingway's *The Sun Also Rises*.

Glassco, John (1909–1981), came to Paris from Canada at the age of eighteen, was befriended by McAlmon, and wrote one of the funniest accounts of life in the Quarter, *Memoirs of Montparnasse* (1970). In his later years a man of letters and public figure in Canada.

Guggenheim, Peggy (1898–1980), heiress; married Laurence Vail. Later a famous art collector.

Hamnett, Nina (1890–1956), English painter and bohemian.

Heap, Jane, co-editor of the *Little Review*.

Hemingway, Ernest (1899–1961), born in Oak Park, Illinois; wounded in Italy in 1918; came to Paris in December 1921. His first published books, *Three Stories and Ten Poems* and *in our time*, both appeared there in 1923, and his first novel *The Sun Also Rises* (*Fiesta*) was published in 1926. Subsequently achieved international fame and won the Nobel Prize for Literature (1954).

Hemingway, Hadley, born in 1891, first wife of Ernest Hemingway and mother of his son John ('Bumby').

Hiler, Hilaire, painter, pianist, and proprietor of the Jockey Club in Montparnasse.

Jolas, Eugene (1894–1952), co-editor of *transition*.

Joyce, James (1882–1941), Irish novelist; published *A Portrait of the Artist as a Young Man* serially in 1914 to 1915; *Ulysses* appeared in its complete form in 1922. Lived in Paris from 1920 until 1939. Published *Finnegans Wake* in 1939.

Kiki (Alice Prin), model and mistress of Man Ray during the 1920s.

Kohner, Frederic, biographer of Kiki; in Montparnasse himself during the 1920s.

Lewis, (Percy) Wyndham (1882–1957), painter and writer, friend of Ezra Pound. Author of several novels and critical studies.

Loeb, Harold (1891–1974), born into a wealthy New York family and educated at Princeton; worked in industry, ran a New York bookshop, then came to Europe in 1921 to edit *Broom.* Original of Robert Cohn in Hemingway's *The Sun Also Rises.*

Loy, Mina (1882–1966), British-born poet; lived in Paris making and selling lampshades during the 1920s. Her verse is collected in *The Last Lunar Baedeker* (1982).

Martin, Florence (Flossie), former New York chorus girl; self-elected 'Queen' of the Dôme.

McAlmon, Robert (1896–1956), born in South Dakota; came to New York, founded the magazine *Contact* with William Carlos Williams, married Bryher, and set off for Paris in 1921. His books include *A Hasty Bunch* (1921) and *Being Geniuses Together* (1938).

Miller, Henry (1891–1980), New York-born author of *Tropic of Cancer* (1934) and other autobiographical novels. Lived in Paris from 1930 until 1939.

Monnier, Adrienne, proprietor of a bookshop in the rue de l'Odéon, close friend of Sylvia Beach.

Monroe, Harriet (1860–1936), editor of the Chicago magazine *Poetry,* which she founded in 1912.

Moorhead, Ethel, former suffragette, co-founder with Ernest Walsh of *This Quarter.*

Perkins, Maxwell (1884–1947), editor at Scribner's publishing house in New York.

Pound, Ezra (1885–1972), poet, ringleader of the Modernist movement; lived in Paris from 1921 until 1924. Best known for his *Cantos,* published between 1925 and 1970.

Putnam, Samuel (1892–1950), literary journalist; lived in Paris in the 1920s and 1930s and translated Kiki's memoirs.

Smith, Bill, friend of Hemingway; went on the Pamplona trip that inspired *The Sun Also Rises.*

Stearns, Harold (1891–1943), edited *Civilization in the United States* (1922) and came to Paris, where he worked as a racetrack tipster.

Stein, Gertrude (1874–1946), came to Paris from California in 1902 and began to collect paintings with her brother Leo, befriending Matisse and Picasso. Wrote *Three Lives* (1909), and *The Making of Americans,* which did not appear in book form until 1925. Her many other writings include *The Autobiography of Alice B. Toklas* (1933).

Stein, Leo (1872–1947), brother of Gertrude Stein.

Stewart, Donald Ogden (1894–1980), humorist, friend of Hemingway; came on the Pamplona trip that inspired *The Sun Also Rises.*

Toklas, Alice B(abette) (1877–1967), San Francisco-born companion of Gertrude Stein.

Twysden, Lady Duff, habituée of Montparnasse during the 1920s; original of Brett Ashley in Hemingway's *The Sun Also Rises.*

Vail, Laurence (1891–1968), married Peggy Guggenheim, and later Kay Boyle.

Walsh, Ernest (1895–1926), poet described by Hemingway as 'marked for death'. Was rescued from Claridge's in Paris by Ethel Moorhead and founded *This Quarter*. Father of Kay Boyle's daughter Sharon.

Williams, William Carlos (1883–1963), New Jersey poet, friend of Ezra Pound from college days. Best known for *Paterson* (1946–1958). Usually avoided Paris.

Appendix B: Bibliography

The following are the books most frequently cited in the notes which follow, arranged alphabetically by the abbreviation I have used for each item.

Anderson   Michael Fanning (ed.). *France and Sherwood Anderson: Paris Notebook, 1921*, Louisiana State University Press, 1976

Baker   Carlos Baker. *Ernest Hemingway: a life story*, Collins, 1969

Beach   Sylvia Beach. *Shakespeare and Company*, Harcourt, Brace, 1959

BGT   Robert McAlmon. *Being Geniuses Together, 1920–1930*, revised, with supplementary chapters and new afterword by Kay Boyle, Hogarth Press, 1984

Bowen   Stella Bowen. *Drawn from Life*, Virago, 1984

Callaghan   Morley Callaghan. *That Summer in Paris*, MacGibbon & Kee, 1963

Charters   Jimmie the Barman (James Charters) with Morrill Cody. *This Must be the Place: Memoirs of Montparnasse*, Herbert Joseph, 1934

Civilization   Harold E. Stearns (ed.). *Civilization in the United States: an inquiry by thirty Americans*, Harcourt, Brace, 1922

Cowley   Malcolm Cowley. *Exile's Return* (first published in 1934), 3rd edn., Bodley Head, 1951

DLB   Karen Lane Rood (ed.). *Dictionary of Literary Biography, Volume Four, American Writers in Paris, 1920–1939*, Gale Research Company, 1980

Dear Scott/Dear Max   J. Kuehl and J. R. Bryer (ed.). *Dear Scott/Dear Max: the Fitzgerald–Perkins correspondence* [between Scott Fitzgerald and Maxwell Perkins], Scribner, 1971

Essential Hem.   Ernest Hemingway. *The Essential Hemingway*, Triad Panther, 1977

Fitch   Noel Riley Fitch. *Sylvia Beach and the Lost Generation*, W. W. Norton, 1983

Ford   Ford Madox Ford. *It Was the Nightingale*, William Heinemann, 1934

Glassco   John Glassco. *Memoirs of Montparnasse*, Oxford University Press (Toronto), 1970

Hamnett   Nina Hamnett. *Laughing Torso*, Constable, 1932

Hem. CH   Jeffrey Meyers (ed.). *Hemingway: the critical heritage*, Routledge & Kegan Paul, 1982

Hem. Letters   Carlos Baker (ed.). *Ernest Hemingway Selected Letters, 1917–1961*, Scribner, 1981

Kiki   Kiki [Alice Prin]. *Kiki's Memoirs*, translated by Samuel Putnam, Edward W. Titus, Black Manikin Press (Paris), 1930

Knoll   Robert E. Knoll (ed.). *McAlmon and the Lost Generation*, University of Nebraska Press, 1962

Kohner   Frederick Kohner. *Kiki of Montparnasse*, Cassell, 1968

Loeb   Harold Loeb. *The Way It Was*, Criterion, 1959

Mellow   James R. Mellow. *Charmed Circle: Gertrude Stein and company*, Phaidon, 1974

Meyers   Jeffrey Meyers. *Hemingway: a biography*, Macmillan, 1985

MF   Ernest Hemingway. *A Moveable Feast* (first published in 1964), Panther, 1977

Nick Adams Stories   Ernest Hemingway. *The Nick Adams Stories*, Scribner, 1972.

Poli   Bernard J. Poli. *Ford Madox Ford and the Transatlantic Review*, Syracuse University Press, 1967

Putnam   Samuel Putnam. *Paris Was Our Mistress*, Viking, 1947

SAR   Ernest Hemingway. *Fiesta/The Sun Also Rises* (first published in 1926), Grafton Books, 1976

Sarason   Bertram D. Sarason. *Hemingway and 'The Sun' set*, NCR/Micro-card Editions (Washington DC), 1972

Smoller   Sandford Smoller. *Adrift Among Geniuses: Robert McAlmon*, Pennsylvania State University Press, 1975

Stein   Gertrude Stein. *The Autobiography of Alice B. Toklas*, Penguin, 1966

Svoboda   Frederick J. Svoboda. *Hemingway and 'The Sun Also Rises': the crafting of a style*, University Press of Kansas, 1984

Williams   William Carlos Williams. *Autobiography*, MacGibbon & Kee, 1968

Appendix C:
Notes on Sources
(abbreviations refer to the Bibliography)

Prologue: 'A denser civilisation than our own'

Quotations from Benjamin Franklin are chiefly drawn from Ronald Clark, *Benjamin Franklin, A Biography*, Weidenfeld & Nicolson, 1983; those from Thomas Jefferson are taken from Merrill D. Peterson, *Thomas Jefferson and the New Nation*, Oxford University Press (New York), 1970. Other sources are Nathan G. Goodman, *Benjamin Franklin's Own Story*, University of Pennsylvania Press, 1937, and Hugh Brogan, *Longman History of the United States*, Longman, 1985. Quotations from Henri Mürger's *Scènes de la Bohême* are taken from the translation by Norman Cameron, published as *Vie de Bohème*, Folio Society, 1960. Du Maurier's *Trilby* was reprinted as an Everyman by J. M. Dent in 1956, though to see the illustrations it is necessary to consult earlier editions. The textual change designed to disguise Whistler is recorded by Leonée Ormond, *George du Maurier*, Routledge & Kegan Paul, 1969. Quotations from Henry James's accounts of his life in Paris are taken from Leon Edel, *Henry James*, volumes 1 and 2, Hart-Davis, 1953 and 1962, and from *Henry James Letters* (ed. Edel), volumes 1 and 2, Macmillan, 1974 and 1978. Quotations from James's *The American* come from the 1921 Macmillan edition.

Part One: The Introducers

1 *'Slowly I was knowing that I was a genius'*

Principal sources are Stein and Mellow. Quotations are also taken from John Malcolm Brinnin, *The Third Rose: Gertrude Stein and her world*, Weidenfeld & Nicolson, 1960; Elizabeth Sprigge, *Gertrude Stein: her life and work*, Hamish Hamilton, 1957; and Alice B. Toklas, *What Is Remembered*, Holt, Rinehart & Winston, 1963. Gertrude Stein's *Three Lives* was reprinted by Peter Owen in 1970. *The Making of Americans* was published in a trade edition by Harcourt, Brace in 1934. The word-portraits are quoted from Mellow as is Sherwood Anderson's comment on them. Picasso's comment on the portrait is found in Roland Penrose, *Picasso*, 3rd edn., Granada, 1981. Edmund Wilson's disparagement of *The Making of Americans* comes from his *Axel's Castle* Fontana, 1961. Hemingway's response to Gertrude and Alice is recorded in *MF*.

2   *The Amazon Entertains*

The principal source is George Wickes, *The Amazon of Letters: the Life and Loves of Natalie Barney*, W. H. Allen, 1977. The excerpt from Natalie's poems comes from Natalie Barney, *Poems & Poèmes*, George H. Doran & Co (New York), 1920. Djuna Barnes's *Ladies Almanack* was issued in a trade edition by Harper & Row in 1972. Quotations from *The Well of Loneliness* by Radclyffe Hall are taken from the Virago edition (1982). Truman Capote's observations are recorded in Wickes's biography of Natalie (see above). Ezra Pound's remark about her comes in Canto 84, p. 539 of the 1975 edition.

3   *Sylvia and Company*

Principal sources: Beach, Fitch, Anderson, Mellow. Quotations are also taken from Ray Lewis White (ed.), *Sherwood Anderson/Gertrude Stein: correspondence and personal essays*, University of North Carolina Press, 1972. Gertrude Stein's poem about Shakespeare and Company is in *Painted Lace*, the fifth volume of the Yale edition of her posthumous pieces.

Part Two: **Being Geniuses Together**

1   *Melancholy Jesus*

Principal sources: Beach, Fitch, Anderson. I have also, of course, been indebted to Richard Ellmann, *James Joyce*, Oxford University Press, revised ed, 1982.

2   *'The fastest man on a typewriter'*

Principal sources: Fitch, Beach, Charters, *Hem. Letters*, Baker, *MF*, Meyers. Other quotations are from Michael Reynolds, *The Young Hemingway*, Blackwell, 1986, and the passages from Hemingway's early short stories are taken from Peter Griffin, *Along With Youth: Hemingway, the early years*, Oxford University Press, 1985.

3   *'No fat, no adjectives, no adverbs'*

Principal sources: *MF*, Baker, Meyers, *Hem. Letters*, Stein, Beach. 'Up in Michigan' is printed in Hemingway's *The Fifth Column and the First Forty-Nine Stories*, Cape, 1939. His remark about wanting to write like Cézanne painted is in *Nick Adams Stories*, p. 239. Wyndham Lewis's account of the boxing lesson and Hemingway's statement that Pound had taught him to write come from Noel Stock, *The Life of Ezra Pound*, Routledge & Kegan Paul, 1970. Pound's phrase 'the touch of the chisel' appears in a letter to Arnold Gingrich, 28 August 1934 (University of Pennsylvania Library).

4   *McAlimony*

Principal sources: *Hem. Letters*, Williams, Glassco, Beach, Knoll, Smoller, *BGT*. Hemingway reporting the pregnancy to Gertrude Stein and Alice Toklas is described in Stein. Eliot's recollection of wanting to settle in France and write in French is in Peter Ackroyd, *T. S. Eliot*, Hamish Hamilton, 1984; Eliot's observations to McAlmon about Paris are in *BGT*. Joyce's comment on McAlmon's writing is in Richard Ellmann, *James Joyce* (see Part Three, Chapter 1 above). McAlmon's *Hasty Bunch* was printed by Darantière in 1921 or 1922; there is a copy in the Bodleian Library, Oxford. Ford Madox Ford's comment on Contact Editions is in Ford; the Contact prospectus is quoted in Baker.

5 'Summer's just started'

The principal source is *BGT*, where McAlmon describes at length how he spent the night of 13 to 14 July 1923. I have also drawn on his earlier version of this account of Bastille night, entitled 'Truer Than Most Accounts' and published in Ezra Pound's magazine *Exile* in the Autumn 1927 issue. This uses pseudonyms for most of the people named; I have silently substituted their real names. The remaining material in the chapter is drawn chiefly from *Hem. Letters*, *MF*, *SAR*, Charters, Hamnett (augmented by Denise Hooker's *Nina Hamnett: Queen of Bohemia*, Constable, 1986, which contains a lot of information about Quarterites), Svoboda, Loeb, Kiki, Kohner, Williams, Glassco, Beach, and *DLB*. Margaret Anderson's account of Parisian cultural life comes from her book *My Thirty Years' War*, Alfred A. Knopf, 1930. Picabia's description of *Relâche* is quoted in *The Concise Oxford Dictionary of Ballet*, Oxford University Press, 1982. Apollinaire's comments on Montparnasse are from Roland Penrose's *Picasso* (see Part 2, Chapter 1 above), and Marcel Duchamp's from Charters. Harold Stearns's description of the Dôme in 1921 comes from his book *The Confessions of a Harvard Man* (a new edition of *The Street I Know*), edited by Hugh Ford and published by Paget Press (California) in 1984. Sinclair Lewis's description of the Dôme is quoted in Brian N. Morton, *Americans in Paris: an anecdotal street guide*, The Olivia & Hill Press (Ann Arbor), 1984. Douglas Goldring's *The Façade* was published by Jarrolds in 1927. Mina Loy's poem on Gertrude Stein is quoted from the omnibus edition of her poetry, *The Last Lunar Baedeker*, Jargon Society, 1982. Margaret Anderson's remark about Ezra Pound is from Barbara Guest's biography of H.D., *Herself Defined*. Peggy Guggenheim's reminiscences are from her book *Out of this Century: confessions of an art addict*, Deutsch, 1980. Eliot's letter to McAlmon is quoted in *BGT*.

Interlude: The oldest country in the world

Principal sources: Cowley, *Civilization*, Anderson, Glassco. Quotations are also taken from Baker, *BGT*, *Hem. Letters*, Knoll, Loeb, *MF*, *Nick Adams Stories* (the latter is the source of Hemingway's remark about Joyce inventing some new tricks). Details of Hemingway's school curriculum are from Peter Griffin, *Along With Youth* (see Part 2, Chapter 2 above). Comments on Princeton attitudes are from F. Scott Fitzgerald, *This Side of Paradise*, book 1, chapters 1 and 2. Information on E. E. Cummings is from Richard Kennedy, *Dreams in the Mirror: a biography of E. E. Cummings*, Boni & Liveright, 1980. The hostile comment on the Dadaists is by Emmy Veronica Sanders and was published in *Broom*, November 1921. Gertrude Stein's remark about America comes from *transition*, fall 1928. Henry Miller's comment on Paris life is from George Wickes, *Americans in Paris*, Doubleday, 1969. Cowley's poem on the dying farm was published in *Broom*, May 1922.

Part Three: **Fiesta**

1   *Iceberg principle*

Principal sources: *Hem. Letters, MF, Hem. CH, Nick Adams Stories, Essential Hem.*, Bowen, Poli, *Dear Scott/Dear Max*. Quotations are also taken from Loeb, Stein, Glassco, Ford, *BGT*, Baker, Svoboda, and the *transatlantic review*. Sisley Huddleston's description of Ezra Pound doing the Charleston comes from his *Bohemian, Literary & Social Life in Paris*, George Harrap, 1928. The *New York Times* article from which Hemingway took the *in our time* chapter is in the issue dated 20 December 1922. Hemingway's rude remarks on the expatriates, originally published in the *Toronto Star*, are reprinted in Hemingway, *The Wild Years*, edited by Gene Z. Hanrahan, and published by Dell (New York) in 1962. The parody of Gertrude Stein published in *Der Querschnitt* is reprinted in Nicholas Joost, *Ernest Hemingway and the Little Magazines*, Barre Publishers (Barre, Massachusetts), 1968. Fitzgerald's mention to Gertrude Stein of the 'slick drive' comes from Arthur Mizener, *The Far Side of Paradise*, William Heinemann, 1969.

2   *La vie est belle*

The source for this chapter is Kay Boyle's narrative in *BGT*.

3   *Some fiesta*

The principal source is Loeb. Quotations are also taken from *Hem. Letters, SAR, BGT*, Sarason, Svoboda, Callaghan, Baker, and Donald Ogden Stewart, *By a Stroke of Luck!*, Paddington Press, 1975.

4   *'Just a damn journalist'*

Principal sources are Svoboda (for the early drafts of the novel, and the history of composition) and Sarason (for the comments by the real people who appear in the novel). Quotations are also taken from the published text of *SAR*, and from *Hem. Letters, Hem. CH*, Callaghan, Loeb, Glassco, *MF*, Cowley, *DLB*, and *Nick Adams Stories*. Material about Harold Stearns comes from Stearns's *The Confessions of a Harvard Man* (a reissue of his 1935 book *The Street I Know*), Paget Press (California), 1984. John Dos Passos's comment on Stearns is from his autobiography, *The Best Times*, Andre Deutsch, 1968. Hemingway's *The Torrents of Spring* was reprinted by Crosby Continental Editions (Paris) in 1932.

5   *These rocky days*

The principal source is Kay Boyle's narrative in *BGT*. Quotations are also taken from *Hem. Letters*, Glassco, Meyers, and Beach. McAlmon's comments on the Quarter, to Kay Boyle and Ethel Moorhead, are taken from his observations in *BGT*.

6 *Summer's almost ended*

The source is Kay Boyle's narrative in *BGT*.

Epilogue: **Homeward trek**

Sources: *BGT*, Williams, Putnam, Callaghan, Glassco, *MF*, Meyers, Stein, Kiki, Charters, *DLB*, Beach, Loeb, Sarason, *Hem. Letters*, Mellow, Stearns, Cowley. There are also quotations from Richard Ellman's life of Joyce (see Part Three, Chapter 1 above), and from Deirdre Bair, *Samuel Beckett: a biography*, Jonathan Cape, 1978. 'The Snows of Kilimanjaro' is reprinted in *Essential Hem*. Alfred Kazin's remarks come from his book *On Native Grounds*, 2nd ed, Harcourt, Brace, 1942. Leon Edel's account comes from his introduction to Glassco.

Appendix D:
Acknowledgements

Today, the crossroads at Métro Vavin is one of the noisiest spots in Paris. By day, traffic rushes past on its way to and from the *périphérique* motorway; by night, the lights of the cinema arcades and the Tour Montparnasse skyscraper bear more resemblance to Times Square than to the district that McAlmon and Hemingway knew so well. The Dôme, its terrace uninvitingly glassed in, is an expensive restaurant selling shellfish, usually closed for some reason; the Rotonde and Coupole are snazzy and unalluring, and only the Sélect has the faint look of a 'local' where one might meet a friend. However, many quarters of Paris remain hospitable and unspoilt, and my first thanks must be to Malcolm and Jane Van Biervliet for the extraordinarily generous loan of a flat in one such spot, a quiet little street on the Île St Louis, a few yards from where Bill Bird printed *in our time* and Ford Madox Ford presided magisterially over his Thursday tea parties. My family provided stimulating companionship during the time I spent there, and so did Ian Smith, whose criticisms of the first draft of this book, particularly the passages on Hemingway's style, have done much to improve the finished product.

Rayner Unwin – always my best source of ideas – first suggested that I write it, and generously provided the means for visits to Paris in the course of it; Mary Butler at Unwin Hyman gave much encouragement and help; and Hazel Orme worked miracles with her editorial pencil. The manuscript was read by several kind and wise persons who have saved me from many errors: Hugh Brogan, Edward Mendelson, George Wickes, and Kay Boyle, who scrutinised what I had written about her and corrected the grosser mistakes. Jean Preston and the staff of Princeton University Library provided photographic prints from the Sylvia Beach Collection, and George Wickes kindly lent pictures of Natalie Barney. The Estate of Man Ray gave permission for his photographs to be reproduced, Chatto & Windus and North Point Press permitted me to quote extensively from *Being Geniuses Together* by Robert McAlmon and Kay Boyle, Malcolm Cowley generously allowed me to use his *Exile's Return*, and Jonathan Cape Ltd and Charles Scribner's Sons gave permission for quotations from the writings of Ernest Hemingway. When it was not possible for me to be in Paris, the Bodleian Library, as always, proved a more than acceptable substitute.

When I read the chapter 'Summer's just started' at the 1986 Cheltenham Literary Festival, someone in the audience asked if I knew where a lifestyle like that of the Quarter could be found today. I wish I did; perhaps somebody could tell me.

Index

LEFT BANK PARIS
IN THE 1920's

0   ½ kilometre

RUE JACOB

Natalie Barney

Les Deux Magots

St-Germain des Prés

Brasserie Lipp

BOULEVARD SAIN

RUE DE SEVRES

RUE DE L'ODEON

St-Sulpice

BOULEVARD RASPAIL

RUE DE RENNES

Shakespear and Company (No. 12)

RUE DE SEVRES

Palais du Luxembourg

Jardin du

RUE DE FLEURS

Gertrude Stein (No. 27)

Luxembourg

MONTPARNASSE

("THE QUARTER")

AVENUE DU MARNE

BOULEVARD DU MONTPARNASSE

RUE NOTRE DAME DES CHAMPS

Sélect

Ezra Pound's studio (No.70 bis)

Coupole

Rotonde

Falstaff

RUE DU MONTPARNASSE

Dingo

Dôme

★ Metro Vavin

Hemingway's apartment, (1924-26) (No. 113)

BOULEVARD SAINT MICHEL

RUE DELAMBRE

Gare Montparnasse

BOULEVARD EDGAR QUINET

BOULEVARD RASPAIL

Jockey Club

Closerie des Li